The Captain's Guide to Alternative Energy Afloat

The Captain's Guide to Alternative Energy Afloat

*Marine Electrical Systems, Water Generators,
Solar Power, Wind Turbines & Marine Batteries*

by

Bill Morris

SEAWORTHY PUBLICATIONS, INC. • MELBOURNE, FLORIDA

The Captain's Guide
to
Alternative Energy Afloat

Marine Electrical Systems, Water Generators,
Solar Power, Wind Turbines & Marine Batteries

Copyright © 2019 by William V. Morris

Published in the USA by:
Seaworthy Publications, Inc.
6300 N. Wickham Rd.
#130-416
Melbourne, Florida 32940
Phone 310-610-3634
email orders@seaworthy.com
www.seaworthy.com - Your Bahamas and Caribbean Cruising Advisory

All rights reserved. No part of this book may be reproduced, stored in a retrieval system, or transmitted in any form or by any means, electronic, mechanical, photocopying, recording, or by any storage and retrieval system without permission in writing from the Publisher. All photography in this book is by the author, unless otherwise noted.

Library of Congress Cataloging-in-Publication Data

Names: Morris, Bill, 1957- author.
Title: The captain's guide to alternative energy afloat : marine electrical
  systems, water generators, solar power, wind turbines, marine batteries /
  by William Morris.
Description: Cocoa Beach, FL : Seaworthy Publications, Inc., [2016] |
  Includes bibliographical references and index.
Identifiers: LCCN 2016029893 (print) | LCCN 2016030432 (ebook) | ISBN
  9781892399823 (e-book (part I)) | ISBN 9781892399830 (e-book (part II)) |
  ISBN 9781948494236 (hardcover : alkaline paper) | ISBN 9781948494236
  (hardcover: alkaline paper) | ISBN 9781948494243 (paperback: alkaline
  paper)
Subjects: LCSH: Yachts--Energy consumption--Handbooks, manuals, etc. |
  Sailboats--Energy consumption--Handbooks, manuals, etc. |
  Yachting--Handbooks, manuals, etc. | Offshore sailing--Handbooks, manuals,
  etc.
Classification: LCC VM331 (ebook) | LCC VM331 .M67 2016 (print) | DDC
  623.822/3--dc23
LC record available at https://lccn.loc.gov/2016029893

To Marilu and Yasmin

Foreword

I FIRST MET BILL MORRIS SEVERAL YEARS AGO IN FIJI WHEN HE WAS CLOSE to midway on his mostly singlehanded world circumnavigation, and his decades of experience and tens of thousands of offshore miles are readily apparent.

His new book, *The Captain's Guide to Alternative Energy Afloat: Marine Electrical Systems, Water Generators, Solar Power, Wind Turbines & Marine Batteries*, is a guide for sailors interested in outfitting their sailing vessels with energy-saving systems in order to save money and also to contribute toward a cleaner and healthier ocean environment.

Bill covers a wide range of topics, from engines, generators, and electrical systems to a detailed review of alternative power systems, including solar, wind, water, and even hydrogen fuel cells as a way of increasing one's cruising range, saving money and decreasing reliance on diesel fuel.

The helpful insights on provisioning, anchoring to avoid damaging coral, and rubbish disposal will be welcomed by cruisers wanting to have a minimal impact. This book will prove valuable to both folks shopping for an ocean voyaging boat and those who are nearly ready to depart.

John Neal
Mahina Expeditions

Acknowledgments

EVERY BOOK WORTH ITS SALT IS A COLLABORATIVE EFFORT. NO MATTER how knowledgeable, experienced, or dedicated the author, it is simply beyond the ability of any one person to know everything about a given topic, particularly the finer details of an energy-independent offshore sailing yacht. In researching and writing this book, I depended heavily on the technical expertise of the Curry Family of Hydrovane, West Vancouver, British Colombia; marine engineer Leif Johansen, Marina del Rey, California; John and Amanda Neal, Mahina Expeditions, Friday Harbor, Washington; Ramsey Fawzy, AC/DC Marine, Torrance, California; Kit Rogers, Jeremy Rogers Yachts, Lymington, Hampshire, U.K.; and Sean Vattuone, San Pedro, California. For their critical reviews of this book, I thank my brothers Robert and Al Morris; my old school chum Jim Le Berthon; and fellow sailors Ron Durham, Jean Louis Fallon of the Cheoy Lee 35 *Walkabout*, and Joao Nicolau of the Contessa 35 *Simple Pleasures*, all based in San Pedro, California. Although my earliest ambitions of sailing around the world were the inspiration of my father Tom Morris, it was not until after my friend and colleague Dr. Roger Morgan of the Tayana 37 *Doc Holiday* talked me into taking a sailing class with him through the Red Cross that I knew what the rest of my life would be about and for that I sincerely thank him. In addition, I would like to express my gratitude to Seaworthy Publications for their expert care in publishing *The Captain's Guide to Alternative Energy Afloat: Marine Electrical Systems, Water Generators, Solar Power, Wind Turbines & Marine Batteries*, and to sailing guru John Neal of Mahina Expeditions for his kind, thoughtful words in the Foreword. Finally, I wish to thank my wife Marilu for her assistance with computer graphics in this book and for her patience, and our daughter Yasmin for her patience as well, during the many months of research and writing to complete this book.

Contents

Foreword vii
Acknowledgments viii
Introduction 1
Main Power Plant 3
    Gasoline Engines 3
    Diesel Engines 5
    Repowering with Diesel 7
    Electric Propulsion 9
    Hybrid Electric Power 10
Engine Alternators 13
    How Generators and Alternators Work 13
    Selecting an Alternator 16
    External Controllers 17
    Basic Troubleshooting 18
Gas & Diesel Generator Sets 20
    Optimum Power 21
    Dimensions and Layout 23
    Engine Manufacturer 24
    Engine Performance 24
    Load Surge Protection 25
    Sound Shield 25
    Traditional Genset: Westerbeke 25
    Belt Drive: Next Generation 26
    Asynchronous: Fischer Panda 26
    Fuel-Injected Gasoline: Kohler 26
    Hybrid Genset: Mastervolt 27
    Got Juice? 27
Alternative Fuels 28
    Petroleum Distillates 28
    Ethanol 29
    Low Sulfur Diesel 30
    Biodiesel 31
    Home-Made Biodiesel 31
    Complications of Biodiesel 32
    Liquid Petroleum Gas 33
    Gasoline-LPG Conversions 34
Cranking and House Batteries 36

  Cranking, House, and Dual-Purpose Batteries 36
  Battery Ratings 37
  Flooded Batteries 39
  AGM 39
  Carbon Foam 39
  Gel 40
  Lithium-Ion 40
  Fuel Cells 41
  Optimum Combinations 42
  Installing Batteries 44

Solar Panels 46
  Photovoltaic Energy 46
  Rigid Solar Panels 47
  Flexible Solar Panels 48
  Non-Marine Panels 48
  Electrical Installation 49
  Mounting Techniques 50

Wind Generators 53
  Theory 53
  Design Features 54
  Leading Models 55
  Deck and Arch Mounting 58
  Installation Kits 59
  Other Considerations 60

Hydro Generators 61
  Advantages of Water Power 61
  Design and Construction 62
  Towed Water Turbine 63
  Wind-Water Conversions 64
  Towline-Free Hydro Generators 66
  Experimental Technology 67

Voltage Regulators and Controllers 69
  Voltage Regulators 70
  Smart Controllers 73
  Switches, Isolators, and Solenoids 74

Monitoring Systems 77
  Analog and Digital Monitoring 78
  Engine Monitoring 81
  Battery Monitoring 82

  Monitoring Charge Sources 83
  Additional Monitoring Devices 84

Lighting, Navigation, and Communication 86
  Navigation Lights 86
  Cabin Lights 87
  Navigation 88
  Charting 89
  Communications 90
  AC Appliances 92

Refrigeration 94
  Assessing Refrigeration Needs 94
  How Refrigeration Works 96
  Refrigeration and Climate 97
  Air-Cooled Systems 97
  Water-Cooled Systems 97
  Keel-Cooled Refrigeration 98
  Cruiser Options 99

Windvane Self-Steering 101
  Windvane Versus Autopilots 101
  Servopendulums 102
  Trim Tabs 104
  Wind-Powered Auxiliary Rudder 105
  Matching Windvane to Boat 105
  Installation Tips 107
  Emergency Rudder Capability 108

Autopilots 111
  Operating Theory 111
  Above-Deck Systems 112
  Below-Deck Systems 114
  Sailing With an Autopilot 115

Manual Windlasses 117
  Overview of Manual Windlasses 117
  The Simpson-Lawrence Legacy 120
  New Manual Windlasses 122

Electric Windlasses 124
  Overview of Features 124
  Horizontal 126
  Vertical 127
  Drawbacks of Electric Windlasses 128

    Electric Windlass Advantages..128

Tools, Spare Parts, and Maintenance Supplies............................ 130
    Engine and Drive Train..130
    Electrical..131
    Plumbing 133
    Hand Tools 133
    Power Tools 135
    Hull and Deck 137
    Rigging Materials 137

The Essence of Green Voyaging 140
    Bilge 140
    Marine Sanitation Device 141
    Gray Water 141
    Garbage Overboard 142
    Anchoring and Mooring 142
    Sailing Versus Motoring 143
    Going Ashore 144
    Responsible Fishing 145
    Establishing Personal Standards 145

Energy Efficiency: Three Cruising Yachts 147
    Going the Distance 147
    Contessa 32 148
    Tayana 37 151
    Hallberg-Rassy 46 153

References 156

Appendices 158
    Appendix 1: AWG Battery Cable Sizes 158
    Appendix 2: AWG Wire Gauge Sizes 158
    Appendix 3: Beaufort Scale 159
    Appendix 4: Cruiser's Ham Bands 160
    Appendix 5: Marine Fire Extinguishers 160
    Appendix 6: Sailboat Specifications Decoded 161

Special Thanks 162

Index 164

About the Author 168

Introduction

INDEPENDENCE IS THE ONE THING THAT ATTRACTS US MORE THAN ANYTHING else to offshore sailing. Once you disconnect the shore power, slip the dock lines, and set sail toward the horizon, you are on your own, free of the day-to-day grind of shore life. If properly equipped, your waterborne home can see to your every need: fresh water, cold beverages, hot food, navigational stability, self-steering, communication, lighting, and entertainment. With proper planning and effective energy management, you can have 24-hour access to all of these things anywhere on the planet, provided you have a realistic energy plan encompassing charging capability, battery capacity, and daily energy usage.

Installing, using, and servicing the various battery charging systems you select, along with energy-saving devices, will depend on your own tastes and on the space limitations of your vessel. Two vessels of the same model and year can be outfitted in very divergent ways. One skipper may prefer using lots of fuel and dedicating extra space to diesel tanks. Another skipper may carry much less fuel and install solar panels, a wind generator, and a hydro generator to supply the bulk of the vessel's battery charging current. This latter style of generating and managing energy is far more sustainable over a long cruising career. For steerage, one captain may use an autopilot exclusively, spending thousands of dollars a year on fuel because a windvane steering unit would "destroy" his vessel's beautiful lines. At the same time, another skipper may install an energy-saving windvane self-steering device instead of a below-decks autopilot, keeping the house battery topped off for other purposes and more than likely avoiding the need for hundreds of gallons of extra diesel fuel every year in the process. The daily use of fossil fuels, unfortunately, erodes the sense of independence that one seeks on the ocean because freedom is strictly measured in number of days per quantity of fuel consumed. With renewable energy sources, the amount of time you spend off the grid is open-ended. Occasionally, you will want to pull into port to top off the fuel and buy fresh vegetables and libations, but your access to daily electrical power should not depend on those forays ashore.

There are various other ways to reduce fuel consumption and amperage draw, such as relying on mechanical rather than electrical systems to perform essential tasks. Using, for example, a manual anchor windlass instead of a power windlass requires more physical labor but also makes you more self-sufficient and less vulnerable to the fickleness of electrical and fuel-burning machinery. Electric windlasses are quite popular these days, but for solid dependability when your electrical charging system cannot provide the high level of current required by a windlass, a hand-operated windlass can be a true friend. We will look at both electric and manual windlasses, comparing their benefits and deficits in raising the anchor safely and efficiently in the roughest of anchorage conditions.

The more we appreciate the raw reality of offshore voyaging, the more we prepare for things that should not go wrong, but do. If you are preparing for a major ocean passage on a sailing vessel single-handed or with short-handed crew, you will have a greater chance of success by depending as much as possible on mechanical rather than electronic systems. For some of the ship's systems, of course, including navigation and lighting, traditional alternatives (e.g. a sextant and kerosene lamps) are no longer practical. All of today's offshore yachts rely on GPS technology, owing to its dependability, high precision, and affordability. Nonetheless, it is still prudent to carry a back-up sextant with reduction tables, just in case both your main and back-up GPS units fail or there is an extended black-out in the geostationary GPS satellites over your corner of the ocean. Whether you chart your position with paper or electronic charts is purely a matter of choice—one system is just as good as the other.

In the ensuing chapters, a short list of critically important points support the over-arching ideals of energy efficiency and environmental responsibility:

•Whenever possible, use mechanical instead of electrical devices, even if you carry those electrical gadgets on board.

•Maintain an energy plan, adding up all the amp hours used in a given week, and reconcile this sum with the total input you expect from battery charging sources.

•Always follow United States Coast Guard (USCG) and American Boating and Yachting Council (ABYC) guidelines for electrical and plumbing installations.

•Follow U.S. and international laws regarding the disposal of oil, fuel, plastic, glass, human waste, and other refuse.

•Adhere to U.S. regulations for fishing wherever you roam, catching only what you can eat and releasing juvenile fish and crustaceans back into their aquatic environment.

•Wherever you sail or anchor, try to leave the area cleaner than you found it.

•Establish a personal statement, or credo, either written or internalized, about how you intend to interact with the natural surroundings you encounter in your travels.

The foregoing set of basic guidelines should give you a sense of what most contemporary cruisers agree are "best practice" for skippers. And for the most part, doing what is right for Mother Nature is also good for the wallet. If you are trying to save fuel by continuing to sail instead of motoring when your speed drops below 5 knots, you are also saving money and preventing noxious hydrocarbons from sullying the ocean while at the same time reducing wear and tear on your vessel's engine and gearbox.

Some of what you will read here is based on the author's own experiences sailing around the world, singlehanded for two-thirds of the distance, on a 1966 Cal 30 masthead sloop. Tacking up the northern Red Sea and later up the coast of Baja California in full gales with a Fleming windvane self-steering system (no autopilot, no radar, and no fridge) was an instructive and eye-opening experience. One of the greatest lessons learned was to ensure self-reliance by installing equipment that was easy to repair while under sail. Dependence on manual systems made for a difficult yet ultimately successful voyage because there was little of anything to break, and whatever did break was easy to fix with basic hand tools.

Other information for this book has been garnered through research, sailing voyages on a variety of boats, and wisdom gained through many years of dockside conversations with other cruising sailors. One thing you will learn from listening to the opinions of experienced sailors is that they have wide-ranging opinions on what works in terms of hull design, sail rig, self-steering, navigation, you name it. But if you listen long enough, certain consistencies will emerge: the importance of a manual back-up bilge pump, bathing in seawater and rinsing with a small amount of fresh water, manual rather than electric faucets and heads, navigating with paper rather than digital charts to see the "big picture" on major ocean crossings, and other key assertions that just make good sense. By conducting thorough research, listening to experienced offshore cruisers, and sailing as often as you can in a variety of weather conditions, you will develop your own picture of what works best for you and your vessel.

Chapter 1
Main Power Plant

ONLY THE MOST DIE-HARD SAILING PURISTS WOULD INTENTIONALLY SET off on an extended ocean cruise on a sailboat without an auxiliary engine. There's no denying, of course, the allure of sailing singlehanded or with a romantic partner accompanied by the natural music of wind and water, the flutter of sails, the rhythmic clinking of bottles in the galley, and the cawing of sea birds to lull you into an ethereal state of bliss. And the knowledge that even if you wanted to, you could not possibly cause an oil spill or an engine fire, must be hugely gratifying. But when this euphoria is shattered by the pounding of surf on a rocky lee shore, romance vaporizes in an explosion of spindrift as you realize your vessel, and quite possibly your life, could be snuffed out in a matter of minutes. This is where a dependable diesel engine or electric propulsion motor comes to the rescue. With a properly maintained engine or electric motor backed up by a fully charged battery, you still have a chance of clawing your way far enough off that shore to seek a safe anchorage or resume sailing.

The most popular form of auxiliary propulsion for offshore sailing is the ubiquitous diesel engine. Its fuel is relatively stable and affordable, it has fewer moving parts than a gasoline engine, and it requires little maintenance. Here and there you might still see an offshore cruising vessel with a gasoline engine, but it will be a rare occurrence. Some North American coastal cruisers still have gasoline engines in their holds, yet even these sailors usually will admit they are in the market for a diesel, or for a serious offshore cruising vessel that already is fitted with a diesel engine. A third type of propulsion gaining popularity these days is an electric auxiliary motor powered by a generator and conventional batteries or a fuel cell. An electric motor requires little maintenance, produces no noxious smoke, requires no wet exhaust plumbing, and best of all, costs less to operate. And finally, diesel-electric hybrids offer what is likely the best of two worlds: two types of propulsion working alternately and in unison to provide the best combination of power with the greatest savings in fuel consumption. We will look at all four propulsion systems with an eye to durability, safety, maintenance, and fuel economy, the main factors you must consider in selecting an auxiliary power plant for your offshore cruising vessel.

Gasoline Engines

The great expansion of the pleasure sailing industry in the 1960s and 1970s ushered in a parallel growth in the manufacturing of small gasoline inboard auxiliary engines. Universal and Palmer both cashed in on the demand for small, lightweight, dependable engines for coastal sailboats ranging from 25 to 40 feet in length. Rather than converting automotive engines for marine use, Universal was unique in designing the Atomic Four, a four-cylinder, flathead 25-horsepower engine, specifically for use as an auxiliary engine for small sailing craft. This simply designed and constructed engine used raw water cooling, rather than the freshwater heat exchangers included on most diesel auxiliaries today. Built from 1947 until 1985, the Atomic Four accounted for 85 percent of the sail auxiliary engine market, with roughly 40,000 units being sold to sailboat builders. Some 20,000 of the engines are still in use today. If you have an Atomic Four and want to get a few more years of service out of it while you save up money for an offshore-capable diesel, consider installing an after-market heat exchanger and an electronic ignition conversion kit to extend the life of the engine.

The Palmer P-60 is a marinized version of the International Harvester C-60, designed and built by Thermo Electron Engine Corp. in Michigan for tricycle-style row crop tractors, such as the International Cub and Farmall tractors. The 22-horsepower Palmer 60, originally available as either a high- or low-compression version, was installed in the Islander 30, the Coronado 32 and 35, the Pearson 30, and numerous other makes and models of 1960s-era fiberglass sailing craft. Like the Atomic Four, The Palmer 60 has a flat head, four cylinders, and a raw water cooling system, the cause of many headaches with both engines. It doesn't take a chemist or a metallurgist to predict what will happen if we introduce saltwater into a hot, cast iron environment and allow it to sit in the unprotected water jackets for decades. The sides of the engine block eventually rust through, turning the engine into a chunk of scrap metal.

Even if the gas engine is retrofitted with a heat exchanger and filled with anti-freeze, there are other problems inherent with leaving a gas engine in the hold. First, gasoline is highly explosive with a flash point of -45 degrees F, and gasoline fumes are heavier than air. So imagine how easily gasoline fumes build up at a cabin temperature of 80 degrees F. In comparison, diesel has a flash point of 125 degrees F, which is an unlikely temperature in a boat sitting in relatively cool water. With gasoline fumes densely concentrated in a closed space, all it takes is one spark, one strike of a match to light a cigarette or the stove, to make a major change in your cruising plans. Realistically, though, most skippers know this instinctively and air their cabins out well before working with exposed fuel. Before starting a gas engine, remember to run the engine compartment fan for several minutes to clear out fumes.

Gas engines in a marine environment require frequent inspection and maintenance of sensitive electrical parts—ignition coil, distributor, points, spark plugs, and spark plug wires, any of which can corrode and stop functioning right as we cross the bow of a freighter in the narrow confines of a harbor. In a saltwater environment, these items need to be inspected and replaced far more frequently than in an automobile, and the timing needs to be checked on a regular schedule as well. As both the Universal Atomic Four and Palmer P-60 approach antique status, parts are getting harder to find, and many of the mechanics who once routinely worked on these engines have long since retired.

A shop manual for your boat's make and model of gasoline engine is the best source for maintenance information. Regardless of manufacturer, a gasoline engine with an intact block, head, pistons, rings, and peripheral systems can be kept in service by following a few basic maintenance tips:

- Inspect spark plugs periodically for signs of oil or carbon build-up. Excessive oil indicates worn-out piston rings, which must be replaced. Excess carbon may indicate worn-out valves. Also check the gap with a feeler gauge to verify proper clearance, following manufacturer's specifications.

- Using a multimeter, check the resistance of each spark plug wire. Each wire should have a reading of 10,000 to 15,000 ohms per foot, depending on the engine manufacturer's specifications. Also inspect the metal contacts on each wire to verify they are intact.

- Remove the distributor cap and inspect the rotor and the contacts inside the cap. All contacts should be clean and free of excessive wear.

- Inspect the points on the distributor, checking for burn marks or excessive wear. Also check for proper gap, referring to manufacturer specs.

- Change oil and filter per number of hours stipulated by manufacturer; otherwise, change oil and filter at least once a year.
- Change primary and secondary fuel filters following manufacturer's guidelines.
- Change air filter once a year.
- Inspect raw water pump impeller for broken fins and replace impeller if needed.
- Inspect cooling hoses and fuel hose for leakage or excessive abrasion, and change as needed.
- Check hose clamps closely for signs of rust or crevice corrosion and replace as needed.
- Drain water and contaminants periodically from primary fuel filter through release valve at bottom of filter assembly.
- Check oil dipstick frequently and look for signs of emulsification—a creamy, frothy, tan-colored sludge of water and oil, the telltale of water passing from the cooling jacket into the crankcase. If emulsification is present, change the oil and filter and run the engine for 20 minutes. If the sludge reappears, the engine has a rust hole between the water jacket and the crankcase, requiring complete replacement of the block, essentially meaning the whole engine.

Another limitation of gas engines is that they consume more fuel per hour than diesels at a given horsepower yet produce less torque than similarly powered diesel engines. However, a gas engine is lighter and less expensive than a diesel, a point not lost on sailboat builders of the sixties and seventies. Boat builders installed the gas engines to contain manufacturing costs and to mass produce affordable coastal cruising sailboats for a large customer base of modest means. On the plus side, many of these old vessels are worthy sailing craft waiting to be converted into offshore cruisers. If you own an old Cal, Islander, Pearson, Columbia, or other "classic plastic" with a rusted-out gas engine, one of the first steps in refitting your old coastal boat into an offshore vessel will be to install a new or reconditioned diesel engine, electric motor, or hybrid.

Diesel Engines

The operating theory behind a diesel engine is significantly different from that of a gasoline engine. Whereas a gasoline engine uses an alternator to produce electrical current to enable spark ignition, a diesel engine requires no electricity at all to operate. A high-pressure injector pump, operated mechanically by the engine itself, forces diesel fuel through each injector, and the atomized fuel mixes with air. Instead of using a spark plug to ignite the fuel-air mixture, the piston compresses the existing heat in the cylinder into such a confined space that the heat rises to a point where it causes the fuel and air to explode through "compression ignition." Most diesel engines include glow plugs, pencil-shaped heating coils to warm the cylinders and to make the job of initial cranking a bit easier on the operator. The old 8-horsepower Sabb marine engine, built in Bergen, Norway, had an even simpler system: a nipple fitting with a hole in its tip to hold a lit cigarette in order to heat the single cylinder. After heating the cylinder head for a few seconds, the operator would retrieve the cigarette, put it back in his mouth, thread the fitting back into the head, open the pressure release, crank the engine with either the starter motor or a hand crank, and then close the pressure release, allowing the engine to fire. It sounds crazy, but it was so dependable, it was the standard engine in many lifeboats for over half a century. And it is still in use today.

While a gas engine needs periodic tune-ups to change out electrical ignition parts and to check that the timing is correct, the timing of the cylinders, valves, and injector pump in a diesel is rarely a problem. The bottom line with diesels is they are utterly simple yet very powerful and durable machines that can last a lifetime if properly maintained. Fewer moving parts, heavier construction, and a high degree of reliability when compared to gas engines also render diesels significantly more expensive than gas engines of comparable horsepower. At the same time, greater mileage and reliability equate to less money spent per hour of operation over the life of the engine.

Marine diesel engines require little maintenance as compared to gasoline engines. Problems with late-model marine diesels often are traced to either inadequate fuel flow or worn heat exchanger seals. By adhering to manufacturer guidelines and following these tips, you should enjoy many years of consistent service from your marine diesel engine:

Diesel Engine Comparison Chart

Engine Details	Engine Make and Model			
	Beta Marine BD1005	Universal M-25XPB	Westerbeke 30B	Yanmar 3GM30
Block Manufacturer	Kubota	Kubota	Mitsubishi	Engine & Gearbox by Yanmar
Number of Cylinders	3	3	3	3
Rated Power @ 3000 rpm	28hp	26hp	27hp	27hp
Displacement	1 liter	1 liter	.95 liter	.95 liter
Weight	335 lbs. with gearbox	295 lbs. without gearbox	275 lbs. without gearbox	300 lbs. with gearbox
Fuel Filter	Spin on	Spin on	Disassembly required	Disassembly required
Fuel Pump	Mechanical	Electric	Electric	Mechanical
Water pump access	Fore	Fore	Aft	Aft
Shut Off	Push button solenoid	Manual	Manual	Manual
Alternator	40 Amp / 100 Amp optional	51 Amp / 72 Amp optional	50 Amp	55 Amp

- Change oil and filter at intervals stipulated by manufacturer; otherwise, change oil and filter at least once a year.
- Change primary and secondary fuel filters following manufacturer's guidelines.
- Change air filter once a year.
- Inspect raw water pump impeller for broken fins and replace impeller if needed.
- Inspect cooling hoses and fuel hose for leakage or excessive rub wear, and change as needed.
- Check hose clamps closely for signs of rust or crevice corrosion and change as needed.
- Check coolant level before each time you start engine. Low coolant level may be due to worn heat exchanger seals and raw water passing into the engine's water jacket. If level drops persistently, drain engine coolant to change heat exchanger seals. After removing and disassembling the heat exchanger, clean raw water tubes to remove debris and zinc oxide from pencil zinc, making sure seal seats are clean and smooth. Reassemble heat exchanger and refill with coolant.
- Add a sufficient amount of biocide to fuel supply, following product instructions, to keep fuel tank and primary fuel filter clear of algae.
- Drain water and contaminants periodically from primary fuel filter through release valve at bottom of filter assembly.

Repowering with Diesel

If your current vessel has all the promise of a great ocean cruiser, except for the presence of a gas engine, repowering with a new or used diesel can prevent having to shop around for another boat, which can take many months and a lot of money that might be better spent on upgrading your boat. Before running out and grabbing the first bargain you see just because it's rated at the same horsepower as your gas engine, take ample time to educate yourself on a variety of diesels, paying close attention to their overall dimensions and adaptability to your boat's engine hold. If your boat is currently powered by an Atomic Four, you have the advantage of being able to choose from a number of diesels with engine mount patterns designed specifically to replace this engine. The space occupied by these diesel engines is also more or less in line with the Atomic Four's profile.

One company offering Atomic Four replacement diesels is U.K.-based Beta Marine, which marinizes Kubota tractor engines by adding a proprietary heat exchanger with wet exhaust fittings, a raw water pump, a modified oil filter base, and a Hurth gearbox to produce its line of high-quality yet moderately priced marine diesels. The Beta Marine BD722 is a marinized 20-horsepower Kubota D722 that has been designed to fit right onto a pair of engine stringers originally laid for an Atomic Four. However, depending on the design of your engine box, some adjustment may have to be made to accommodate the height of the engine, which is roughly 1 ½" taller than the Atomic Four. The length of the engine and Hurth transmission package should allow the gearbox flange to butt directly up against the shaft coupler with enough space for an added flexible coupler, which is sandwiched between the shaft coupler and transmission flange.

Your vessel will pose its own idiosyncrasies in the repowering process. No two boats are exactly alike, not even two boats of the same model produced side by side in the same yard. Even in this day and age, robotics have yet to take over an industry still fueled primarily by human hands. So expect to make a few modifications here and there to fit your new diesel, along with its electrical harness, control panel, fuel line, and return line in place. Before taking the big dive into an engine repowering project, you should first attend to a few important details:

Engine Space

Measure the inside dimensions of your vessel's engine box, including the mounting pattern, and transfer these measurements onto a rough sketch on graph paper. Include the full length of the engine and transmission, from the drive shaft pulley to the shaft coupler at the aft end of the transmission. Do not worry too much about the fuel line track or the present electrical harness. All that will be replaced. But take into account such potential limitations as a panel or bulkhead that could interfere with installing the new engine. Cross-check your rough sketch and measurements against the new engine's dimensions, preferably by measuring them yourself on the sales floor, if that is possible.

Depending on the make of your original engine and its replacement, you might need to modify or reinforce the engine stringers. In most cases, it is better to have the engine mounts modified to fit the existing pair of stringers.

Horsepower

The horsepower should be in the same general range as the original engine. Downgrading from a 25-horsepower Atomic Four to a 20-horsepower Beta Marine is not a big change, perhaps a loss of ½ knot of maximum speed. But downgrading from 50 horsepower to 20 horsepower just to save money on initial purchase and fuel consumption could leave your vessel seriously underpowered. Hull speed at maximum engine cruising rpm should be close to theoretical hull speed (hull speed in knots = square root of length on waterline in feet × 1.5). For example, a sailing vessel measuring 26 feet LWL has a theoretical hull speed of 7.65 knots, so you should expect a realistic maximum hull speed, not normal cruising speed, of slightly over 7 knots.

Oil Sump

Some installations may require a custom oil pan, or sump, to accommodate a shallow clearance between the top of the stringers and the hull or drip pan. Beta Marine and no doubt other manufacturers offer a choice between a shallow sump and a deep sump. If necessary, you may need to have the sump custom-made by a machine shop, using the factory-provided sump as a pattern. Obviously, the replacement will have to hold enough oil to keep the engine lubricated properly, so some communication with the manufacturer on this matter is essential.

Fuel Tank

If you are replacing a gas engine with a diesel, check the fuel tank to see what material it is made of. If it is stainless steel, it has to go. Period. Stainless steel slowly dissolves in diesel, like Styrofoam in gasoline, but more slowly, taking a few months before the diesel fuel slowly starts soaking right through the stainless. Spend the bucks to have a marine-grade aluminum tank built to the same dimensions as the old stainless tank. Polyethylene and fiberglass are also good options, but polyethylene tanks are molded to standard sizes, and high-impact fiberglass construction is far more expensive than aluminum. The ABYC does allow 316L and 317L stainless for fuel tanks, yet even these alloys are not totally resistant to crevice corrosion, which occurs when stainless is exposed to water in an anaerobic environment. Water can sit at the bottom of a fuel tank undetected for years, except for the portion caught in the primary fuel pump/water separator inspection bowl. With all due respect to the ABYC, that water can wreak havoc on stainless steel and cause multiple leaks at the worst possible time with no way to solve the problem, particularly thousands of miles from a modern haul-out facility. Stick with a heavy-gauge aluminum diesel tank and sleep soundly.

Fuel Filters

Be sure to install a primary fuel filter with water separator, such as those made by Racor, in addition to the fuel filter mounted on the engine. The water trapped at the bottom of a diesel tank is the natural habitat for certain types of algae that actually feed off nutrients in diesel fuel. Sailors refer to their algae farms as "snot," owing to its slimy texture. A Racor filter will collect water and algae in the inspection bowl at the base, where you can empty it with ease through a release valve. Install the filter in an easily accessible spot, either in the engine compartment or on a nearby bulkhead, preferably at a level near or below the bottom of the fuel tank.

Ventilation

Allow ample ventilation around any engine installation. For a diesel engine, a ventilation fan is not required because diesel fuel does not produce flammable fumes. However, humidity in the dank confines of some engine compartments can cause premature corrosion in the mild steel engine mounts, cast aluminum bell housing for the transmission, and stainless hose clamps.

Engine Controls

Teleflex Morse, now owned by SeaStar Solutions, is pretty much the international standard for engines and transmissions on everything from jet skis, to sailboats, to 300-foot megayachts with multiple engines. While other companies, such as Vetus and ZF Marine, certainly offer high-quality accelerator and transmission controls, the default generic term for engine controls and cables, regardless of manufacturer, is "Morse controls," which you will find in such far-flung tropical locations as Suva, Fiji; Papeete, Tahiti; Pago Pago, American Samoa; Abu Tig Marina, Egypt; and numerous locations in the Caribbean area.

Control Panel

After having priced out a new engine, along with a custom fuel tank and the other various modifications your boat will inevitably demand, you might be tempted to skimp on the little things that do not seem very important, like the engine control panel. Just as in everything else involved with the repowering, be prepared to lay out the funds necessary to buy the best option offered with the new engine. The control panel needs to have more than just an ignition keyway, a kill switch, and a couple of warning lights to alert you in the event of low oil pressure or overheating. In order for you to monitor your engine properly, the panel must have a tachometer, engine hour counter, alternator output voltmeter, water temperature gauge, oil pressure gauge, and if possible, warning lights and alarms for high engine temperature and low oil pressure. You never know when a plastic bag or a piece of kelp will lodge itself in the raw water intake and overheat the engine, perhaps destroying it. An extra couple of hundred bucks for a top-of-the-line engine control panel is cheap insurance when you consider the $10,000 or more you will spend installing a new diesel engine.

Electric Propulsion

Another repower option receiving a lot of attention at boat shows is an electric auxiliary motor powered by an array of traditional 8D or 6-volt batteries, lithium ion batteries, or for the latest ground-breaking technology, fuel cells. The arguments in favor of electric propulsion are many:
- No engine warm-up time
- Less maintenance
- Silent motoring
- Various options for producing and storing power
- No changing oil filter or fuel filters
- No fuel tank or diesel jerry cans
- No water intake or wet exhaust

Photos courtesy of Electric Yacht

The QuieTorque 10.0 electric propulsion motor from Electric Yacht replaces a 20 horsepower engine and requires a 200 amp hour battery.

Finding and installing an electric motor with enough power to turn the prop shaft at the same speed as your gas or diesel engine will be your first task. You can set about choosing the motor, designing the coupling yourself, and then hiring out various jobs to machine shops, or you can take the easy way out and install a system designed and marketed to fit your vessel's size range.

Clean eMarine Americas, Elco, Electric Yacht, Mastervolt Aquapella, and Thunderstruck Motors offer electric motor replacements for your existing gas or diesel engine. All of these motors use brushless, permanent-magnet motors and, as their builders claim, are capable of thousands of hours of running time before needing a rebuild. In theory, all of these motors can double as generators while under sail; however, check with each manufacturer to verify whether the model in question offers a battery charging option.

The Thoosa 7000HT, along with the company's full line of inboard electric motors, is set up as a generator to restore batteries while under sail, adding to the model's appeal. Also note that the rpm listed for each motor may or may not be the shaft speed; reduction gears are offered for these models in order to approximate the power and rpm rating appropriate for the vessel's length and displacement.

If you are preparing to repower with an electric inboard motor, your first task will be a tough but joyous one: removing the engine and fuel tank,

Electric Inboard Motor Comparison Chart

Manufacturer	Model	LOA Range	Volts DC	Max Power	Max HP	Recommended Battery Size	Max RPM
Elco	EP-2000	25'-40'	72	14.7kW	25	245Ah	----
Clean eMarine Americas	Thoosa 7000HT	30'-38'	48	6.1kW	18	200Ah	1030
Mastervolt	DriveMaster 5	----	38-60	5kW	----	100Ah	1050
Electric Yacht	QuieTorque 10.0	35'	48	10kW	20	200Ah	----
Thunderstruck Motors	10kW Kit	30'	48	10kW	28	200Ah	2400

along with fuel lines, water intake, lift muffler, exhaust tube, Morse controls, and control panel. Then you can revel in scouring the grease and oil from the engine hold, and then painting it with Awlgrip or Brightside enamel. Inside this glistening space you will bolt in the motor and reduction gear assembly, hook the motor shaft coupler to the original shaft coupler as you would with a gas or diesel engine, install the motor controls in the cockpit, and enjoy your clean, quiet, new phase of cruising life.

The main challenge in using an electric propulsion motor, of course, is having a dependable, long-life source of energy at your disposal, whether it is a battery or a generator, which offers the advantage of fuel savings, meaning fewer gallons of fuel per distance covered while sailing. We will look at gas and diesel generators in Chapter 3, and the main battery technologies—flooded, AGM, gel, and the latest developments in marine fuel cells—in Chapter 5. Between diesel engines and electric motors there is yet another option: hybrid electric propulsion.

Hybrid Electric Power

As large cruise ships shift from propulsion diesel engines to diesel-electric power in order to save money on fuel and engine rebuilding, this trend is beginning to catch on among some cruising sailors as well. On a large diesel-electric ship, crew can direct power from several diesel-electric generators to provide current for propulsion or for other purposes, such as lighting, refrigeration, air conditioning, navigation, and communications. In a cruise ship, this type of propulsion arrangement involves minimal house battery storage, with a steady flow of current from the generators. In contrast, when installing an auxiliary main power plant on a small to midsized yacht, rather than having to choose between a diesel engine and a motor powered by a battery charged primarily by a diesel or gas generator, a hybrid system now makes it possible to have the best of both worlds.

A popular new form of hybrid diesel-electric power for cruising boats is a parallel system designed by Graeme Hawksley of Hybrid Marine on the Isle of Wight in the U.K. Hawksley's hybrid diesel-electric power plant couples a motor-generator to a Beta Marine or Yanmar diesel engine via belt drive, allowing the generator-motor to provide power to the prop shaft either separately or in unison with the diesel engine through "power split," depending on the helmsman's judgment. The helmsman selects the source of power based on battery charge level, using the electric motor as much as possible to reduce wear and tear on the engine and to minimize fuel use. The hybrid also offers the extra advantage of propeller-driven hydroelectric power while the vessel is under sail. As the propeller rotates through the oncoming water current, the electric propulsion motor may be switched to generator mode, isolating the engine and main alternator from this task. With

The Thoosa 7000HT from Clean eMarine Americas cranks out 6.1 kilowatts, or 18 horsepower, with a 200 amp hour battery.

more battery storage and a greater availability of charging current from alternative sources, such as solar panels, a wind generator, or a hydro generator, the need for running the engine decreases.

Beta Marine and Yanmar have well-established reputations for their high-quality marinized diesel engines. Now, with the coupling of these engines with an electric motor-generator option from Hybrid Marine, sailors can benefit from the value added by this unique means of saving money and reducing carbon emissions at the same time. Having the freedom to choose between diesel and electric propulsion, or the simultaneous combination of the two, or hydroelectric battery charging, whatever the situation dictates, adds up to greater independence from fossil fuels on ocean passages.

Jamie Marley of Jeremy Rogers Yachts fits the new Contessa 32 Calypso with a hybrid diesel-electric engine from Hybrid Marine, Island of Wight, U.K. Hybrid Marine's electric motor is coupled with a Beta Marine 3-cylinder engine.

A Thoosa 7000HT sits on its mounts, ready to provide clean, quiet power for this sailing vessel.

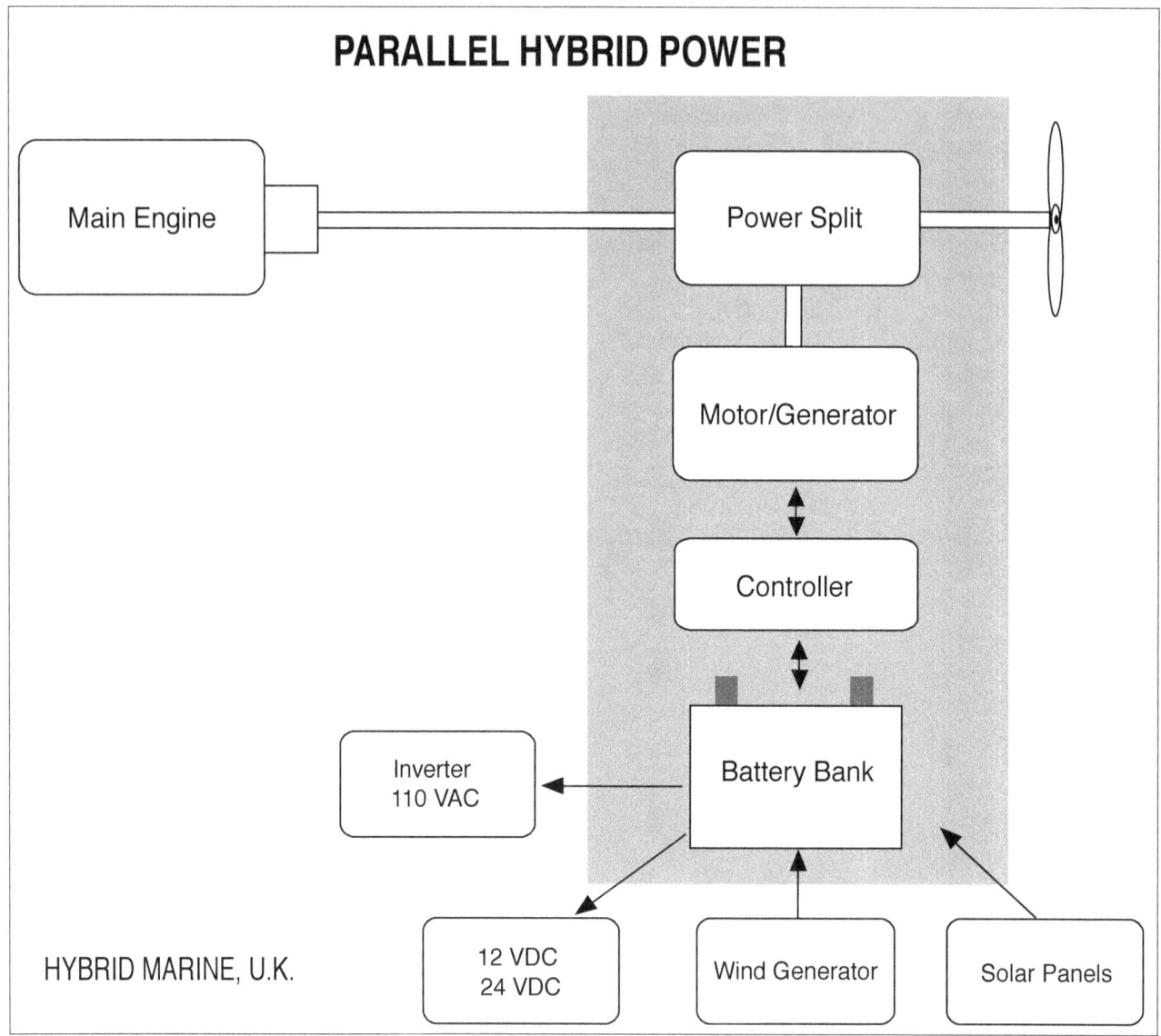

As much as we share a devotion to sailing, most of us can also agree that we need some form of auxiliary power, be it gas, diesel, electric, or hybrid, to keep us on track toward our destination and out of harm's way. The variety of options in propulsion and battery charging power for offshore sailing vessels is making it easier for sailors to enjoy a comfortable way of life on the ocean and at anchor. And the really good news is that these additions and upgrades to our vessels are surprisingly affordable. Take a good look at what is available, and spend time to research the viability of each option for your boat. In choosing a power plant, take into account the manufacturer's business history and product line, online customer comments, and most important of all, dockside advice. Once you have invested in a main propulsion system, it is likely to stay with you and your vessel for many years.

Chapter 2
Engine Alternators

ALONG WITH THE HULL, RIG, SAILS, AND ENGINE, A CENTRAL COMPONENT of an offshore vessel is the engine alternator. This apparatus tops the batteries off in short order, which is frequently necessary, particularly when there is no time for, or availability of, alternative energy sources. Wind generators and hydro generators also use alternators, although much smaller than the one hooked up to your engine, and the basic operating concept applies equally to the smaller alternators. The smaller devices look different at first glance, and their construction and means of control are somewhat different from an engine alternator, but they achieve the same thing: generating alternating current (AC), rectifying it into direct current (DC), and providing power for the batteries and a variety of onboard systems requiring 12-volt or 24-volt DC power. This chapter offers basic information on the function of the alternator mounted on your vessel's engine, plus helpful tips on the selection, installation, and troubleshooting of an alternator. You will also find advice here on sorting out the business of battery isolators and switches, which logically dovetail with your choice and use of an alternator. For detailed instructions on how to troubleshoot and repair an alternator, you may refer to any one of a number of fine references on the subject, one of the best of which is Nigel Calder's *Boatowner's Mechanical and Electrical Manual*.

How Generators and Alternators Work

Alternators, the most immediate source of electrical charging for ocean-going vessels, gradually have replaced traditional generators in most boats and automobiles over the last six decades. While alternators and generators both produce alternating current before converting it to direct current, they achieve this through different means. In simple terms, a generator employs permanent magnets mounted on an armature that rotates within a field winding, using a commutator and brushes to rectify the resulting alternating current into a steady stream of direct current. The commutator is comprised of copper bands lined up lengthwise on the internal, rotating armature. As the armature rotates, a pair of carbon brushes on opposite sides of the commutator direct the rectified current to the battery or load.

The traditional permanent-magnet generator is a dependable system built to last for decades without stressing out the captain with fears of blowing out a delicate, little diode, as found in an alternator. The problem is that permanent-magnet generators do not produce much current. Engine-mounted generators produce a greater amount of power through the use of either partially magnetized coils on the armature, or a small amount of exciter current from the field coil. A self-exciting generator on a small diesel engine with an optional hand crank can be used to charge a low battery. When you crank on the engine, the remaining charge in the battery excites the alternator's field coil, and the generator starts recharging the battery. Sometimes there are big advantages to be had with old-fashioned technology. A modern alternator can be used the same way, as long as it is supplied with enough exciter current to activate charging current.

An alternator uses a rotating field coil within a fixed stator coil to produce AC. If you peek through the vent holes on the alternator with the engine running on your boat or under the hood of your car, you will see the blur of the copper-wired field coil in action. Unlike the carbon brushes and commutator in a generator, an alternator uses diodes, small silicon components that allow current to flow in only one direction, to rectify the current into DC. The diodes are housed in the plastic cap holding the cable contacts at the back of the alternator. Replacement diode caps are available for many makes and models of alternator, but before attempting to repair a malfunctioning alternator, you first need to know how to properly diagnose the device in order to determine whether the problem lies in the diode or in one of the windings. As you will no doubt surmise, it is faster and easier to seek the services of a qualified technician than to attempt such repairs on your own.

Like some generators, alternators use a small amount of exciter field current from the battery to produce a magnetic field in the field winding. In order for an alternator to function, it must be hooked up to a battery that has enough charge to excite the rotating field coil. A permanent-magnet generator or alternator needs no exciter current because the permanent magnetic field is, in itself, an inexhaustible source of electromotive power.

Alternators are smaller and lighter yet tend to produce greater power than generators at lower engine speeds, and also withstand higher rpm than generators can tolerate. Because alternators use slip rings in place of brushes, they produce no sparks, thereby averting a potential fire hazard. If there is one beef with alternators, it is the high-frequency noise from the silicon rectifier diodes that can interfere with radio reception and propagation. For a few bucks you can buy an alternator noise suppressor to eliminate this problem. If possible, be sure the suppressor is rated for marine use.

Generators, although less common on boats today than they were decades ago, are still found on some cruising yachts. Their rugged construction and longevity make them a good choice for diesel engines running at moderate rpm. A generator is generally big and heavy, in some cases requiring a slightly larger engine compartment to accommodate it. Some generators in older yachts serve double duty, working as both a charge source and as a starter motor. The old 8-horsepower Sabb engines used this type of reversible motor-generator system, which unfortunately did neither job very efficiently. In generating mode it produced a very low level of charging power, and in cranking mode it produced barely enough force to turn over the engine. Fortunately, the Sabb included a hand crank for the flywheel as a back-up. You can expect contemporary yacht engine installations with generators to include a dedicated starter motor in order to maximize the efficiency of both devices.

Despite its limited power as compared to a modern, high-tech alternator, the ability of a permanent-magnet generator to produce power without being hooked up to a battery is a major reason for the ongoing demand for this simple, dependable device. If the battery goes out completely, and you can still power a generator, whether by wind, water, or a manually started engine, you have access to electrical power indefinitely. In a small, outlying community with an ankle-deep stream running through town, an automotive permanent-magnet generator hooked up to a wooden paddle wheel and some old bicycle parts for reduction gearing can provide enough current for several light bulbs, a radio, and a refrigerator. Hence the continuing popularity of the permanent-magnet generator among survivalists and many sailors.

Battery charging from generators and older alternators is controlled by an external voltage regulator (the "black box" on the firewall of Grampa's '49 Dodge pickup), which senses battery charge via electromagnetic tension working against a spring adjusted for a specific charge level. As current from the battery increases, an electromagnet activates a potentiometer, or variable resistor (like a dimmer switch), to trim the output current to the battery bank. This simple, low-tech design allows a trained technician to adjust charge control with the turn of a screwdriver. An advantage with the old, external regulators is that when one finally burns out, it is easy and inexpensive to replace. But a newer alternator with a defective internal controller leaves you no alternative but to replace the whole alternator or have it repaired by a qualified technician, and neither option is cheap.

Alternators are divided into two categories: P-type and N-type. The more common P-type alternators are regulated on the positive side of the field winding, and N-type alternators are regulated on the negative side. On an alternator with an exterior solid-state regulator, you can spot the field winding terminal, usually marked F or FLD, on the alternator casing. Determining whether the alternator is P-type or N-type requires a continuity check with a multimeter between the alternator's FLD terminal and ground (anywhere on the engine block). If there is continuity with a reading of zero ohms, the alternator is a P-type. If it reads a high level of resistance, it's an N-type.

When disconnecting the alternator, first disconnect the battery cables to prevent an accidental short. Then clearly label each wire as GRD, FLD, or ST (ground, field, or stator) or POS and NEG, whichever applies, with a piece of tape before you disconnect the wires from the alternator. Also,

This Prestolite 105-amp alternator features a 1-inch single foot mount and a single-vee pulley.

whenever the engine is running, take care never to turn the battery selector switch off. Cutting off the connection between alternator and the battery or crossing the positive and negative leads to the battery during charging will blow out the rectifier diode and require a new or repaired alternator. An Alternator Spike Protector from Balmar is cheap insurance against accidental battery shut-off during engine operation—30 bucks as opposed to a grand or more for a new marine-grade alternator. This simple device consists of a sacrificial diode and connecting wires that you attach to the positive and ground posts on the alternator.

When an alternator is in operation, take care not to touch the cable posts or the wiring with your bare hands. Some large marine alternators produce upwards of 200 amps at 24 volts DC, a scorching amount of power. Because we sailors exist in a confined, bouncing, perpetually damp environment, we must take extra care to watch out for our own safety. Keep the surfaces around you dry, place unneeded tools away from your work area, and take off your watch and jewelry before performing any kind of testing on electrically charged components. Gold neck chains, more conductive than copper wire, are especially notorious for wrapping around small, protruding pieces of metal while someone is leaning over an engine. Just for good measure, it is wise to have a pair of electrical insulating gloves in your tool box. Magid of Romeoville, Illinois, offers a variety of linesman gloves, with a pair of low-voltage gloves starting at around $20 and their highest-rated professional gloves priced near $200.

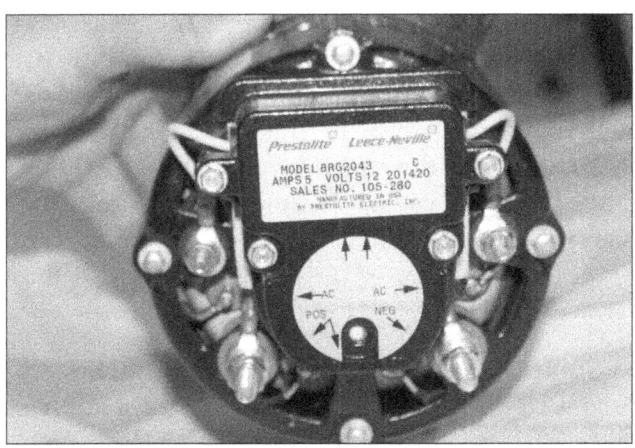

A new Prestolite 105-amp alternator with connection points clearly labeled.

Selecting an Alternator

When you purchase a newly commissioned sailboat, or a new replacement engine for your boat, the engine comes with a stock alternator, more than likely of the lowest power necessary to charge the starter battery. Engine vendors make their wares more attractive to boat builders by making their equipment as inexpensive as possible, knowing fully well that many end users will have to upgrade the alternator and possibly a few other items in order to get the best service out of the engine. Adding insult to injury, if you opt for a more powerful alternator, you will probably end up paying for the stock alternator anyway. If this is the case, ask the boat builder or engine manufacturer to include the stock alternator as a back-up in case of damage to the upgrade unit.

You will need an alternator powerful enough to charge multiple battery banks—at the very least, the cranking battery and a modest deep-cycle battery, which can be a humble Group 31, a pair of 6-volt golf cart batteries, or one or more 8D deep-cycle batteries with many hundreds of amp hours of reserve power. Choosing the appropriately sized alternator for your house batteries will not only charge your batteries faster, but it will use less fuel per amp hour of charge, thereby saving fuel and reducing carbon emissions at the same time.

As a general rule, an alternator should be rated at about 25 percent of the total house battery storage for traditional flooded batteries. So if your house battery is rated at 400 amp hours, you will need a 100-amp alternator. Gel and AGM batteries can accept an alternator rated at up to more than 35 percent of total amp hours. Assuming a 400-amp gel or AGM house battery, the alternator can have an output of up to roughly 140 amps.

Also, you should take into account the size and model of the engine itself, which will indicate the size of alternator belt you will need. A single 3/8-inch vee belt will fit an alternator only up to about 80 amps, and that single belt will be found only on smaller engines. Larger engines may have a shaft pulley for two 3/8-inch vee belts, one ½-inch vee belt, or either a 5-groove or 6-groove serpentine belt. Mounting hardware kits, including engine shaft pulleys and associated hardware, are available for alternator upgrades on some marine diesel engines. If you cannot locate the pulleys you need, you may need to seek the services of a precision machine shop to produce the parts.

Some alternator upgrades may require that modifications be made to the existing mounting system on the engine. Installing a new bracket could entail making further modifications to ensure proper alignment of the alternator belt pulley with the engine shaft pulley. Most likely, though, you will want an upgrade that fits the mounting system already in place. With the variety of high-quality marine alternators available on the market, you should have little trouble finding an upgrade to fit your engine's existing mounting system. Higher alternator output could also require a heavier-gauge wiring harness to prevent overheating and a potential fire hazard. Wire gauge must be rated for the length of wire between the battery bank and alternator, and for the maximum amount of current that will pass through the harness. The installation instructions provided with the alternator should include a chart indicating the proper wire sizes for different distances between the alternator and battery.

Another thing to consider in an alternator upgrade is the present size and shape of the engine compartment, along with amount of airflow around the engine. The increased physical size of an upgrade alternator and the air circulation required to keep the alternator within its optimum temperature range may require alterations to the existing engine box. If the alternator gets too hot, the heat sensor will lower the output to prevent further overheating. Some skippers find themselves having to increase the size of the engine box or build a new enclosure to accommodate the larger alternator, along with the thicker engine pulleys. In some cases, the upgrade ultimately demands more time and energy for the custom cabinetry than for the alternator job itself to make sure the whole configuration blends in naturally with the cabin design.

Some shoestring sailors may be tempted to install a standard automotive alternator in place of a more costly marine unit. With new automotive alternators starting at around $100 and the least-expensive Balmar units running

A reconditioned marine alternators, such as this 125-amp marine alternator from AC/DC Marine in Torrance, California, is a good option for increasing charge amperage while saving money.

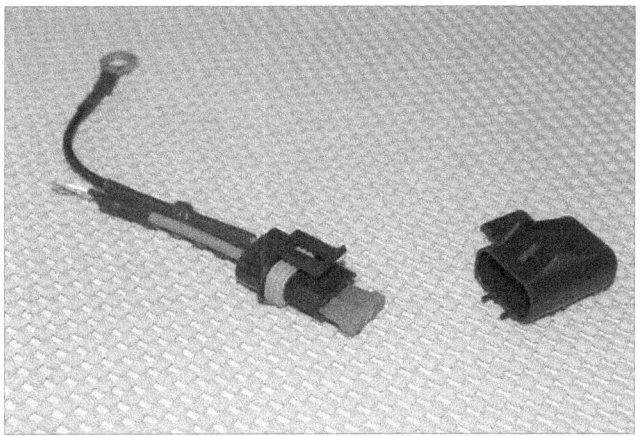

The Balmar Transient Spike Protector includes a 10-amp fuse in addition to the diode embedded in the negative lead.

about $700, it is easy to see how some skippers may be tempted to go the cheap route. After all, an automotive alternator typically produces up to 100 amps at roughly 2000 rpm to keep up with onboard computers, halogen lights, a multifunction entertainment system, the ignition system, and an electric fuel pump. So a typical automotive alternator will have no trouble keeping up with the demands of a 400-amp house battery bank. For a while, anyhow. The difference with a cruising vessel, or any boat for that matter, is the harshness of a marine environment and the long periods of disuse, no doubt the hardest thing a boat alternator must endure. We trust the alternator to survive many years in a tropical marine environment, where it may be splashed with saltwater and left unused for long periods in a cramped, poorly ventilated wooden box, and then we expect it to perform flawlessly with full output and a perfect sine wave at a moment's notice. Automotive alternators are not built to withstand such abject conditions because they lack the humidity resistance and heavier construction that a marine environment demands of an alternator.

A number of reputable manufacturers produce alternators specifically designed for marine applications. Aside from those alternators sold by engine manufacturers under the same company name, such as Volvo Penta, Cummins, and Yanmar, a long list of high-quality, after-market marine alternators are available from Balmar, Mastervolt, Delco, and Prestolite. Balmar alternators are known for their highly durable bearings, epoxy-coated casings, wide range of sizes and amperage ratings, and flexible adaptability to virtually any marine diesel engine. For cruisers who want to save money on a spare alternator, Balmar also offers repair kits, including bearings and seals. The company's alternators are available in the four basic mounting systems used by the majority of marine engine manufacturers:

- 1" single foot (Motorola mount)
- 2" single foot (Delco mount)
- 3.15" dual foot (Hitachi mount)
- 4" dual foot (J-180 mount)

External Controllers

Some basic marine alternators include internal, single-phase controllers, a simple system with a fixed cut-off battery charge voltage ranging from 14.1 to 14.4 volts. You can get greater charging efficiency and longer battery life by adding an external, multi-phase controller to regulate alternator output. Multi-phase smart controllers begin charging a deeply discharged battery with a "bulk" charge, drawing on the full output of the alternator. If the alternator is rated at 100 amps, the controller will permit a severely starved battery to receive the full 100 amps. Once the battery reaches approximately 80 percent charge, the controller shifts to an absorption or "taper" charge of less amperage. Finally, once the battery is almost fully charged (85 to 90 percent), the controller shifts to a "float" or "trickle" charge, which is low enough not to overheat the battery bank.

Some of the latest external controller designs include output amperage control, battery and alternator temperature sensing, dual-alternator control capability, and a selector switch for standard flooded, deep-cycle flooded, AGM, or gel batteries. A highly practical system that will fit many a cruiser's needs is Balmar's Max Charge external controller, which replaces battery selector switches and isolators while the engine is running. Connected directly to the house bank, the Max Charge senses both the starter and house charges simultaneously, making sure the banks are topped off at the operator-set voltage. Some skippers prefer the traditional but less effective manual approach to controlling each bank, keeping an eye on separate charge levels and switching the selector switch to keep up with two different charging demand levels. Since the alternator has a regulator or controller to prevent overcharging, the manual method will not hurt the batteries but could waste fuel and fall short of ensuring a maximum charge in each battery bank.

As you will read further along in this book, alternative charging sources eliminate much of our dependence on the engine alternator and the trouble of having to worry about differential charging requirements. However, it still pays to lay out a few extra bucks for a beefy engine alternator with the latest microprocessor charge control technology for situations where we need to "cheat" by rapidly recharging a nearly depleted battery bank with a high-capacity engine alternator (more on controllers in Chapter 9).

Basic Troubleshooting

If the engine has been running for an hour or more and you discover that the selected battery bank is not charging, you need to figure out which device is not functioning: the alternator, the controller, or the battery. A few simple procedures will help you troubleshoot the malfunction and save you a few bucks on a diagnostic fee.

First of all, remember that a diesel engine can run indefinitely after the alternator gives up the ghost. So here we are, motoring across the equator in a dead calm, the alternator dies, and we are blissfully unaware that the only charging system left on our boat is a pair of solar panels. This would play out quite differently with a gasoline engine, which needs a constant source of 12-volt current to power the alternator and spark plugs, plus any other ancillary systems required to keep the engine running. Usually the first symptom of a dead alternator on a gas engine is when the engine just stops. In a modern automobile, an onboard computer will first shut off the radio, then the headlights, and finally the engine, but on a gas-powered boat, they all shut down at once. In the case of a diesel engine, all you need is enough battery power to get it started (except in the case of an electric fuel pump, which requires a constant source of current), and it will run faithfully until you cut off the fuel supply to shut it down. So in the case of an alternator on a marine diesel engine, we can exclude the engine in the process of elimination.

The most basic rule in diagnosing electrical problems is to start at the source, in this case the cranking battery. With the engine off and one battery cable disconnected to ensure a zero load on the battery banks, test the battery charge with the DC voltage setting on your multimeter. If the cranking battery voltage reads less than 12 volts, the battery probably needs replacement. Just to make sure, reconnect the battery and jump-start the engine with a spare cranking battery or portable starter battery. Turn off all loads, such as lights, radios, and navigation systems, to ensure maximum charging output to the cranking battery. Also, take care NOT to disconnect the alternator or turn the battery switch off while the engine is running, or you will blow out the alternator rectifier immediately because the current will have nowhere to go. With the engine running, test the output at the positive post on the alternator. If it is producing at least 14 volts DC, the culprit is more than likely a worn-out battery. If the alternator output is showing a very reduced voltage while trying to charge a partially charged battery, then the alternator or controller is likely the problem. Nine times out of ten, the problem is a worn-out battery. If you are still not sure, hook the questionable battery up to another charge source, such as a wind generator. If several hours of vigorous charging are still yielding no increase in battery voltage, then the matter is settled: time for a new battery.

Excessive or exclusive use of an engine alternator to maintain battery banks is a costly practice, consuming large amounts of fuel and putting more wear and tear on both alternator and engine. Furthermore, running the engine produces carbon monoxide and carbon dioxide, one of the chief culprits in the warming of Earth's thin, vulnerable atmosphere. That being said, we sailors live in the world of the immediate. Storms, crosscurrents, reefs, and pirates temporarily relegate environmental concerns to the back seat as we desperately motor out of harm's way. Our thoughts are with our loved ones and our personal safety. In better times, though, we owe it to our shared biosphere, and to our wallets, to turn off the iron jib, harness natural sources of power, and revel in the pure joy of sailing.

Chapter 3
Gas & Diesel Generator Sets

EVEN THE BEST-MANAGED ALTERNATIVE BATTERY CHARGING SYSTEM, BE it solar panels or power from the wind and water, will have a hard time keeping up with the power needs of a large sailing vessel. Adhering as much as possible to alternative energy is still a must, but there are often situations where natural sources of energy are not in sufficient supply. In a dead calm with heavy cloud cover, you will find that the solar panels, wind generator, and hydro generator are of little use. However, on a larger yacht, where the guarantee of a comfortable lifestyle may have been the deal breaker in convincing a special someone to join us, ensuring an immediate source of 12-volt or 24-volt DC current to power a wide range of modern conveniences might not be negotiable. And certainly on the largest yachts, alternative energy cannot keep up with massive, constant demands for electric power that rival those of a house on land. Pressurized hot and cold water, a high-volume watermaker, plus a bevy of navigation systems with color graphic displays, not to mention an entertainment system befitting a large yacht, all point to the necessity of an onboard generator in addition to the propulsion engine alternator, at least during hours of peak electrical usage. Fortunately, the genset industry is responding evermore to the demand for fuel-efficient generator systems specifically designed for cruising yachts.

At the humbler end of the yacht spectrum, some crews are content with a back-up, portable, gas-powered generator for charging the battery banks just in case the engine alternator gives up the ghost, or for using power tools. A key advantage of a portable gasoline genset is, of course, its portability. A Honda 2000i 1600-watt generator would be ideal for a dinghy-building project or a lighting and sound system for an evening beach party. However, for anything beyond, say, 3 kW for onboard use, you are wise to invest in a permanently installed diesel or gas genset. By the way, if you do choose a portable, make sure it is sitting as far downwind as possible from the crew, preferably near the transom. If the unit sits on top of the cabin near an open hatch during a calm, the rapid accumulation of carbon monoxide (CO) in the cabin can bring your cruising days to an abrupt end.

Low-sulphur bio diesel and low-CO gasoline engines (See Chapter 4, "Alternative Fuels") in some genset models will ease some of the guilt you may feel from not being a 100 percent "green" voyager. And the fact that your genset will be using less fuel to crank out more kilowatt hours per unit of fuel than your main engine easily qualifies the genset as a genuine component of an alternative energy system, right along with the solar panels and wind generator. Gasoline is highly flammable, something to keep in mind when shopping for a genset. Safe gasoline generators are available for small yachts, but make sure the overall installation meets ABYC and USCG standards and fuel is stored with proper ventilation and spark prevention.

Before embarking on a search of the wide variety of makes, models, and output levels to be found on the market, you need to compose a short list of basic needs. First on your list is determining your requirement for power in kilowatts, plus the space available on your vessel for a genset, and the maximum noise level you expect—the industry gauges genset noise in decibels at 7 meters with the sound cover fastened in place. To be sure, you will need to weigh a number of other factors as well to make the best choice. As for deciding between diesel and gas, it makes sense to stick with the fuel already stored in your vessel's tanks, as you can tap into the main engine's fuel line, eliminating the need for a dedicated genset fuel tank. If you find a quietly operating gasoline model that fits your space requirements perfectly, you will need to install a separate gas tank, which must be free of leakage and fumes and safe from static electricity.

Optimum Power

Generators are more than a mere after-thought in the design of your power-generating matrix. So you need to establish whether you need a genset in the first place. Before making that assumption, calculate how much electricity you expect to you use over a 24-hour period, and then assess, on average, how many amp hours of current you expect to receive from your non-fuel power inputs. Calculate for a whole week, both at sea and at anchor, to account for a variety of weather conditions—sunny, cloudy, rainy, windy—and combinations thereof. Divide the total by seven and see if that realistically covers your daily needs for electrical power. If it comes up significantly short, you can either add to your current array of alternative power generators or invest in a genset.

"Sometimes folks come into my shop asking what size genset to buy," said Don Peters of S&W Diesel, a Nor'pro genset distributor near the Port of Los Angeles. "I tell them, first do your homework. Assume you have everything on at once and see what it adds up to. That's the minimum amount of power you need." Don's plain-spoken advice will work in most situations. But what if the hole you have set aside for the genset is too small for the size and power rating of the machine you have in mind? And what about load surges, especially from an old, worn-out motor in a refrigerator or watermaker, which can draw up to three times its rated power on start-up? As you will read, in order to meet such challenges, you do not necessarily need to move up to the largest, most powerful generator you can fit into your yacht. As a matter of fact, having too big a generator is actually counterproductive.

In some cases, a generator can produce too much power. Not just too much for the vessel's needs, but also too much for the generator itself if it is underutilized. Leif Johansen of Marine Diesel Engineering in Los Angeles pointed out the potential damage done to a genset if its output greatly exceeds a vessel's amperage draw. "When a genset has too light a load or no load," Johansen explained, "it's just like running your main engine out of gear. There is inadequate heat in the chambers to burn fuel properly. This causes carbon to build up and shorten engine life. So it's important to select the generator you really need, not the biggest you can afford or squeeze into your boat." It is important to be realistic in assessing power needs along with the overall daily capacity to generate power, and again, that includes alternative charging sources, which often produce more current than we realize.

The conventional genset operates in the same manner as the smaller engine alternators discussed in the previous chapter. The main difference is that a genset alternator is larger and far more powerful. Just like an automotive alternator, a genset alternator has a rotating field winding within a magnetic stator winding to generate alternating current, plus slip rings rather than the carbon brushes of a generator to transfer power to the load. And instead of using a mechanical commutator to rectify AC to DC as in a generator, an alternator uses a set of diodes to rectify the current in DC gensets.

A constant level of alternator output is maintained primarily by fixed engine speed, which is guaranteed by mechanical governors in older gensets or by a microprocessor in newer models. Engine rpm and electrical output are held steady

Marine Genset Comparison Chart

Make/Model	Peak kW	Weight (lbs.)	LxWxH (in.)	dBa	Engine	RPM	Ltrs. Per Hr.
Entec West 4200-D	4.2	234 w/c*	23.25x16x20	63 @ 1m	Farymann 1 cyl. diesel	3600	----
Fischer Panda 4200 Plus	4.1	230 w/c	20.5x14.6x20.5	54 @ 7m	Farymann 1 cyl. diesel	3600	.42-1.121
Kohler 5EKD	5	120 w/o**	27.2x18.4x17.5	----	Kohler 2 cyl. gas	3600	2.57-3.52
Mastervolt GPX-6	6	176 w/c	19.7x17.7x25.6	----	Steyr 2 cyl. diesel	3000	----
Next Generation UCM1-3.5	3.5	160 w/o	30x18x16.5	----	Kubota 1 cyl. diesel	2800	.8-1.6
Northern Lights	5	360 w/c	28.5x20x20.4	----	Lugger 3 cyl. diesel	1800	1.1-2.2
Onan	5	365 w/c	26.1x20.1x20.6	71 @ 1m	Cummins 2 cyl. diesel	2900	.7-2.1
Westerbeke	5.5	356 w/o	27.8x16x20.6	69 @ 7m	Westerbeke 3 cyl. diesel	1800	2.3

Notes: Fuel consumption estimates vary upon load. These gensets are rated at 120 VAC/60 Hz.
*W/c: dimensions and weight with sound cover
**W/o: dimensions and weight without sound cover

also through closed coupling between the engine and alternator. At least one manufacturer runs belt coupling between the engine and alternator, making the whole genset smaller and lighter while permitting optimum engine speed for a specified level of alternator output. By running the engine at its most efficient speed, you save fuel and extend the life of the engine. Adjustable amperage, an advancement allowing the tailoring of a generator to the precise power needs of a given yacht, can be found in some new genset models.

Many of today's genset manufactures advertise brushless alternators and solid state voltage regulators to produce 120 volts of AC at 60 Hz, but in fact, "brushless" and "solid state" apply to all large, late-model gensets. These include the popular models from Beta Marine, Westerbeke, Cummins Onan, and Northern Lights. A few of these, to include those from Mastervolt and Fischer Panda, feature an asymmetrical, or "skewed," stator to produce a pure symmetrical sine wave, well suited for refrigerator condenser motors, laptop computers, and other sensitive equipment.

Some models are engineered to provide 12 volts DC instead of the usual AC. Fischer Panda builds DC generators, in addition to its popular line of high-tech alternator gensets, for those who want to feed DC power directly to their onboard systems and battery banks. Small and light, Fischer Panda boasts a 100 percent freshwater cooling system, eliminating the need for an extra through-hull fitting and worries about maintaining a heat exchanger. The Polar Power PDC-8080VP-13 5.5 kW diesel DC generator incorporates an inverter to turn out more amperage while conserving fuel. Powered by a Volvo Penta D-1 diesel engine, the Polar Power genset produces 5.5 kW of 24 or 48 volts DC, supporting such heavy loads as "a bow thruster, water maker, air conditioning, refrigeration, radar, autopilot, and entertainment systems." The whole unit weighs 246 pounds and may be ordered with a unique "soft enclosure," a flexible box composed of individually removable pads.

Dimensions and Layout

As a rule, the larger the genset, the more kilowatts it kicks out. Not always, though. Space-saving engine-generator couplings, high engine rpm, and water-cooled generator windings can yield astounding levels of power in small packages. The Fischer Panda 8 Mini DP, for example, weighs a modest 350 pounds and fits into a space of only 23.7 by 17.7 by 23.7 inches, yet it reportedly produces up to 62 amps at 120 volts, or roughly 7.4 kW. This compact, high-performance genset involves cutting-edge engineering and costs a pretty penny, but again, it is only one option in a wide and varied market.

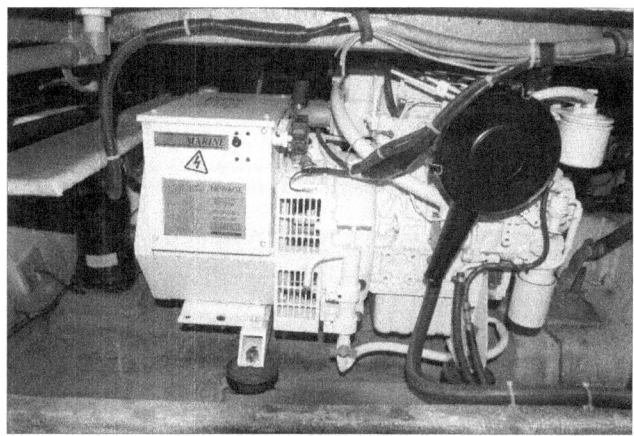

The Beta Marine 7kW genset is powered by a reliable 3-cylinder Kubota diesel.

When matching a genset to the space you have designated, make sure you have unobstructed access to everything on the unit that may require your attention. You should find all the main points of operator contact located on one side, but check just to make sure. Imagine where each checkpoint on the engine and generator will be located once the unit, along with its electrical harness, fuel lines, and wet exhaust, is permanently installed in its hold. That means having access to such vital points as the controller, circuit breaker, fuses, raw water pump impeller, heat exchanger pencil zinc, oil dipstick, and hopefully the hose clamps on the wet exhaust. Can you imagine having to extract a 300-pound genset just to get a wrench around a faulty injector?

Engine Manufacturer

The majority of marine genset engines have been designed for some sort of propulsion, not for operating at one fixed speed to power a high-output alternator. When we hear names like Kubota, Isuzu, Westerbeke, Yanmar, and Volvo-Penta, our minds drift to bow waves, not microwaves, yet you can find all these names cranking out power in gensets as well. Kohler, for example, manufactures both the gasoline power plant and the generator side of its gensets, rather than partnering with another manufacturer, to produce a self-contained generator. Designing a genset as an integrated apparatus straight from the drawing board has allowed Kohler to claim a level of efficiency that reduces engine CO emissions by 90 percent.

Just as there are preferences among sailors for various propulsion engine manufacturers, so too are there biases favoring certain genset power plants over others. Feel free to apply what you have gleaned from experience and dockside advice about noise, vibration, cooling, bearing life, and so on while weighing various brands and models of gensets. The ideal choice of engine will offer the longest life with the least amount of hassle from oil leaks or prematurely burnt-out main bearings due to, for instance, a tendency toward inadequately lubricated crankcases. On the bright side, at least with this engine, you won't have to worry about prop shaft alignment, packing gland, or cutlass bearing.

This 1970s-era 8kW Westerbeke genset, rebuilt by Leif Johansen of Los Angeles, will provide many more years of dependable service.

Engine Performance

Few genset manufacturers advertise the horsepower of the engines in their gensets. However, virtually all the major brands list the number of cylinders, operating speed, and fuel usage per hour. Compare two or three gensets with the same engine and check for significant discrepancies in power output and fuel consumption. Is fuel usage more or less the same across the different units at equal engine speed? The same make and model of engine may run at 1800 rpm in one unit and at 3600 rpm in another to generate two different levels of amperage at the same 60 Hz for the North American market. If so, which engine can we expect to use less fuel and last longer?

Speed consistency is the most critical demand we place on a genset engine. Manufacturers use two main strategies to achieve stable rpm. The traditional method is to employ an extra-heavy flywheel and governor springs specially designed for constant speed. The other solution for regulating speed is a microprocessor-controlled servo motor, which reduces the need for a heavy flywheel and, arguably, ensures more precision than governor springs can deliver.

On the other hand, as Johansen pointed out, one big splash of seawater can render the microprocessor, its related wiring, and the remainder of the high-tech wonder useless until you can order new parts. Life is not always easy for a genset aboard an offshore cruising yacht. You never know when a plastic bag will lodge itself in the raw water intake hose, or when a heat exchanger tube will spring a leak, or when a voltage regulator will fizzle. In other words, it faces most of the same challenges as the main power plant during its tenure on a cruising yacht. So in a rough setting, such as a commercial fishing vessel, a burly, rebuilt Westerbeke genset with mechanical governors may be the best choice.

Late-model gensets offer a lot more than microprocessor control of speed and current output. When you see the phrase "automatic monitoring and shutdown" advertised, you can expect the late-model genset to offer comprehensive monitoring of battery charge, engine speed, voltage regulation, fuel consumption, emissions, oil temperature, and other diagnostic and protective capabilities. The unit should offer automatic shutdown capability for, at the very least, high coolant temperature and low oil pressure. The unit may also feature auto shutoff for high exhaust temperature, over-speed, lack of raw water flow, and starter motor over-crank.

Load Surge Protection

In calculating power demands, we might overlook start-up surges from heavy-duty loads like an electric anchor windlass or even a watermaker or refrigerator motor. Rather than installing a genset rated for the highest possible combination of surges, consider installing an inverter that distributes the momentary surge to an array of other charging sources. Victron Energy's microprocessor-controlled DC-to-AC inverter system picks up the slack when the genset cannot keep up with sudden extreme draws of wattage. This may allow you to select a smaller genset, saving you money in initial cost and fuel consumption, and cutting down on extra weight and space dedicated to the unit. Theoretically, coupling a more limited size of genset with a surge inverter can also add to a genset engine's life by ensuring a better-matched load. Netherlands-based Victron explains, "The on-board energy system, with several inverters, effortlessly selects the most efficient combination of available energy supplies: solar panels on the roof, a diesel generator in the hold, a shore side supply, or a…battery bank."

Sound Shield

All internal combustion engines, particularly diesels, are noisy if not properly shrouded. Most gensets come with a removable noise-dampening cover, even if the unit is displayed uncovered in its advertising literature and website. The cover itself is generally constructed of stainless steel, powder-coated aluminum, or molded fiberglass lined with acoustic foam, and held in place with stainless clamps. Some manufacturers offer the cover as an option, allowing you to construct an enclosure custom-fitted to your vessel if you so desire. Ensuring adequate air circulation for cooling is one of the primary aims of a well-designed sound cover. A small, high-performance genset (Fischer Panda is a prime example) may use fluid coolant for fixed alternator windings, reducing the need for air circulation and thereby permitting a smaller sound cover and mounting hold.

Genset manufacturers are far too numerous to be given equal time in this chapter. However, the following five examples should give you a rough idea of the breadth of technology currently available on the market.

Traditional Genset: Westerbeke

Founded in 1937, Westerbeke builds propulsion engines and gensets that have become a staple in recreational, commercial, and military vessels. Westerbeke's high-quality gensets range from 4 kW for small pleasure craft to 95 kW for commercial ships. Their 5.5 kW genset weighs 356 pounds, making it slightly heavy for its class, but its durability and dependability make up for the added pounds.

Still based on traditional 1:1 ratio solid coupling, this warhorse has kept pace with the digital age by incorporating a full text display control panel and digital controls. You may also opt to install this genset within an NMEA 2000 communications network to permit monitoring on your boat's multi-function chart plotter. The Westerbeke 5.5 runs at

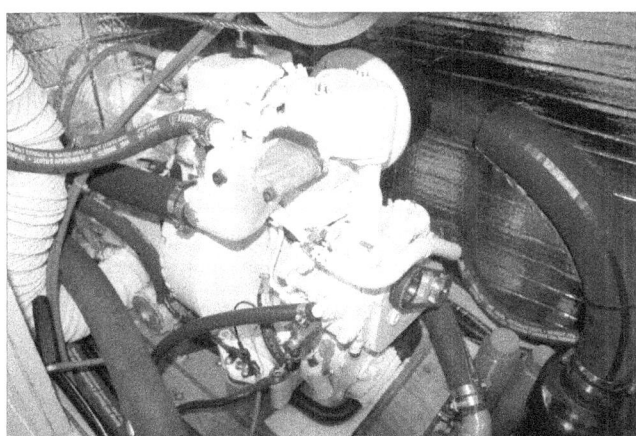

Don and Mary Ellen Leithiser cruised the Pacific on their Norseman 447 Island Time *with this Entec West 4200-D, which they installed new in 1992. A bit of paint has peeled from the exhaust manifold, but the genset still performs faithfully.*

a conservative 1800 rpm fixed speed and consumes an average of 2.3 liters of fuel per hour.

Belt Drive: Next Generation

In case you think gensets are strictly for the privileged, even my Cal 30 *Saltaire* could find room for Next Generation Power Engineering's UCM1-3.5, which achieves its diminutive size and weight through a parallel-mount coupling system for engine and alternator. This 3.5 kW unit, powered by a 7-horsepower, single-cylinder Kubota diesel, sips .8 to 1.6 liters of fuel per hour, weighs only 160 pounds, and fits in a space measuring just 28 by 15 by 15 inches. The optional enclosure expands those dimensions to a mere 30 by 18 by 16.5 inches.

The two secrets behind this unit are the rigid attachment plate and belt-drive system joining the two halves of the genset. The two pulleys are optimized for an engine speed of 2800 rpm, and an elastic, helical drive belt saves you the trouble of checking and adjusting belt tension. Gino Kennedy, the company's president, explained from his home in northern Florida, "Keeping the engine at 2800 rpm gives the best torque, the best fuel efficiency, and maximum lifespan." He added, "We don't use any fancy electronics that you would have to look for if they were to break down in the middle of the ocean. The Kubota engine has dependable mechanical speed control that lasts for years and years."

Asynchronous: Fischer Panda

Fischer Panda, based in Paderborn, Germany, offers a line of freshwater-cooled, asynchronous marine diesel gensets, which they claim are "smaller, lighter, quieter, and more fuel-efficient than the conventional synchronous generators." The company claims that their asynchronous technology produces a "perfect sine wave," which is necessary for the operation of sensitive motors in air conditioning units, refrigerators, and watermakers, and for powering laptop computers. This new wave of gensets uses no windings, brushes, or diodes, requiring less maintenance of the generator assembly. Fischer Panda is so confident in its asynchronous technology that it

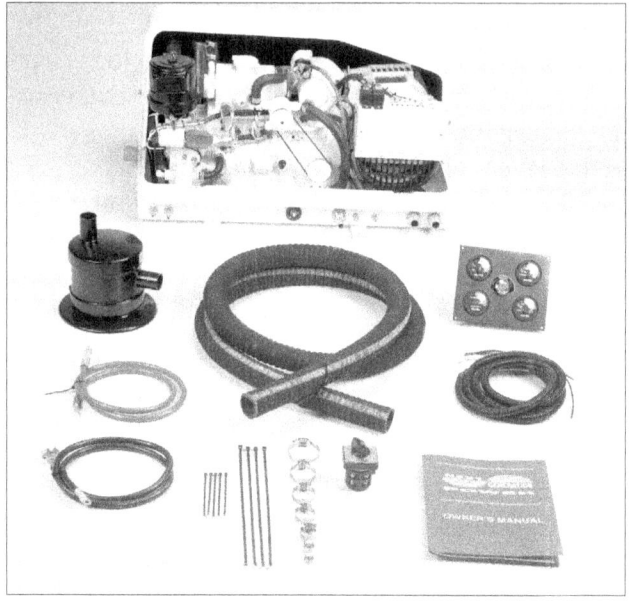

Photo courtesy of Next Generation
The Nexgen UCM1-3.5
(also shown with install kit)
The Next Generation UCM1-3.5 puts out a peak 3.5 kW of power, burns about 1 liter of diesel per hour and weighs a mere 160 pounds without its sound cover.

offers a lifetime guarantee on the rotor, the most vulnerable component in a generator. Freshwater coolant flows through a water jacket in the alternator casing, minimizing the amount of space required for airflow around the whole genset unit and reducing the amount of space required for its installation. Fischer Panda's AC and DC gensets range from 4 kW to 20 kW and also include models using conventional synchronous technology.

Fuel-Injected Gasoline: Kohler

Kohler provides ocean vessels with technology derived from its three industries: electric generators, gasoline and diesel engines, and plumbing fixtures. Ranging from 4 horsepower to 64 horsepower, Kohler's long list of Aegis, Kohler Diesel, Command PRO, Courage PRO, Magnum, and Triad engines power mini tractors, lawnmowers, irrigation pumps, and other small applications. The Kohler, Wisconsin-based firm manufactures low-CO electronic fuel-injected gasoline marine generators in 5 kW, 7.5 kW, and 10 kW models, covering a wide range of vessel sizes. In addition to the standard array of monitoring and shutoff systems, each Kohler engine also features automatic shutoff for excessive levels of CO.

Hybrid Genset: Mastervolt

The Mastervolt Hybrid GPX-6 Generator goes a step further in tailoring output specifically to fluctuations in electrical loads, and in sharing its work with alternative power from the solar panels and wind generator. The GPX-6 produces up to 10 kW of start-up power and then supplies continuous 2 kW from Mastervolt batteries via the GPX unit. Whenever a continuous load exceeds 2 kW, the generator turns on automatically to fill the power void. Mastervolt claims fuel savings of 30 to 40 percent, a message that certainly resonates with the cost-conscious sailor in this era of unpredictable fuel costs.

At 176 pounds with the sound cover and roughly the size of the Fischer Panda 4200, the GPX-6 is one of the lightest permanent-mount marine gensets on the market. A 2-cylinder Steyr diesel engine powers a brushless permanent magnet alternator at 3000 rpm to produce a "perfect sine wave" in a package that looks more like a sleek, new photocopier than a diesel genset.

Got Juice?

Making fair comparisons of gensets based on cost is difficult, to say the least. Genset prices fluctuate, and they vary even more when we factor in such options as electrical harness, sound cover, frame mounts, repair kit, NMEA 2000 capability, and with one manufacturer, the grade of paint your prefer. When you go to verify costs, remember to leave a margin for the unexpected. Or as Johansen emphasized, "It's a really good idea to run your finger down a list of replacement parts and prices before whipping out the plastic." As we breeze past rows of numbers denoting genset output levels, it is easy to become desensitized to the sizzling power behind those numbers. Twenty kW at 120 volts AC equates to 167 amperes, a large amount of current for a cruising yacht. One-fifth of that, only 4 kW, yields 33 amps, slightly higher than the common rating for house wiring. To put it in perspective, a 1200-watt microwave consumes only 10 amps at 120 volts AC.

The environmental purist will find ways to live without the luxury of a genset. But for skippers on vessels measuring 50 feet LOA or more and carrying a refrigerator, freezer, radar, autopilot, and a full complement of electronic navigation equipment, life is a lot easier with a genset because it precludes dependence on the main engine and therefore saves fuel. Whether you choose AC, DC, gas, diesel, direct drive, belt drive, synchronous, or asynchronous, an efficient, fuel-saving genset can be a liberating, fuel-saving, ecologically correct upgrade to your cruising lifestyle.

Chapter 4
Alternative Fuels

IF WE CANNOT COMPLETELY ELIMINATE THE BURNING OF LIQUID FUEL to propel our sailing vessels through calms and charge our batteries when alternative power is lacking in supply, the next best thing is to find fuel that is less harmful to the ocean, and perhaps a bit easier on our pocketbooks. The options in alternative fuels are numerous. Some engine fuels are variations of standard diesel but with lower sulfur or with an admixture of biodiesel. Some skippers may opt for pure biodiesel, or for the really daring, even homemade biodiesel. Ethanol is another alternative fuel for the main power plant, although it is primarily an admixture to gasoline and to a limited extent diesel as well. Rounding out our list is liquid petroleum gas (LPG), the principal fuel for galley stoves and an alternative to gasoline for the outboard motor. So that we are all on the same page with regard to fuel technology and terminology, let us first briefly review, in lay person's terms, the spectrum of petroleum distillates.

Petroleum Distillates

When crude oil is boiled, a succession of products emerges from the distillation process, from the most volatile, with the lowest boiling point, to the least volatile at the highest boiling point. At the top of the hydrocarbon scale are the aromatics, including methane, propane, butane, acetone, and light paint thinners, all of which evaporate easily and must be protected from spark to prevent them from igniting. Next are the naphthenics, comprised of liquid fuels and light oils, such as gasoline, kerosene, diesel, fuel oil, and light machine oil. If you have visited a British Commonwealth country, you no doubt have seen the word *naphtha* used in place of *gasoline*. At the heavy end of the scale are the paraffinics, including heating oil, heavy gear oil, paraffin, and at the very bottom, asphalt.

Through sophisticated processes of re-distillation, purification, and chemical treatment, petroleum distillates end up as products we would never think had started out as crude oil, such as car wax, cleaning solutions, soaps, hand lotion, cosmetics, and mineral oil, which is safe to swallow when properly filtered and commonly used as a laxative.

As sailors, we use substances from all three levels of petroleum distillates. Even if we find ways to avoid gasoline and diesel, the polyester resins in our boats' sails and fiberglass hulls are also petroleum-based. So are the Lexan portlights, varnish, paint, hull cleaner, water hoses, wax, and other items. As much as we would like to imagine a petroleum-free utopia, unless we are prepared to go back to wooden hulls, hemp sails, and whale oil lamps, petroleum products in one form or another will continue to shape our way of life on the water.

Ethanol

One type of fuel gaining popularity as an alternative to petroleum-based fuels is ethanol, digestible alcohol usually produced from corn or sugar cane. Ethanol, as we all know, is first produced through fermentation, the process through which bacteria, or yeast, consume carbohydrates and water, and excrete alcohol and carbon dioxide. Distillation captures the ethanol and leaves behind water and residual solids from the mash used in fermentation. Ethanol's popularity as a fuel has grown from its lack of carbon emissions, which are known to cause global warming, along with a number of health issues.

Ethanol is being added to gasoline throughout the U.S. in ever-greater concentrations, ranging from 15 to 85 percent ethanol, rated E15 to E85 respectively. According to the U.S. Energy Information Administration, most of the gasoline sold in the U.S. contains ethanol, and all gasoline-powered automobiles can use E10 without modifications. Ethanol blends are known for reducing engine knock in gasoline engines but yield lower mileage than pure gasoline. In fact, pure ethanol contains 33 percent less energy than gasoline. Some argue that if ethanol ever does replace gasoline, ethanol will end up being more expensive because of the limited area to produce enough sufficient sugar cane and corn for growing demand. For the meantime, ethanol-gasoline mixtures cost less than pure gasoline, but with the lower mileage, the savings, if any, are not much.

A potentially serious complication with ethanol is that it is hygroscopic: it attracts water. Water drawn from the surrounding atmosphere and blending with fuel can cause corrosion in fuel tanks, fuel injection systems, and internal engine components. The automobile industry has taken notice of this inherent problem with ethanol and has begun to redesign engines and fuel systems accordingly. Many newer automobiles, specially designed for flex fuel, can use ethanol concentrations of more than 50 percent. Older autos and presumably all marine inboard gas engines, which date from an earlier era, should stick with pure gasoline or a maximum blend of E15.

Some experimental ethanol-diesel blends exist, but they are limited to 15 percent ethanol in the U.S. and are permitted only for off-road vehicles. Experimentation with ethanol-diesel mixing has shown best results when diesel is first injected into the cylinder and then is joined by air infused with atomized ethanol provided by a separate tank. Combining diesel and ethanol in this manner produces less smoke and generally enhances performance. However, levels of uncombusted hydrocarbons, carbon monoxide, and nitrous oxide are higher with this pre-mix, suggesting that faster-burning ethanol causes combustion before the diesel has a chance to burn completely. Modifying the injection timing of the fuel mix can improve these results somewhat, but all of this begs a question: why not simply leave out diesel and burn ethanol in its place? As pressure mounts to lower the cost of diesel and new limits are enforced on particulate matter in diesel exhaust, no doubt we can look forward to higher ethanol limits for diesel and an end to the prohibition of E-diesel for passenger cars, trucks, buses, and yachts.

Other potential limitations of ethanol's utility are its by-products, formaldehyde and ozone. Formaldehyde, of course, is embalming fluid. Whether current atmospheric concentrations of this substance are cause for alarm is still a debatable

Flashpoints of Common Fuels

Fuel	Degrees Fahrenheit	Degrees Celsius
Methane	-306.4	-188.0
Propane	-155.0	-104.0
Butane	-76.0	-60.0
Gasoline	-45.0	-43.0
Ethanol (E100)	61.9	16.6
Kerosene	100.0	38.0
Diesel	125.0	56.0
Biodiesel (B100)	266.0	130.0

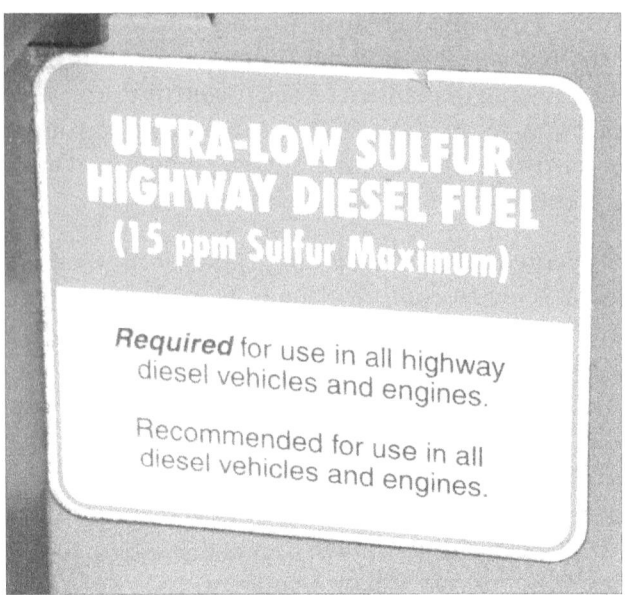

Though no law establishes fuel specifications for pleasure craft, diesel for fuel docks arrives on the same trucks as that for automobile service stations, which must adhere to the high standard of a maximum 15 parts per million sulfur.

matter, as was the case with gasoline engine exhaust before the 1960s. Ozone, on the other hand, is a greenhouse gas that we have been trying to reduce for several decades. Studies on ethanol combustion in Brazil have revealed high levels of ground-level ozone, which can cause severe respiratory problems. So which is the lesser evil, energy-packed fossil fuels with their high levels of hydrocarbons, or lower-energy ethanol with its formaldehyde and ozone? Further empirical research and consumer feedback will continue to generate answers to this question.

Low Sulfur Diesel

In 2006, the U.S. Environmental Protection Agency began rolling out its Ultra Low Sulfur Diesel (ULSD) program, permitting diesel fuel for commercial and passenger vehicles to contain no more than 15 parts per million (ppm) of sulfur. The EPA estimated that by converting to this fuel, total emissions would drop by 90 percent. The following year, the EPA released a corollary law, the Clean Air Nonroad Diesel Rule, limiting heavy equipment, locomotives, and large ships to 500 ppm. Though not specifically listed, small vessel diesel engines, by virtue of their size and purpose, apparently fall under the more stringent 15 ppm rule. Compliance with this regulation entails modifying engine design and alloys, so full adaptation to the new fuel standards will take many years to bring to fruition. Owners of pre-2007 diesel engines have found themselves in the same situation as owners of older automobiles that were forced to run on unleaded gas beginning in the early 1990s. Classic cars required upgraded valve seats in their engines to keep them from burning out from the lack of lead lubricant.

Older diesel engines face a somewhat similar problem. When it comes to the internal combustion process itself, an older diesel engine will have no trouble burning ULSD. The weak link is the injection pump, which relies on sulfur as a lubricant. Diesel refineries are experimenting with alternative lubricants for older engines, but there is no consistent standard to ensure the mechanical integrity of older diesel fuel injection pumps. The solution would appear to be ULSD-compatible replacement pumps, but this alternative does not appear to have taken root yet. Diesel engine owners have experimented with such fuel additives as 2-stroke engine oil to increase mileage and have reported some success. No doubt such additives increase emissions, so this practice is a battle between conscience and expedience.

ULSD also yields another dubious outcome: lower mileage. As with ethanol in gasoline, one wonders what the trade-offs are between lower emissions per unit of fuel, and more units of fuel per mile or hour. In other words, if we are burning greater amounts of lower-emission fuel, are we really reducing emissions? With the new EPA rules, this is no longer up to debate. However, in the developing world where you will probably spend most of your cruising career, you might have a choice. If you can choose between two fuel docks, one that sells ULSD and another that sells regular diesel, which do you choose? To play it safe, if the engine is a 2007 or later model, fill up the tanks with ULSD. If it's an older model, stick with standard diesel until you can find a low-sulfur-tolerant injection pump replacement for your engine. You can pretty well guarantee that when you tie up to a fuel dock in Latin America or virtually anywhere in Asia, the sulfur content in diesel will be 500 to 1000 ppm well into the future. In the U.S. and most developed nations, there is yet another solution to providing lubricity to your diesel engine's injection pump and internal combustion system: biodiesel.

Biodiesel

Biodiesel, in simple terms, is the product of converting vegetable oil or animal fat into a fuel that has combustion traits comparable to those of standard, petroleum-based diesel. Most biodiesel is produced by using virgin vegetable oils that pass through a process called transesterification, in which the oil reacts with methanol or ethanol, producing biodiesel and glycerol. The remaining glycerol is either reprocessed through subsequent transesterification, or used in the food and pharmaceutical industries.

Using biodiesel offers the advantage of eliminating carbon emissions and reducing our dependence on oil imports in a perennially fragile international economy. It also means less fracking and offshore oil exploration, the kind that led to the BP Deepwater Horizon oil field disaster in the Gulf of Mexico in 2010, and fewer oil tankers, such as the infamous *Exxon Valdez*, which broke up on a reef in Alaska in 1989. Produced solely from vegetable matter or mixed with conventional diesel, biodiesel offers us an inexpensive alternative that may, arguably, promise the cleaner environment for which we yearn.

Rather than pure biodiesel, blends of biodiesel are what we are most often seeing available at our local filling station or fuel dock. The most commonly available on today's market is B20, or 20 percent biodiesel, 80 percent diesel. This conservative blend offers more or less the same performance and mileage as regular diesel, or petrodiesel, but without the complications associated with higher blends of biodiesel. One big plus for biodiesel, either pure or mixed with petrodiesel, is its lubricating quality in the injection pump and cylinders, which is lost in non-bio, low-sulfur diesel.

Home-Made Biodiesel

Some home enthusiasts, including sailors seeking a greater degree of freedom from having to purchase high-priced conventional diesel, have developed methods for making their own biodiesel from fresh, unused vegetable oil or from used oil disposed by fast food restaurants. Biodiesel kits and instructions for converting fresh or used vegetable oil into biodiesel abound on the Internet. The following information is provided only as a simplified overview to familiarize you with the process, and not intended as actual step-by-step procedures. If you intend to undertake the manufacture of biodiesel in your home or vessel, please conduct thorough research into this process before embarking on your project. You will need to know the acidity testing procedures and specific ratios of the required ingredients, which are not included here. Work in a well-ventilated area away from pets and children, and use chemical-resistant gloves and goggles, and a charcoal filter respirator to protect yourself from harmful chemicals.

1. Collect oil and remove as much debris as possible with cheese cloth or a coffee filter. Large chunks of foreign matter can not only clog filters, they may contain water, which will throw off the delicate chemical balances you will need to maintain throughout this process.

2. Transfer the filtered oil into a large pot for heating. Using an electric stove or hotplate, no flame,

Biodiesel Blends

Blend	Biodiesel	Petrodiesel
B100	100%	0%
B85	85%	15%
B20	20%	80%
B10	10%	90%
B5	5%	95%

heat the oil to about 140° F, maintaining temperature for 15 minutes in order to allow water to settle to the bottom. Allow the oil to cool off and settle for 24 hours.

3. After having tested the oil for its acidity level, calculate how much lye (sodium hydroxide) you will need, given the oil's pH level, and pour the lye into a separate glass or plastic container.

4. Add the appropriate amount of methanol to the lye. Stir the methoxide solution carefully, as this is a dangerous, corrosive substance.

5. Warm the oil to 130 degrees.

6. Combine the oil and methoxide solution and mix vigorously for five minutes.

7. After waiting for at least half an hour, decant the biodiesel from the top of the mixture, leaving the remaining glycerin and solids at the bottom of the container. The mixture will need further washing with distilled water and further decanting to purify the biodiesel, but you now have a fuel that can cost you pennies on the dollar when compared to commercially produced biodiesel.

After finishing your batch of biodiesel, you can use it straight or mix it with petrodiesel in the fractional amounts you desire. Pure biodiesel has limited shelf life, so the sooner you pour it in the tank and take a test ride around the harbor, the better.

A simpler alternative fuel is straight vegetable oil (SVO), also called pure plant oil (PPO). Most diesel engines will run on SVO with some minor changes to the fuel system. To prevent sludge build-up in the injectors and cylinders, some home mechanics run petrodiesel upon starting and again just before shutting off the engine to clear out remaining SVO. Another strategy is to preheat SVO so that it atomizes properly without gumming up the tiny hole in each injector nozzle. Instead of using straight SVO, the oil can be cut by petrodiesel to break the surface tension of the SVO, preventing the sludging effect sometimes caused by SVO. The optimum portions of each fuel are a matter to be ferreted out by research and experimentation. SVO is not just for your eccentric neighbor with the Mercedes Benz exhaust smelling like french fries as it passes by.

In times of fuel shortages in remote areas of the world, SVO in the form of coconut oil, rapeseed (canola) oil, used cooking oil, and other biofuels has kept whole economies alive by keeping busses, trucks, municipal generators, and small, commercial, ocean-going craft in motion.

Complications of Biodiesel

Under most conditions, biodiesel performs the same as conventional diesel. Biodiesel has a significantly higher flash point, making it safer to store than regular diesel, yet consistently combusts at the same compression ratios and temperatures as petrodiesel. However, biodiesel has certain limitations in its use as a fuel, and in its supposed advantages to our natural environment.

Biodiesel is a strong solvent, aggressively scrubbing carbon deposits and sludge out of the cylinders and crankcase, and sending the dislodged debris to the oil filter. Plan on changing the oil filter more frequently after switching to biodiesel in order to prevent early clogging. After a few oil filter changes, the excess sludge in the filter should subside. Biodiesel also attacks standard rubber fuel hoses, so the old hoses should be replaced with a biodiesel-safe alternative. Utah Biodiesel Supply markets synthetic fluoroelastomer fuel line hose from 1/8 inch ID to ½" inch ID, which should cover your engine's requirements.

Another problem with biodiesel is the presence of sterol glucosides and bacteria, which block fuel filters. Sterol glucosides are a type of fine particles naturally occurring in biodiesel. These particles impart a cloudy appearance to the fuel at low temperatures yet burn along with the rest of the fuel during combustion. The presence of sterol glucosides with certain bacteria that are at home in a vegetable-based liquid may have you changing fuel filters more often than you are accustomed with petroleum diesel. Furthermore, the presence of these substances only compounds the gelling of the fuel that occurs at low temperatures, making it difficult to store in cold climates, all the more reason for some mechanics to deride biodiesel with the pejorative *greasel*.

The effects of biodiesel on performance tend to show anywhere from slightly to significantly

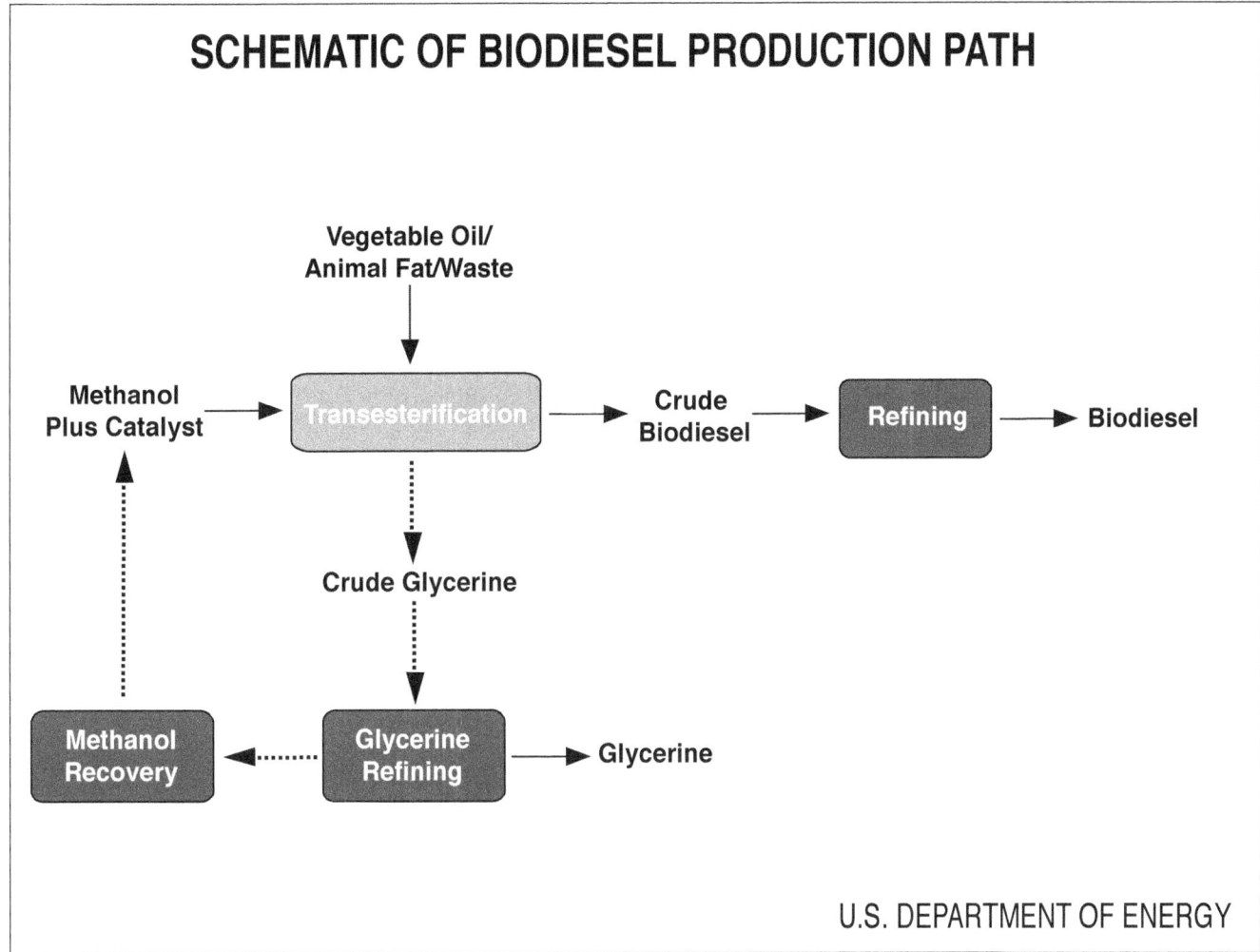

lower efficiency and torque. As biodiesel is available as a stand-alone fuel or as a blend with standard diesel, the proportions of each fuel can have a demonstrable effect on power output. Differences also exist among types of vegetable matter used, with pure cotton seed oil biodiesel performing almost as well as standard diesel.

Aside from weaning ourselves off dependence on fossil fuels from countries that are less than accommodating toward the U.S. and its allies, we are searching for cleaner sources of energy to serve our needs for comfort while cleaning up our atmosphere. A major selling point of biodiesel has been its reputation for producing less carbon than diesel, or being carbon-neutral, since it returns carbon that it has taken from the air in the form of carbon dioxide. However, biodiesel also releases nitrous oxide, which contributes to acid rain and global warming, and causes the same health complications as those associated with carbon monoxide resulting from the burning of fossil fuels.

Research in performance, storage, production costs, and engine maintenance is ongoing and changing as this new technology matures, so keeping up with the most recent research will help you make informed decisions about this promising yet complex substitute for standard diesel fuel.

Liquid Petroleum Gas

LPG is available worldwide as either propane or butane. In North America, propane is gaining popularity as a safe, clean fuel for outboard motors. In parts of Europe and the South Pacific, including Australia and New Zealand, a similarly clean and safe form of LPG, butane, is the preferred pressurized fuel. Lying near the top of the petroleum distillate chart just under methane, propane and the slightly heavier butane are best known to sailors as fuel for the gimbaled stove in the galley and for the barbecue on the stern pulpit. Propane, with a flash point of -155° F and a boiling point of -44.05° F, is much lighter and more volatile than butane, which has a flash point of -76°F and a relatively high boiling point of 30° F.

So, to dispel a common misunderstanding among cruisers—I too have been guilty here—neither fuel is cleaner or dirtier than the other. If you refill your American propane bottle with butane in Mexico, you will see black soot under your pots the rest of the way around the world until you reach Canada or the United States again. This is because the regulator on your fuel tank and the jets in your stove are calibrated for propane, not butane, which happens to be the choice of the majority of the world. The opposite happens to the Aussie cruiser in Los Angeles Harbor who finds himself stuck with what he sees as dirty Yank propane. You can switch from a 37-millibar propane regulator to a 28-millibar butane regulator, but going from higher to lower pressure may leave your stove a bit underpowered since there is no practical way to change to larger jets. Conversely, cooking with butane on a propane stove forces a heavier fuel at higher pressure to pass through smaller jets, there again causing inefficient burning and its natural consequence, soot.

Propane-powered outboard motors allow you to enjoy the latest advancements in propane-powered outboard motors, as long as you have consistent access to LPG. Lehr of Culver City, California, manufactures an innovative line of propane-powered outboard motors that are gaining considerable popularity among cruisers and weekend sailors. The engines combine the advantages of clean fuel, low emissions, and low maintenance in the same power levels found in other well-known outboard brands. Along with the difference in fuel, of course, comes a big difference in how these outboards connect to their fuel source. Their two smallest motors, 2.5hp and 5.0hp, use a hose fitting for a one-pound camp stove bottle and an auxiliary adaptor for larger tanks. Their 9.9hp, 15hp, and 25hp motors use only the standard hose fitting.

Cruisers heading out of North American waters with a Lehr outboard typically have questions regarding the use of butane in place of propane. Lehr spokesman Darrel Evans explained that aside from some slight—he emphasized slight—tweaking of the idle adjustment, we need not worry about any problems with carburetion. The hose connector for the high-impact composite Lehr fuel tank, or standard 20 lb. fuel tank, might need a special adaptor just like your stove tank in certain countries. In French Polynesia, plan on purchasing a brand new tank and an adapter for your fuel hose, and storing the other tank for future use. Again, you will be playing musical tanks and adaptors throughout your cruising career just to keep the stove and barbecue going, and the Lehr outboard is just one more appliance to add to the list. On a positive note, propane tanks rarely if ever leak, so your dinghy will be liberated from the chaos of splashy, unwieldy, red plastic gasoline bladders and their inevitable spills. And if you have been accustomed to mixing oil and gas for a two-stroke motor, you can forget about that chore too with Lehr's clean-running four-stroke engines.

One particular caveat from Evans at Lehr resonates with similar warnings you may hear about sourcing butane in developing countries. Some large butane tanks at filling stations accumulate a sticky residue over the years, either from impurities added to the fuel supply, or from the heavier butane fuel itself. Over time, filling your LPG tank at such facilities can cause a waxy, gooey build-up in the fuel hose and bronze fittings. Since there is no practical way to clean an LPG hose, it is always wise to carry one or two spares.

LPG-powered generator sets are currently manufactured for home use, so we can expect to see marine versions of this technology becoming available in the near future. This will offer us yet one more option and more flexibility in designing the overall fuel and power matrix for our yachts. Small back-up gensets powered by propane or butane could provide just the right amount of added power to fill in the gaps with non-fuel alternative power sources.

Gasoline-LPG Conversions

Converting gasoline engines to LPG is the dream of many automobile owners who are tired of paying high gas prices and getting their cars smog-checked regularly. Just as this is impractical for most automobile owners, skippers of vessels with gasoline-powered auxiliary engines can probably forget about this option as well. Conversion kits to switch gas engines to LPG do exist, but remember, gas engines, just like diesels, are designed from the drive shaft out to accommodate their original design fuel. This includes cylinder size, compression ratio, torque, valve clearance, spark plug gap, timing, horsepower, operating temperature, cooling rate, and so on. The conversion process from gasoline to LPG is very costly and, for this reason and more, irrelevant to contemporary cruising sailors. If there exists a kit for converting an old Palmer 60 or Atomic Four to propane or butane, it never surfaced in the research for this book. Theoretically, it can be done, but it is beyond the scope of practicality for today's cruising yacht.

What we offshore sailors seek are fuels that are inexpensive, harmless to our fuel systems and engines, safe to handle in the confined space of an offshore yacht, and benign to our aquatic and atmospheric environment. Ethanol, biodiesel, and LPG are all ahead of the curve in reducing atmospheric hydrocarbons while ensuring adequate power for the needs of modern cruising yachts, be it in the galley, the main engine, or the dinghy outboard. With proper planning and technical expertise, we can implement the best of these alternatives to achieve our goals as cruisers. At the same time, a convincing argument can be made for sticking to the fuels we know best, but using them sparingly. As long as there is wind in our sails and we are making progress on open water, why crank on the engine? What's the hurry? Let's conserve fuel in order to save money, wear and tear on the engine—and Mother Earth.

Chapter 5
Cranking and House Batteries

YOUR BOAT'S CRANKING AND HOUSE BATTERIES ARE THE NERVE center of your entire cruising career. And our assumptions about what is best in power storage are rapidly being challenged by newer technologies that have matured from the experimental stage to stable systems that will serve our cruising needs over the long haul. Beyond the standard flooded, AGM, and gel batteries, lithium ion, fuel cells, and the latest technological breakthrough—carbon foam batteries—are rapidly changing the way we design our vessels' battery and charging systems.

Cranking, House, and Dual-Purpose Batteries

There are three broad classes of marine batteries, as you probably have seen in your favorite marine hardware catalog: cranking, house, and dual purpose. A marine cranking battery is designed to withstand huge amperage draws over brief periods of time, usually only a few seconds, to start a high-compression diesel engine. A small number of thick lead plates with a minimal amount of antimony, a brittle metallic element, provide enough structure for the standard flooded cranking battery's lead alloy to stand upright and provide a large amount of power at an instant. Despite its high power, the cranking battery's limited purpose means it has limited reserve amperage, which is provided by the house bank. The standard cranking battery for most diesel engines is a Group 24, although some larger engines require the higher current of a more powerful Group 27 battery. A Group 27 battery is only slightly bigger and more expensive than a Group 24 but ensures significantly higher initial current and reserve power, thus adding to the life of the starter bank and more than likely saving money in the long run. As always, though, check your engine manual to make sure you are complying with the manufacturer's recommended battery specifications.

The house battery provides 12-volt or 24-volt current, depending on the model, for everything but the main engine and generator set. House banks are deep-cycle batteries comprised of numerous thin lead-alloy plates containing a high amount of antimony, adding more lifespan to the battery but dampening the speed at which electrons are released to provide current. The house battery is capable of much deeper discharges, up to 75 percent of charge through hundreds of cycles while still accepting a full charge. Up until the mid-1990s, when affordable GPS systems opened up the world's oceans to a whole new generation of nouveau riche gadget heads, a deep-cycle Group 27 or 31 battery sufficed for the limited demands of a couple of cabin lights and navigation lights, the latter of which never needed a separate battery in the first place because they were used only while motoring in or out of the marina at night. The only exception might have been a VHF radio, which was used only in emergencies. Now you are considered a caveman if your boat doesn't have a stereo and 250-watt speakers, refrigerator and deep-freeze, trash compacter, pressurized hot and cold water, washer and dryer, hydraulic steering with a below-decks autopilot, fully integrated navigation system with color graphic display, satellite telephone, remote-controlled anchor windlass, and for chrissakes don't forget the wi-fi. I don't know about you, but some of us go cruising to get away from all that stuff.

For the minimalist like yours truly, you can still get by with a Group 31 house battery as *Saltaire* did for an entire five-year circumnavigation. However, a modest upgrade to a small refrigerator, radar, and electronic charting system will demand more battery storage, along with new cables, connectors, switch panel, battery monitoring system, and extra room to house a considerably larger battery bank, more than likely a single 4D or 8D deep-cycle battery, or a pair of 6-volt golf cart batteries connected in series. Along with the larger bank, there must also be an adequate, consistent charging system, including an alternator properly matched to the battery, plus a set of alternative, non-fuel energy sources (see chapters 6, 7, and 8).

A dual-purpose battery is in a separate category from cranking and house batteries, essentially a compromise between the fast power of a cranking battery and deep-cycle capacity of a standard house bank. For most boats, particularly offshore cruising craft, dedicated cranking and house banks are the safest, surest means of guaranteeing power for the engine and keeping it separate from all other duties. However, in some smaller craft with only minimal lighting, a no-frills GPS, a VHF radio, and a sparingly used ham set, a sound argument can be made for combining these functions with a pair of identical dual-purpose Group 27 or Group 31 batteries. As long as both batteries are kept charged, they can be used interchangeably as cranking and house batteries. However, as with many systems on our vessels, we need to anticipate how we plan to replace the batteries in a country that is not familiar with our comparatively exotic technology. You can purchase a Group 24 cranking battery in virtually any auto parts store in the world. And where there are 18-wheel trucks, there are 8D batteries, though probably not of the deep-cycle variety. But a dual-purpose battery with thick lead plates and high antimony is probably something you can forget replacing outside North America, the U.K., Australia, or New Zealand. If you are heading for the "little latitudes," stick with dedicated cranking and house batteries. This way, if you have to replace an AGM or gel 8D battery after many years of cruising, and your vessel is anchored on the Malabar Coast of India, you can replace it with a new truck battery. This beast will not offer the same number of cycles, but it will fulfill its purpose until you reach the Mediterranean—where you can buy another truck battery.

Battery Ratings

Batteries are rated in cold cranking amps (CCA) and cranking amps (CA), which is the same thing as marine cranking amps (MCA) in a boat battery. CCA is the maximum amperage that a battery can deliver at a minimum of 7.2 volts for 30 seconds at 0°F. CA, or MCA, is the same rating but at the freezing point of water, 32°F. You will notice that MCA is always higher than CCA on a given battery because batteries release current faster at higher temperatures. A battery's reserve capacity is the number of minutes for which 25 amps may be drawn at 80°F before the battery's voltage dips below 10.5 volts. For example, an 8D battery rated at 480 reserve minutes will drop to a 10.5 volts charge after eight hours of a steady 25 amp load, while a brand-new, fully charged Group 24 with a reserve rating of 90 will last only 1.5 hours.

When selecting your house bank, make sure the battery has at least four times the reserve power as the maximum amount of power your boat might use in a day. If your boat is capable of drawing 150 amp hours per day with everything in use, including the running lights, autopilot, refrigerator, bilge pump, and occasional use of the 100-watt single sideband transmitter, then your deep-cycle house battery bank needs to be rated for at least 600 amp hours, easily covered by a pair of 8D batteries run in parallel. As long as your alternative energy inputs are keeping up with the demand, you should have little reason to worry about draining the house batteries. As a general rule, sailors look at four numbers when comparing batteries: group number, CCA, reserve minutes, and price. We want not only the best we can afford, but also the best we can justify and the one that fits the

Deep Cycle/Dual-Purpose 12V 8D Batteries

	Manufacturer	CCA	MCA	Capacity in Amp Hrs.	Length	Width	Height (in inches)	Weight in pounds
Flooded	Interstate	1050	-----	455	20.75	11.0	9.63	124.00
	Powerstride	1300	1600	250	20.75	11.0	10.0	161.00
	West Marine	1400	1730	185	20.75	11.0	10.0	127.00
AGM	Deka	-----	-----	245	20.75	11.0	10.63	161.00
	Lifeline	1350	1675	255	20.76	10.89	8.64	156.00
	Mastervolt	1300	-----	225	20.6	9.4	9.5	140.00
	Northstar	2250	3150	222	20.75	11.0	8.79	185.00
	Trojan	-----	-----	460	20.47	10.64	9.08	161.00
	UPG	-----	-----	250	20.47	10.55	8.66	160.94
	West Marine	1450	1800	245	20.75	11.0	10.0	161.00
Gel	Deka	-----	-----	225	21.03	11.0	10.82	157.00
	Trojan	-----	-----	500	20.69	10.95	10.82	168.00
	UPG	-----	-----	250	20.47	10.55	9.65	172.00
	West Marine	1150	1470	225	20.75	11.0	10.0	166.00

application, given the specific needs of our boats and the design of our charging matrix.

Flooded Batteries

The traditional flooded battery, be it cranking, house, or dual purpose, is the most simply constructed, most powerful, and usually least expensive of all the battery types. A top-of the-line flooded cranking battery has higher CCA and MCA than any other type of construction of its group, with roughly the same reserve minutes. And though it is full of water, it is also lighter than others of its size. One big drawback is its highly corrosive sulfuric acid, which can considerable damage and personal injury if not mounted and housed properly. A flooded battery must be installed standing straight up to prevent leakage, and it must be placed in a plastic well in case of rupture, overheating, or overfilling.

Deep-cycle 6-volt flooded batteries offer several benefits over other deep-cycle options, regardless of construction. First and foremost, since they are designed to propel small cars across golf courses all day long, they are capable of over 1,000 cycles, more than twice the next-best rating among 8D deep-cycle batteries. Second, since they work in series as a two-piece, 12-volt battery, you have more options for installation. Last, weighing less than 100 pounds each, they are much easier to carry than a single 160-pound 8D battery. The Trojan J305P-AC, the Rolls Royce of 6-volt batteries, is a flooded battery with a reserve of 711 minutes, and stands 14.42 inches high. Owing to its extra-thick lead plates, it weighs 96 pounds, more than 30 pounds heavier than the typical marine 6-volt battery. And because it is sealed, spill-proof, and valve-regulated, it can be mounted in any position, a rare feature among flooded batteries. A pair of Trojan 6-volt batteries may cost you a few bucks more than a couple of less-expensive knock-offs, but they will pay off in the long run.

AGM

Absorbed glass mat (AGM) batteries are constructed of sandwiched boron-silicate mat that keeps the electrolyte stable in any position, except

This Deka 8D AGM marine battery is rated for 245 amp hours and weighs 161 pounds.

upside down. AGM batteries are spill-proof, valve-regulated, and highly resistant to vibration. They are also capable of accepting a charge much faster than flooded batteries, a key selling point when we consider the amount of fuel, or time from a solar panel or wind generator, to recharge a deep-cycle house bank. And whereas a flooded battery needs to have at least four times the capacity as the biggest combined house load on a vessel, an AGM battery reduces the requirement to a 3 to 1 ratio. AGM batteries are available in all three marine applications—cranking, deep cycle, and dual purpose. They are available in every marine size, from Group 24 to 8D, including a smaller version of the 6-volt golf cart battery. AGM is steadily becoming the preference of more sailors for stable house bank power. As a matter of fact, even though flooded batteries are still considered the "standard," you will probably find more AGM 8D deep-cycle batteries available on the market than gel or traditional flooded batteries.

Carbon Foam

A new twist in AGM technology is Firefly Energy's Oasis Group 31 carbon foam battery, built around carbon foam plates containing a small amount of lead within an AGM environment. This ground-breaking advancement in battery design severely reduces sulfation on the plates while tripling the number of cycles capable in the unit. The carbon foam construction permits discharges of up to 100 percent of rated capacity without any loss of performance, a claim unheard of in traditional flooded batteries.

The Firefly Group 31 rates about equal to a standard AGM 31 in terms of amp hours (101-116), but somewhat higher in reserve minutes—225 amp hours versus the 200 amp hours associated with standard group 31 banks.

Sailing guru and nautical author Nigel Calder tested a set of Firefly Group 31 batteries during a two-month cruise off the west coast of Scotland and was highly impressed by the results of this new carbon foam AGM platform. "The kind of operating regime I followed spells death for most lead-acid batteries," explained Calder. "In contrast, after two months of intensive cycling, the Firefly batteries tested out with 100 percent of the capacity with which they started."

Gel

If you need a battery that will recover unscathed from deep discharges, you might want to consider a gel battery. A silica gel battery can sit completely discharged for up to a month yet still accept a full charge. What's more, it is highly resistant to overcharging and can keep a full charge for long periods in extreme cold. Of all marine batteries, this is the only type than can be placed completely inverted and even submerged without incurring damage. Like AGM batteries, gel batteries are completely sealed, so they never leak and require no maintenance.

On the down side, these cold-loving batteries suffer from a dislike of excessive heat. Any gel battery installation should be away from the engine compartment in order to prevent an early death to this bank. Another limitation is their sensitivity to charging voltage. A cheap battery charger, or an alternator not producing the exact voltage required by a gel battery, will soon destroy the battery, which otherwise could last many years. In selecting a shore power battery charger, regardless of the type of battery, a good rule is to make sure the charger can supply 35 percent of the total reserve capacity of the battery bank being charged within roughly an hour. Another potential challenge to consider is that with a variety of inputs from your alternative energy array, it is doubtful that each charge source will be able to consistently produce the same, precise 14.1 volts required by most gel batteries. When in doubt, it is best to consult with a marine electrician to verify that your batteries and charging sources are properly matched and installed to guarantee safety and long battery life.

Lithium-Ion

Lithium-ion batteries have come a long way from the early 1980s, when they were known for their instability and, in some highly publicized cases, spontaneous combustion and serious bodily injury. Now we take the safety of lithium-ion batteries for granted in our cell phones, laptop computers, and other personal electronic devices. Today's marine lithium-ion batteries pair up one or more anodic metals, such as manganese, with lithium as a cathode to produce deep-cycle batteries for house banks and electric outboard motors.

The chief advantages of lithium-ion batteries are significantly lower weight (some can actually float) and the capacity to discharge and fully recharge

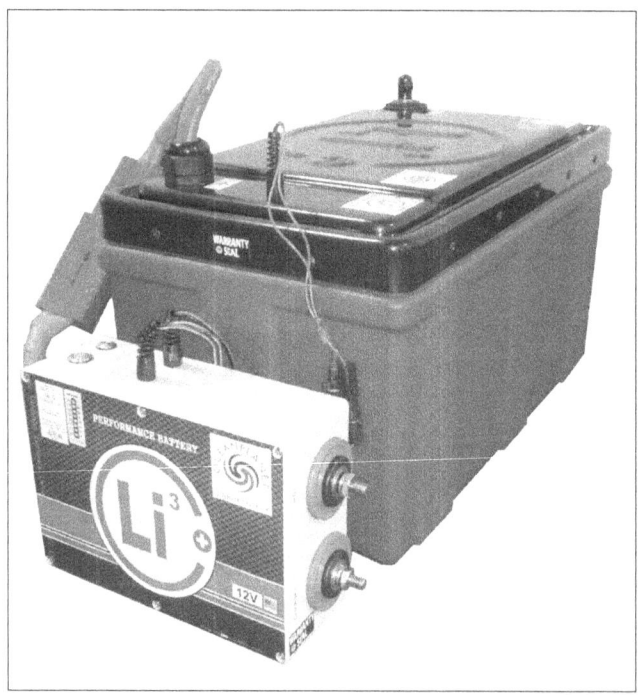

Photo courtesy of Oceanplanet Energy

The OPE Li-3 lithium battery comes with Oceanplanet's signature Battery Management System, which features automatic shut-down in the event of over- or undercharge.

hundreds of times over. Also, lithium-ion batteries can maintain a full charge for up to a year, adding substantially to their dependability and to their cost effectiveness for cruisers. The stability of lithium-ion batteries is critically dependent on the purity of metals in the battery and the isolation of the batteries' contents from impurities. A tiny crack in the battery casing could allow minute amounts of saltwater, along with microscopic flecks of metal, to enter the battery's core and start an unstoppable chain reaction resulting in an explosion or fire, the total destruction of your vessel, and ultimately loss of life.

The solution to a lithium battery's volatility is to isolate the cells into separate compartments, preventing extensive damage due to puncture. The OPE Li-3 lithium battery, developed by Bruce Schwab, America's first Vendée Globe finisher, in conjunction with Lithionics of Clearwater, Florida, contains nano-ceramic separators within each cell to enhance charge rates and to act as a "shut-down curtain" in the event of cell failure or penetration by a sharp object. Schwab claims a 100 percent safety record for the OPE Li-3 battery over the last four years, an impressive record for this new battery concept.

An added feature of the OPE Li-3 is a separate Battery Management System (BMS) module featuring "dual-channel battery management," in which the charge side of the battery is isolated from the side leading to the switch panel. This configuration prevents a problem on one side from interfering with the other. Both channels have high and low cut-off points for charging. If the charge climbs too high or drops too low, the BMS automatically shuts off the battery, which cuts off all inputs to the bank, be they from the engine alternator, wind generator, or other charging source. To resume supplying power to a load when the battery is overcharged, you simply press either the manual or remote reset button to bypass the shut-off.

Installing multiple banks on separate BMS units running in parallel offers ample reserve power while protecting each bank from the others. This improves the chances of having a functioning battery bank intact after a hit by lightning, which actually occurred to one of Schwab's clients. "There's strength in numbers," he emphasized.

The OPE Li-3's lithium-ion-iron-phosphate electrolyte offers six to eight times longer life and greater safety than flooded lead-acid batteries, and is "four to seven times lighter than any other battery" in a given size range, according to Lithionics. The OPE Li-3 battery line is available in eight sizes, from a 12-volt Group 31 (G31EXT) to a 48-volt 9D (9DR).

The sticker price of a lithium-ion battery can be five times as much as an AGM battery of similar amp hours, and more than ten times the cost of a flooded deep cycle of the same amp hour rating. However, if we consider the longer life, greater cycling resistance and new safety features of the OPE Li-3, the cost over its lifetime is less than that of a flooded battery.

Fuel Cells

Hydrogen fuel cells are another battery technology attracting a lot of attention among ocean cruisers. Rather than receiving a charge from an alternator or other power source, a fuel cell combines hydrogen and oxygen within what is called an "electrochemical energy conversion device," which continuously produces electrical power in the process.

In a fuel cell, hydrogen forms the positive cathode, and oxygen from the surrounding air forms the negative anode, unlike in a conventional battery with its dissimilar metals submerged in an acid solution. A solid membrane serves as the electrolyte as power is collected at the positive and negative plates within each cell. As long as hydrogen and oxygen are introduced steadily to produce the chemical reactions essential to creating electrical power, the "battery" never wears out. In its most common form, it produces a steady stream of water as its exhaust while producing electricity.

This all sounds wonderful, except that compressed hydrogen is both highly expensive and potentially dangerous, as hydrogen is extremely explosive. Hydrogen, if you will recall, was the buoyant gas inside the dirigible Hindenburg before it hit a power line and detonated in 1937. Fortunately, by storing hydrogen in a solid or liquid

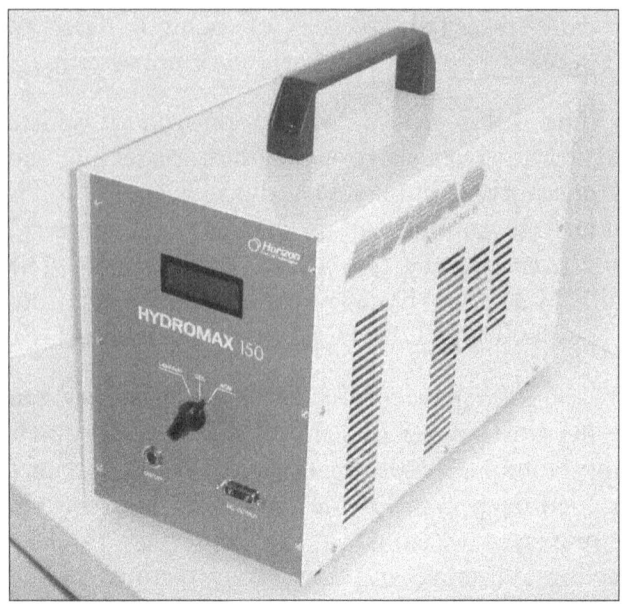

Photo courtesy of Hydrovane

The Hydromax 150 hydrogen fuel cell is helping to revolutionize how we generate electrical power on cruising boats.

form, this volatile substance can be used safely to power a fuel cell, which can take the place of an alternator in charging batteries.

Harnessing hydrogen and turning it into a practical, simple electric generating system is what Dynad International has achieved with its Hydromax 150 hydrogen fuel cell. Two plastic tanks of powdered chemicals, one with malic acid from apples, the other with a salty compound, produce hydrogen on demand, and the fuel cell dispenses the spent HydroFuel, which is harmless and may be disposed overboard. An integrated voltage regulator controls battery charge by combining the chemicals as needed to keep batteries topped off.

The Hydromax 150's main unit weighs a mere 22 pounds yet is capable of generating 12 volts at 360 amp hours per day silently and consistently, as long as it has fuel. Hydrovane of British Columbia, makers of the Hydrovane self-steering system, is the North American distributor for the Hydromax 150 fuel cell system.

An alternate form of fuel cell technology is found in the Efoy Comfort, a user-friendly fuel cell generator gaining popularity among offshore sailors. This system is packaged in a self-contained unit much like the Hydromax but uses methanol, or wood alcohol, as its source of hydrogen. The fuel, packed in Efoy's M10 fuel cartridge, emits harmless carbon dioxide gas rather than water during use. One 18.5-pound, 2.64-gallon fuel cartridge will produce approximately 11 kilowatt-hours of power; the life span of the cartridge depends on the amount of current drawn over time.

The 12-volt Efoy is available in three sizes, labeled by their approximate amp-hour days: Models 80, 140, and 210. Offshore racer and 2010 Route du Rhum winner Andrea Mura installed an EFOY Comfort 210 fuel cell to provide auxiliary power aboard his Open 50 *Vento di Sardegna* during the Two Handed Transatlantic Race ("TWOSTAR") 2012 and has reported that the Efoy has lived up to his high expectations for electrical power.

Easily charged fuel cells open up the possibility of eliminating diesel and gas auxiliary engines from sailing craft altogether, leaving the engine box to a small electric motor producing the same rpm and horsepower as its gas or diesel predecessor. Fuel cells could keep our battery banks perennially charged, powering every electric device on our vessels, including the refrigerator and autopilot. For the foreseeable future, though, most of us will continue to include a diesel engine in the mix to charge our battery banks and to provide main propulsion power, applying the best combinations of available technology to meet our vessels' needs.

Optimum Combinations

When considering the various battery types available to us, it is tempting to optimize each battery selection, including the particular type of battery, for a particular set of tasks. This is okay, but with one great caveat: avoid turning the battery selector switch to ALL while running the engine if the batteries are of dissimilar types unless you are using a smart controller capable of detecting different battery charges separately and automatically shifting charging current to the battery in most need. Flooded, AGM, and gel batteries have different charging times, temperatures, and flow curves from bulk, to taper, to float charge. By charging all at the same time, you risk over- or undercharging at least one of the banks and possibly damaging one of them. An added solution to this problem is to install a second alternator, dedicating one to the cranking bank and the other to the house, which, again, may be composed of two or more banks, each with a different storage medium.

For the starter motor, the best bet is to adhere to the engine manufacturer's specifications regarding minimum size cranking amps. This one battery, with its singular purpose to provide a quick burst of energy to turn over a high-compression diesel engine while powering an electric fuel pump and a set of glow plugs, is almost always a traditional flooded Group 24 or Group 27 battery. New developments in AGM batteries, though, have proven this to be a sound alternative technology for starter batteries, not just dual-purpose house banks. AGM cranking batteries are available from several manufacturers and are the preference of sailors who do not mind paying a little extra for what these batteries offer: low discharge rates, resistance to vibration, safety from acid spills, and versatility in installation. Lifeline, Mastervolt, and Northstar are just a few of the companies that offer AGM starter batteries.

Northstar's thin-plate pure lead AGM batteries are in a category of their own. These cranking batteries offer an astounding amount of initial power: their smallest battery, the Group 24, produces 840 cold cranking amps, beating or matching any other battery of its size. This battery offers 160 minutes of reserve power and, like all AGM batteries, shorter recharging time than flooded batteries and zero maintenance. AGM batteries are typically, though not always, higher priced than flooded batteries of the same size, so be prepared to shell out at least three times the price of a flooded battery for a top-of-the-line Northstar or other battery in its class.

On the house side, the old entry-level standby is a single flooded battery, anywhere from a Group 31 to an 8D, depending on the demands of the vessel's electrical loads. An AGM battery can easily replace that old standby, offering the advantages of rapid charging and structural stability in a bouncing, hard-heeling sailing vessel. Another option, in lieu of or in addition to another house bank, is a pair of 6-volt golf cart batteries. Then again, perhaps you desire a house bank that can serve as a cranking battery in case of loss of the main cranking bank.

The most popular set-up I have observed on yachts over 40 LOA includes a Group 27 flooded cranking battery and for the house either one 8D flooded dual-purpose battery or two run in parallel, or a pair of Trojan 6-volt golf batteries run in series. Larger yachts dedicate different house banks to perform specific functions. It would be convenient, say, to run the lights and electronics off one house bank and the refrigeration and plumbing off another bank, but the average yacht would need

A pair of Trojan T-125 Plus 6-volt deep cycle batteries, rated at 240 amp hours each, offers a flexible, durable alternative to the standard 8D house battery.

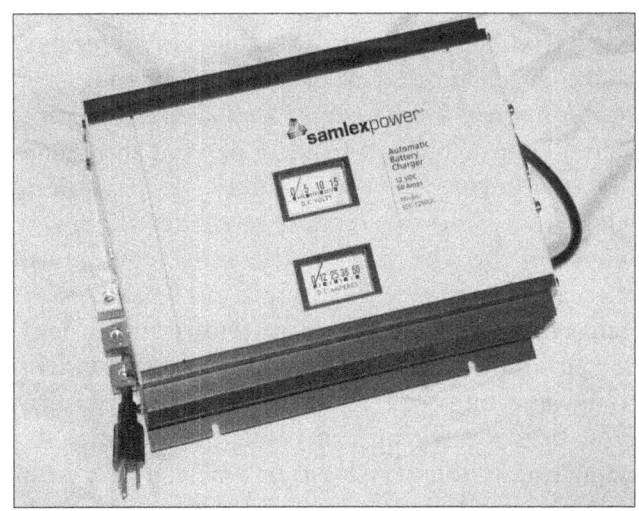

A 12-volt, 50-amp automatic shore battery charger from Samlex America.

to have a compelling need for such an option, plus have its switch panels rewired to accept such a configuration.

Installing Batteries

When installing a battery, take care to protect it from impact, ensure sufficient ventilation, and isolate it from the surrounding structure in case of leakage. Plastic boxes molded for Group 24, 27, and 31 batteries are sold with lids to protect the batteries from dust, spray, and dropped objects, such as wrenches and screwdrivers, which could short out a battery and produce sparks. You can dispense with the lid as long as you have some kind of cover, such as a plywood battery compartment lid, in place. You can even opt for building a plywood box and sealing it with waterproof glue, caulking compound, or strips of fiberglass with epoxy resin. Some skippers install the batteries with no container at all, placing the batteries on stringers epoxied to the hull. If a battery starts leaking, though, the bilge will be contaminated with sulfuric acid, posing danger to metal fittings and possibly inviting a large fine during a Coast Guard inspection. Space always seems to be in short supply on sailing yachts, but the batteries do need to be placed in some kind of drip-catching container. Along with containing the batteries, they also must be strapped firmly in place to keep them from breaking loose during a knockdown or capsize.

The wire gauge of the battery cables should be the minimum recommended by the ABYC for the given amperage and length of cable run, preferably a size larger in order to prevent overheating and fire. American Wire Gauge (AWG) guidelines are stated in both 3 percent and 10 percent amperage drops. Allowing for only a 3 percent drop requires a larger size, but this reduces resistance along the length of the wire during large amperage draws. Increased resistance resulting from smaller wire gauges results in higher wire temperatures, and the hotter the wire, the greater the resistance. This spiraling of resistance and temperature in undersized wiring can result in melted cable insulation at the very least, or worse, a fire. As a rule, the smallest size of wire used by experienced boat owners from the control panel to individual loads is 16 gauge. Carrying two sizes of wire, commonly 14 gauge and 16 gauge, ensures a greater expectation of safe wiring, saves space in wire spool storage, and requires only two sizes of connectors, which you can purchase in bulk to save money. Maintain a healthy store of snap plugs, butt connectors, and ring terminals, plus a soldering iron kit with solder and acid-free flux onboard—all of this will come in handy during your cruising career.

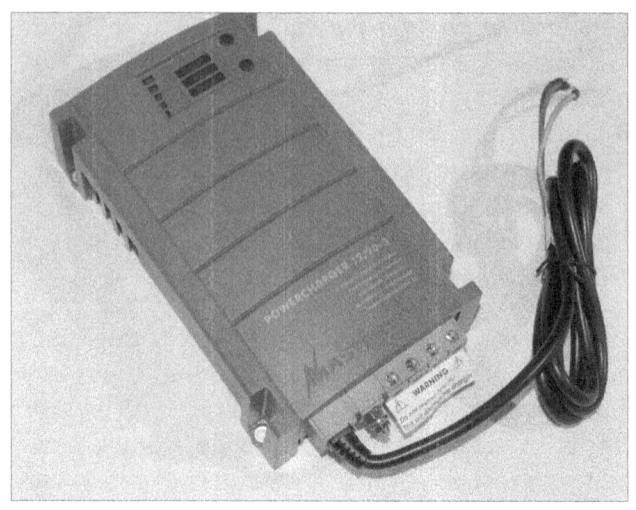

The Mastervolt Powercharger 12/20-3 automatic battery charger can operate on 110 or 220 volts AC (60 or 50 hertz) and charge lead acid, gel, AGM, or spiral batteries.

How you design your electrical storage and charging system will play a major role in the success and enjoyment of your voyage. This is especially true if there are crew members who delight more in watching videos and eating ice cream than in trimming sails, which is the real stuff of sailing. The availability of a few electric creature comforts, in addition to the enhanced safety from having proper communication and navigation systems in place, can go a long way toward making a long ocean crossing a truly memorable experience for everyone on board.

AWG Battery Cable Sizes
12 Volt; Vessel Current in Amps (3% Drop)

Round-Trip Length in Feet	Amperage							
	60	80	100	120	140	160	180	200
15	4	4	2	2	2	1	1	1/0
20	4	2	2	1	1	1/0	2/0	2/0
30	2	1	1/0	2/0	2/0	3/0	3/0	4/0
40	1	1/0	2/0	3/0	3/0	4/0	4/0	
50	1/0	2/0	3/0	4/0	4/0			
60	2/0	3/0	4/0	4/0				
70	2/0	3/0	4/0					
80	3/0	4/0						
90	3/0							

AWG Wire Gauge Sizes
12 Volt; Vessel Current in Amps (3% Drop)

Round-Trip Length in Feet	Amperage								
	5	10	15	20	30	40	50	60	70
15	16	12	10	10	8	6	6	4	4
20	14	12	10	8	6	6	4	4	4
30	12	10	8	6	4	4	2	2	2
40	12	8	6	6	4	2	2	1	1/0
50	10	8	6	4	2	2	1	1/0	1/0
60	10	6	6	4	2	1	1/0	2/0	2/0
70	10	6	4	2	2	1/0	2/0	2/0	3/0
80	8	6	4	2	1	1/0	2/0	3/0	3/0
90	8	4	4	2	1/0	2/0	3/0	3/0	4/0

Chapter 6
Solar Panels

IF WE WERE TO ENCOUNTER BUT ONE FORM OF ALTERNATIVE POWER on a small yacht, it would be the ubiquitous solar panel, silently doing its job wherever and whenever the sun shines. A solar panel has no moving parts—no bearings or bushings to wear out, no liquids to top off, no maintenance protocols to follow, and no chance of blade cavitation, as with some wind generators if the apparent wind rises above 30 knots. The unassuming, flat, gray panel just lies there facing the sun, pouring pure DC power into the batteries. A solar panel is not intended to provide direct power to any of your vessel's systems. And though a large solar panel should be able to revive a starting battery enough to where it turns the engine over after a day of charging under a cloudless sky, that is not really the purpose of solar energy. The main job of solar panels is to top off house banks, assuming an engine generator, a genset, a wind generator, or a hydrogenerator is providing the primary charge current. If all your charge current is coming solely from an engine alternator and solar panels and your only loads are cabin lights, a basic GPS, and a couple of radios, you will need to run your engine for only an hour or so two or three times a week to keep up with your vessel's DC power demand. But more equipment means a bigger amperage diet and an aggressive charging system to keep up with that diet.

The big variable for purposes of this discussion is how many amp hours you expect to draw from your solar panels. You are limited only by the amount of horizontal space available on your vessel's decks, arch, and aft pulpit, plus any other space you create on the boom while at anchor, on mounting masts, or conceivably, embedded right into the deck laminates themselves. If you choose wisely, install your solar panels strategically, and protect them from impact, the panels will shoulder their share of the boat's battery charging task silently and consistently. Treat your solar panels well, and they will serve you for decades.

Photovoltaic Energy

"Photovoltaic" refers to light plus electrical pressure, or volts. Photovoltaics is the process of converting light into electrical current through the use of silicon wafers, or cells. Each cell is sandwiched in a thin layer each of boron and phosphorous. When a photon passes through a silicon cell, the phosphorus in the "N-type" layer produces a negative charge, and the silicon in the "P-type" layer produces a positive charge. The close proximity of the positive and negative charges induces galvanic action, in which electrons pass from the N-type anode layer to the P-type cathode layer, since electricity always flows from negative to positive. This current then flows through thin metal strips connecting the cells so that power comes together at a junction box and passes on to a load or a battery bank. A layer of tempered glass sealed in rubber protects the silicon wafers from dust and humidity.

Rigid solar panels are fabricated from either monocrystalline or multicrystalline cells. Monocrystalline photovoltaic cells are cut from a single cylindrical rod of silicon, whereas multicrystalline cells are cut from a square rod and are less expensive to manufacture. Monocrystalline cells tend to be more isolated from each other and therefore are less likely to short each other out the way multicrystalline cells occasionally do. In order to economize on space, mono cells are generally trimmed square with rounded corners for better fit, and modern manufacturing techniques have eliminated most of the problems with shorts between these cells. Mono cells were the original type of solar panel marketed to the public, and they still offer the highest quality, and cost, of photovoltaic panels.

The principal variables affecting solar panel output wattage are the size of each cell, the number of cells (usually 36), and the intensity of sunlight. The larger the cell, the more light it can collect, and therefore the more amperage in can produce. A dependable way of estimating solar charge output in the tropics is first to divide the panel's rated wattage by 14 volts, which will give you the amperage. Since a normal full day in the tropics is 10 hours, multiply the amperage by 10. Finally, because most solar panels produce only about half of their rated wattage, divide that result by two and you have a good estimate of the panel's amp hours. Using a 40-watt panel as an example, 40 watts divided by 14 volts gives us 2.86 amps. When we multiply 2.86 amps by 10 hours, we get 28.6 amp hours, which we divide by two in order to yield a more realistic 14.3 amp hours per day, or about 100 amp hours per week. Not enough power?

Okay, let's try two 65-watt panels, a combination that is becoming popular on cruising boats these days. Assuming we have only half the amperage available, we calculate thus: $(65 \div 14) \times 10 = 46.4$ am hours per day, or 325 amp hours per week. This is 3.24 times the current from a single 40-watt panel and a major contribution to your house bank's reserve power. A 70-amp alternator producing 30 amps at idle speed will need to run for nearly 11 hours per week, or a little over an hour and a half per day, to keep up with the two 65-watt panels. At $3.50 per gallon of fuel, that comes to roughly $38.00 per week, so a pair of 65-watt solar panels costing $500 will have paid for themselves after about 13 weeks, or three months. Another thing to think about: as diesel prices have gradually risen, solar panels have come down in price over the last 30 years (if we correct for inflation), and we can probably expect these trends to continue.

Rigid Solar Panels

Top-of-the-line, marine-grade solar panels, like those produced by Siemens, are constructed of monocrystalline cells with a thick polymer coating on the back of the panel. These panels are secured to a strong anodized aluminum frame that can be mounted on a fixed structure or an adjustable base. *Saltaire* has had the same Siemens 38-watt panel mounted on her aft pulpit for nearly 20 years, and after countless dousings in tall breaking seas, the panel is still faithfully keeping the house bank topped off with a small charge controller to prevent it from frying the Group 31 battery. The panel is mounted onto one-inch stainless steel tubing with a pair of plastic clamps with an adjustable arm allowing the panel to be dropped in close quarters, as it was when *Saltaire* was side-tied to another vessel during a transit of the Panama Canal.

A generation ago, rigid, high-quality aluminum-framed solar trickle chargers were available in sizes as small as 5 watts. Today, a lot of cheaply built polycrystalline solar panels fill that niche with small units touted as "marine" quality but leave us with considerable doubt. They range from 10 watts to 30 watts or more but may not include tempered glass, anodized aluminum framing, or waterproofing in their advertising, leaving some doubt as to their quality. These panels are best left for home or RV use, where they serve an adjunct rather than critical role in the overall charging matrix.

Sunsei, a prominent player in the marine charge controller industry, also manufactures high-power solar panels. Its largest panel is rated at 130 watts with a daily output of roughly 46 amp hours each, equating to an impressive 650 amp hours per week.

All that power from a space of 60.24 by 28 inches. A pair of these panels could easily find a home atop an arch on a vessel of over 35 feet and, with a solid 10 hours of direct sunlight per day, provide enough juice to power a small refrigerator, a color chart plotter, and running lights while having enough amperage left over to rag chew on your favorite ham or marine SSB cruiser net every day.

Flexible Solar Panels

Another type of photovoltaic cell, amorphous thin-film silicon, is less efficient than its predecessors but is capable of being mounted in a flexible plastic structure. Flexible solar panels usually serve as back-ups to the main panels, or as trickle chargers for boats left unattended for long periods. Some flexible panels are thin enough to be rolled up for easy storage until they are needed for back-up while the crew is away from the vessel for an extended period. Because of their use primarily as trickle chargers, most of the flexible and semi-flexible solar panels you will see slung over mainsail covers in cruiser anchorages are limited to 25 watts, although a few are rated as high as 50 watts. Owing to their complex construction, a flexible panel of a given amp hour rating is generally twice the price of a rigid panel of the same power.

Despite their greater expense, flexible panels pay for themselves through their high impact resistance and the creative ways in which they can be installed. Whereas an errant spinnaker pole could shatter the tempered glass covering of a rigid solar panel, it will bounce off a well-constructed flexible panel. Flexible panels can be sewn onto weather cloth, dodgers, biminis, mainsail covers, and dinghy covers, completely out of the way of crew traffic.

Uni-Solar, Spectra, Nature Power, and PowerFilm all produce flexible panels with cruising sailors as their primary market. Uni-Solar's panels may be rolled up for storage and also offer the benefit of lower prices. Spectra produces three semi-flexible panels of 5, 10, and 20 watts respectively. Nature Power's panels range from only 7 to 28 watts but offer the unique advantage in that they may be rolled up like a chart and stored in a tube. These panels won't keep up with the demanding daily regimen of a cruising yacht but are effective as trickle chargers for weekend boats or cruising vessels left unattended for long periods. One big benefit of low-output panels is that they usually do not require a controller to prevent them from toasting a battery.

Non-Marine Panels

The "off-grid" movement gaining traction with landlubbers over the last few years has spawned a whole new market for purveyors of solar panels and related equipment to install 110-volt AC electrical systems completely independent of power lines and utility bills. While such systems are laudable, they are hardly a substitute for the 30 amps of power available in any room of a house, 24 hours a day, 365 days a year. To the manufacturers' credit, though, these systems have come a long way in quality from where they were 20 years ago. You can go to your local chain hardware store and purchase a kit containing a 1.25 kilowatt set of panels, a large battery, a full sinewave AC inverter, plus a set of house outlets, all for under two grand. Pretty impressive.

For the cruising sailor, such self-contained kits pose two problems: one, they may include "marine" in their advertising, though let's face it, they are not marine-grade equipment; and two, they are no less expensive and sometimes actually more expensive than comparable marine panels. Indeed, some kit panels will be cheaper than marine solar panels, but that is all the more reason to stick with the real thing. Shore solar equipment can be expected to have inferior UV and weather resistance, and the panels, although touted as "impact resistant," cannot compare to a high-quality marine panel with a thick layer of tempered glass and a waterproof junction box. As with virtually all equipment on a long-range cruising vessel, we want marine-grade hardware. We want our vessels to comply fully with Lloyds of London, the ABYC, and the U.S. Coast Guard with respect to wiring, connectors, radio interference, impact resistance, AC and DC control panels, fuses, inverters, safety standards, and the list goes on. If your vessel has no hull insurance, you have no room to take chances with flimsy shore equipment. If your vessel does have hull insurance, your underwriter definitely requires strict compliance with a nationally recognized set of electrical safety standards.

Electrical Installation

The steps to installing a solar panel are fairly straightforward and easy to follow. However, first having some understanding of the materials and components involved will ensure a solid installation. On the back of any marine-grade panel you will find a junction box where you will connect the positive and negative wire leads. The junction box, although generally hidden from direct sunlight, is constructed of a highly UV-resistant polymer. The lid joins the box with a rubber seal to prevent water intrusion, and the wire ports are rubber-sealed in like manner. Inside the box there should be diodes to keep electrical current from running back into the panels and discharging the battery at night. You will also find wire clamps to connect the leads to the battery. Make sure you use high-quality, tinned, marine-grade wire and connectors, such as those produced by Ancor/Marinco—NOT the cheap stuff you find at a home hardware store—and the size recommended by the panel manufacturer. Undersized wire, especially over long runs, can get hot enough to melt the plastic cover, short out, and cause a fire. For long runs you might want to step up the size, probably from 18 gauge to 16 gauge, just to be on the safe side. There should be no wire splices, not even with heat-shrink butt connectors, anywhere outside the cabin for any electrical installation. Period. And although installation instructions will not require it, you may want to tin the exposed tip of each wire with solder to keep the strands in one solid piece. This adds extra protection from corrosion and makes it a lot easier to install the wires.

Some solar panel sales literature advertises "self-regulating" panels. Fortunately, this type of misleading sales pitch occurs mainly outside the marine solar power industry. Just to put the matter to rest, there is no such thing as a self-regulating solar panel. When the sun shines, the panel cranks out DC current until the big, flaming ball of plasma dips below the horizon, and that's all there is to it. In order to regulate the solar panel charge properly, you can choose from a number of surprisingly affordable microprocessed charge controllers to keep the solar panels from frying your battery and leaving the lead posts looking like charcoal. I'm not kidding. This happened to *Saltaire*'s house battery before I purchased a Sunsei solar panel controller to regulate the charge coming from the 38-watt Siemens panel. The tiny microprocessed controller is so small, it fits in the palm of my hand. The Sunsei controller cost me about what I pay for a taco plate, two margaritas, and a tequila shooter at The Green Onion in San Pedro, and the device has more than paid for itself by doubling the lifespan of the house battery.

A microprocessor-based solar panel charge controller senses battery charge and temperature and regulates charging through the three standard phases used by contemporary battery chargers:

This panel is neatly mounted over the aft lifeline, out of the way of foot traffic.

These two large panels are firmly mounted over the lifeline yet safely out of the way of crew.

These two solar panels on swivels offer versatility, desperately needed on a narrow stern.

bulk, taper, and float. On the Sunsei, you can see where the charge process is by the green LED light: a steady green light is bulk, a slow flicker is absorption, and a fast flicker is float. It also has a diode to prevent battery discharge at night, just in case the solar panel lacks such protection.

Mastervolt and a number of other manufacturers offer marine-grade solar panel controllers, although some are a bit larger and more complex than the tiny Sunsei. The Mastervolt Solar ChargeMaster has three-stage charging adjustable for flooded, AGM, and gel batteries and can be used for both 12-volt and 24-volt banks. With its extra features, naturally, the ChargeMaster costs significantly more than the Sunsei and is better suited to larger yachts. Flexcharge offers two small controllers for alternative energy sources, including solar panels and wind generators, also surprisingly small for the job they perform and very reasonably priced (see Chapter 9, "Voltage Regulators and Controllers").

Mounting Techniques

One of the great, alluring aspects of solar panels is their adaptability to a wide range of creative mounting systems. Walk around any cruising yacht marina and you will find yourself shaking your head in amazement at how people utilize dodgers, biminis, arches, aft pulpits, and open space above the decks to create solid, attractive mounts from glimmering, electro-polished stainless steel tubes and connectors. In planning your solar panel installation, there are a number of things to consider. First, the panels must be out of the way so as not to create an obstacle to easy access to all areas of the deck and running rigging. Mounting poles or other supports should be anchored toward the far inner or outer edges of decks to keep decks open for foot traffic. Also, a sharp corner on an aluminum panel frame can inflict injury, the last thing we need while on passage, so either keep those corners away from crew, or find a way to cover the corners with plastic or rubber protectors. Next, when mounting large panels on an arch or atop a dodger or bimini, think of the aerodynamics involved and the possibility of a panel taking flight in a full gale. Every part of the support structure holding the panel, and holding the structure under the panel's support structure, needs to be anchored solidly to the deck. If you currently live and sail in a region that generally has mild weather, such as Southern California, it is easy to lull yourself into believing the rest of the world is more or less the same way. Yet many cruising grounds around the world, including the Med, the Caribbean, and the South Pacific west of Tahiti, are famous for gales that can linger for days, sometimes weeks, without reprieve. Last, take care to see that the panels are more or less free of shadowing in order to ensure a steady stream of charging current. Contrary to popular belief, minimal shadowing will not cut off a solar panel's charging action. When you see a shadow across a panel's black glass surface, it appears as if not a single photon is hitting that portion. But in reality, the half-inch-wide dark line from the backstay is not completely blotting out light, only some of it. That narrow portion of the panel is definitely receiving light and producing electrical current, just not as much as the rest of the panel.

Designing and fabricating a strong, attractive solar panel mounting structure will require some careful planning with regard to the shape, styling, and positioning of the apparatus. Some installations are quite simple, requiring little more than a hacksaw, a short length of stainless tubing, and a few tube connectors. Stainless U-bolts or UV-resistant clamps made of durable marine plastics, such as polypropylene, PVC, or high-density polyethylene, can help make use of an aft pulpit, an arch, or the hand rails above a bimini. For a somewhat more elaborate structure,

This pair of solar panels shares an arch with a KVH Tracvision satellite television dome.

This pair of solar panels shares space atop an arch with a Raymarine radar dome.

a separate, dedicated mast tube supported by a diagonal pair of stainless tubes for lateral support can be fitted with a crossbar at the top, allowing one or two swiveling panels to be mounted on the crossbar. A pair of diagonally mounted support tubes set 90 degrees apart gives amply strong support to a mast carrying a solar panel or a wind generator. This free-standing equipment mast, anchored to a swivel base, allows you to disconnect the diagonal supports and lash the mast to the deck during severe storms.

In selecting stainless tubing, it is tempting to purchase the unpolished variety in order to save money. Using electro-polished stainless tubing, though, is not only about vanity. The tighter surface grain structure produced by electropolishing puts up a stronger defense against attacks by saltwater ions than the more porous surfaces of lower-grade tubing. Electropolished tubing is certainly more expensive, but it will resist oxidation and keep its magnificent mirror shine while brown splotches of oxidation mar the lesser grades.

Larger, more elaborate installations may involve tube bending and welding, both of which demand considerable practice, if not professional training. For mounting panels to an existing structure, such as a bimini or dodger frame, or for creating a complex platform, such as a swiveling mast or an arch, you are best advised to seek the services of a shop specializing in the design and fabrication of stainless steel marine structures. The home welder accustomed to fabricating with a wire-feed arc welder or an oxyacetylene torch may not have the equipment or skill to handle stainless fabrication, which requires a TIG (tungsten inert gas) welding outfit. An experienced stainless steel artisan can design, shape, weld, and polish a beautifully gleaming sculpture that will have your cruiser cocktail party guests spinning their heads in awe. However, get ready to dig deep into your cruising kitty to pay for such services.

If you wish to design and build your own mounting structures, you should be able to use standard stainless tube fittings, the type used for dodgers and biminis, for your solar panel mounting system. The functionality and appearance of your creations will reflect not only your design prowess but also the quality of materials you use in fabricating the structures. By using only electropolished 304 stainless tubing and 316 stainless fittings, you can create structures that will rival a professional installation. Having a machine shop nearby for welding parts and bending stainless tubing will save you time and probably money as well when you consider how easy it is to screw things up and have to start over again. Remember, once you have bent a length of metal pipe or tubing ($10+ per foot for 1-inch OD electropolished 304 stainless tubing), you cannot unbend it. As for specialized fittings, if you cannot find what you need at the local chandlery, sketch the part you desire with precise measurements and find a machine shop to fashion the part from a block of 316 stainless steel or UV-resistant plastic with a DNC milling machine. Many small machine shops enjoy taking on custom projects like this.

For fastening flexible solar panels to canvas, such as the top of the dodger or bimini, you can have your sailmaker sew Velcro strips to the canvas

This pair of solar panels is neatly nestled out of the way on a stainless tube framework above a bimini.

tops, with the outer edges of the Velcro lining up with the edges of the panels. Attach the opposite-side strips to the back edges of the panels so that you have removable panels. If you are worried about losing the solar panels in strong winds, try pulling a Velcro-backed panel from a canvas surface. The Velcro bond is so strong, you are more likely to see the whole dodger or bimini fly away first. While you are designing a flexible panel installation on canvas, make sure you sketch out a plan for the wiring, too. In lieu of unsightly cable ties, theoretically you could run the wires through the canvas seams or inside the stainless tubing, but most sailors stick with the black nylon cable ties. And by the way, you will need to keep a sack of those little black ties on board, as they disintegrate in the sun and break after a year or so of sun exposure.

For all solar panel installations, flexible or fixed, you will probably want to have some way of temporarily removing, or permanently replacing, external wiring. If you need to remove the panels temporarily, you can disconnect the red and black wires from the junction box. But to enable the temporary removal of the wires themselves, use snap plugs at some point along the wiring, and make sure the connections are below decks, not outside. You can run the wires through rubber-sealed deck fittings, such as CableClams from Blue Sea Systems, to protect the exposed metal of the snap plugs from exposure to rain and saltwater.

Many of us subconsciously associate the capacity to generate electricity with movement—pistons,

Four large solar panels, a wind generator, an outboard motor, and an inflatable dinghy all competing for space on a canoe stern might work in a calm marina or anchorage, but not offshore.

turbines, smoke, wads of copper wire spinning around—so it is hard for some of us to make a connection between stillness and power. But let us not be fooled. The passive, stationary profile of solar panels easily belies their hidden capacity to provide sometimes astonishing amounts of power for your vessel's battery banks. Some cruisers report having drawn upwards of 200 amp hours in a single day from a large solar panel array, more power than most yachts can use. For that kind of power, you might have to buy an extra 8D deep-cycle battery just to have some place to store it. When we factor in the other, more aggressive alternative energy sources available for your home on the water, the possibilities for generating electrical power are unlimited.

Chapter 7
Wind Generators

THE MAJORITY OF VESSELS IN THE WORLDWIDE CRUISING COMMUNITY rely on at least some form of non-fuel-consuming alternative power, and the second most common source of such power, after solar panels, is a wind generator. Small vessels (25 to 30 feet) generally do not have high power requirements, especially that demanded by refrigeration, so they can get away with relying on the engine alternator and perhaps a large solar panel to keep up with a small GPS, a VHF radio, and a single-sideband radio, as long as it used sparingly. At the other end of the spectrum, much larger vessels, measuring 50 feet or more on deck, commonly employ a diesel generator to ensure a consistent source of power, not only for the highly complex array of 12- or 24-volt DC electronics, but also for appliances requiring 110 or 220 volts AC. Battery consumption of 200 amp hours per day is not uncommon on these floating power grids.

Between these two extremes lie the bulk of the world's cruising fleet: vessels measuring 30 to 50 feet LOA and generally having onboard a refrigerator and a ham or marine single-sideband radio, plus an array of electronic navigation systems, which together deplete a battery bank quickly under normal cruising conditions. Boats in this broad category typically consume anywhere from 40 to 100 amp hours per day. Many cruisers on these medium-sized boats avoid the high fuel demands of the main engine or genset by combining several solar panels with a wind generator. The logic speaks for itself: when it's calm and sunny, the solar panels keep the batteries topped off. But as long as there is a breeze of at least 8 knots, the wind generator can provide an impressive amount of power, often far more what than is needed (see table, "Wind Generator Output").

Theory

If you have ever watched a wind turbine, even a toy pinwheel in a fair breeze, you have noticed the blades rarely spin at one speed for more than a few seconds. It will slow down to a near-stop, and then as the wind freshens just slightly, the turbine becomes a blur. This is because the power available from the wind increases as the cube of wind speed. So when the average wind velocity doubles, power is multiplied eight times. For example, a 5-knot zephyr will produce 125 units of power; at 10 knots, the power available zooms up to 1,000 units. However, no matter how efficient a wind turbine's blades may be, according to Betz' Law, the maximum amount of kinetic energy that may be drawn from the wind is less than 59 percent of the wind's total power. This theoretical ceiling results from, first of all, drag, and second, cavitation occurring on the downwind side of rotor blades.

Other sources of mechanical inertia place further limits on the harnessing of wind power. Minor flaws in the design or manufacture of rotor blades, the type of generator employed, wear and tear on shaft bearings, and turbulence caused by nearby objects conspire to make some wind generators perform better or worse than others. Knowing about the different types and builders of wind generators and how to install one of these gems properly can make a big difference in the service you can expect from your selection.

Design Features

Marine wind generators employ an aerodynamic rotor blade, similar to an airplane propeller, up to 48 inches in total length to operate a 12-volt, permanent-magnet alternator. A stabilizer tail downwind of the propeller keeps the prop pattern turned directly into the oncoming air current. A permanent magnet stator is affixed to the interior of the casing, inside which rotates a set of coils on an armature. As with engine-mounted alternators, brushless electrical contacts and a diode are used to rectify the AC into DC and transfer power through a positive and negative wire from the armature windings to the battery or load.

In selecting a wind generator, make sure you match the output to fit the general range of power required by your vessel, and the amount of wind you expect to find in your cruising grounds. One model may promise 2 amps at 10 knots of wind, but will it blow an average 10 knots around the clock where your boat will be cruising? Certainly it would be naïve to plan on consistent 48-amp-hour days with that model. At the same time, a small boat using a conservative amount of power for a well-insulated refrigerator and a minimum of electronics does not require a unit producing, say, 6 amps at 10 knots. The optimum wind generator for this boat produces around 4 amps at 10 knots, or 2 amps at 10 knots with some added input from solar panels and occasional backup from the engine alternator.

Two common complaints with wind generators are interference with AM receivers, and vibration and noise produced at high wind speeds. Radio interference, along with interference to the depth sounder and other electronics, may be caused by electrical spikes from the rectifier diodes in the wind generator or in the engine alternator. The solution to this is an alternator noise filter for each alternator onboard the vessel. You can find a wide selection of noise filter coils starting from under 10 dollars online or in auto parts shops, or you can build one with a capacitor and a short length of coiled copper wire for next to nothing. Seek advice from a radio repair technician before attempting this job.

Vibration from the spinning rotor can be a problem with some models, even at moderate speeds. Find out first from another owner of the model you wish to buy as to whether vibration is a problem. Having anticipated this problem, most manufacturers include rubber mounts with their installation kits.

The familiar, high-pitched "whee" sound in some models is produced by air cavitation on the low-pressure side of rotor blades spinning at high speeds, generally in winds in excess of 30 knots. Orville and Wilbur Wright struggled with blade profiles for maximum efficiency on their historic airplane Flyer I over a century ago. Their research formed the basis for the NACA (formerly, National Advisory Committee for Aeronautics) airfoil shapes used in aircraft, and aeronautical engineers are still pursuing the elusive perfect blade. Adjusting blade pitch is but one strategy gleaned from aviation research in order to

The Air X, with its streamlined styling and automatically feathering blades, is a best-seller among cruisers.

reduce drag and noise. Microprocessor-controlled feathering pitch, available in some models, helps to minimize much of the unwanted screeching, along with overcharging, from rotor blades in high winds.

Besides differences in propeller size and output among the various designs on the market, three types of braking systems distinguish wind generators from each other. The simplest form of braking is performed by a crew member who turns the turbine sideways to the wind and ties off one of the blades to the turbine mast when the wind is blowing too hard or when the batteries have been topped off. This simple approach works only when there is at least one crew member available to perform this chore. The main problem with this system is that crew need to brake the system whenever leaving the boat or risk overcharging and frying the battery bank being charged. A more advanced system incorporates a magnetic brake, which slows the turbine in strong winds or when the battery is fully charged. Finally, at least one major manufacturer uses microprocessed pitch control not only to control noise but to flatten the blades against the wind, bringing them to a near stand-still to prevent overcharging. These last two automatic systems may be left unattended indefinitely, offering crew freedom from babysitting the wind generator as long as the braking system is working as intended.

Leading Models

The wind generator industry is populated by numerous manufacturers, a few of them producing large industrial turbines to be integrated into community and regional power grids. Fortunately, a handful of these companies have found a ready market among us cruising sailors who look for alternative energy sources to save on fuel costs.

The Air-X is one of the world's biggest-selling marine wind generators, and a quick walk around any marina or anchorage in North America, the South Pacific, or the Caribbean will confirm its popularity. The Air-X, previously built by Southwest Windpower in Flagstaff, Arizona, and now manufactured by Primus Windpower in Lakewood, Colorado, lies at the middle of the pack in overall output, but its power curve rises quickly to a respectable 12 amps in 20 knots of wind. A recent improvement in the Air-X's design is its carbon fiber composite blades, spanning 46 inches. This construction renders the Air-X lighter than units with aluminum blades, and more resistant to the ravages of wind, sun, and salt. Earlier versions used plastic blades that stretched as wind velocity increased, operating as a centrifugal governor against excessive, potentially damaging speed. Unfortunately, the old blades were noisy at wind speeds over roughly 20 knots.

The latest-generation Air-X electronically controls rotor speed in high winds, putting the blades into a slow, silent spin until wind speed drops. The unit comes with a sealed, brushless alternator, and an internal, three-phase, microprocessor-controlled voltage regulator instead of the more common shunt regulator, which relies on heat dissipation to bleed off excess power. A three-phase regulator allows a high bulk charge when batteries are low, an absorption charge when the batteries are close to maximum capacity, and finally a float charge at reduced voltage to prevent overcharging. The total installed weight of the Air-X, including bracing poles, is less than 35 pounds, and the

Dick Verbeck stands next to the powerful Red Baron wind generator aboard his 34-foot Bruce Roberts-designed cutter Beatitude, on which he has cruised the Pacific coast of Mexico and Central America. He picked up the used generator for $60 at the Chula Vista Marina cruiser swap meet in San Diego Bay.

installation kit comes with an extra set of rotor blades thrown in for good measure.

The Ampair, built by Boost Energy Systems in the U.K., is in the same size and weight range as most of its competitors, and produces a power curve almost identical to that of the Air-X up to about 27 knots wind speed, after which the Air-X automatically reduces its speed until the wind drops. In a light gale of 32 knots, the Ampair puts out a whopping 25 amps DC. The three-phase Ampair 300 features a sealed brushless alternator, a DC rectifier, and blades constructed of glass-reinforced polypropylene. A key component of the Ampair is its PowerFurl blade pitch control system, which prevents excessive spinning speeds while maintaining power output. This is designed to eliminate the vibration and screaming we associate with improperly designed or managed rotor blades.

The Kiss generator, manufactured in Chaguaramas, Trinidad, is a high-output machine cranking out a full 4 amps in a 10-knot breeze. That comes to 96 amp hours per day, if the wind holds steady, in hardly enough breeze to blow away a house fly. In 15 knots of wind, the Kiss puts out an impressive 10 amps of power, more than most cruising vessels can use if averaged over 24 hours. In 25 knots of wind, it produces 25 amps—that's an amp per knot—or 600 amp hours averaged over a 24-hour period.

The Kiss's one big drawback, if you can call it that, is its lack of tapering blades or automatically braking rotor. A crewmember will have to keep an eye on the battery monitor to prevent overcharging. When the batteries are topped off, the unit may be turned away from the wind manually to prevent overheating and overcharging.

Everfair Enterprises of Punta Gorda, Florida, manufactures what is arguably the highest-producing wind generator available to ocean cruisers. The Fourwinds II/Red Baron beats all competitors in its range at every wind speed from 5 to 20 knots. Only the Kiss produces a higher level of current at 25 or more knots. Most of us want to start tapering off the charging output well before that point anyhow, so these upper-end comparisons are essentially academic.

Southern California cruiser Dick Verbeck picked up a used Red Baron for his 34-foot, heavy-displacement, Bruce Roberts-designed cutter Beatitude for the give-away price of $60 at one of the swap meets held periodically at Chula Vista Marina in San Diego Bay. After purchasing mounting poles and stainless steel fittings, he had invested a mere $200 for a machine that keeps two 6-volt golf cart batteries and two 12-volt 8-D batteries, with a total battery storage of 800 amps, fully charged. Verbeck's refrigerator consumes a maximum of 20 amp hours per day, and navigation lights and instruments deplete another 25 amps for a total of 45 amp hours. He said with anything more than 10 knots of apparent wind, the batteries stay topped off with all these systems running. "At 12 knots, we can bump up to the autopilot for coastal cruising," he added.

A unique option offered with the Red Baron is a conversion kit for deployment as a water generator. This set Verbeck back only another $150, and the configuration covers all daily power requirements with only six hours of charging at a boat speed of 6 knots. Because water is many times denser than air, water generators are capable of significantly higher amounts of current (see Chapter 8, "Hydro Generators"). In 6 knots of wind, the Red Baron produces 1.4 amps, but at 6 knots water speed, that figure jumps to 8 amps. When the batteries

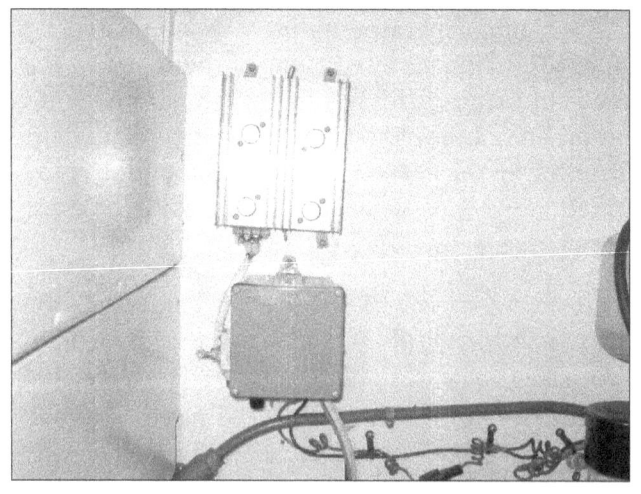

The shiny blue box is the "smart" microprocessor-controlled regulator that came with Dick Verbeck's previously loved Red Baron wind generator. Below is the junction box he assembled containing a discharge-preventing diode and a fuse.

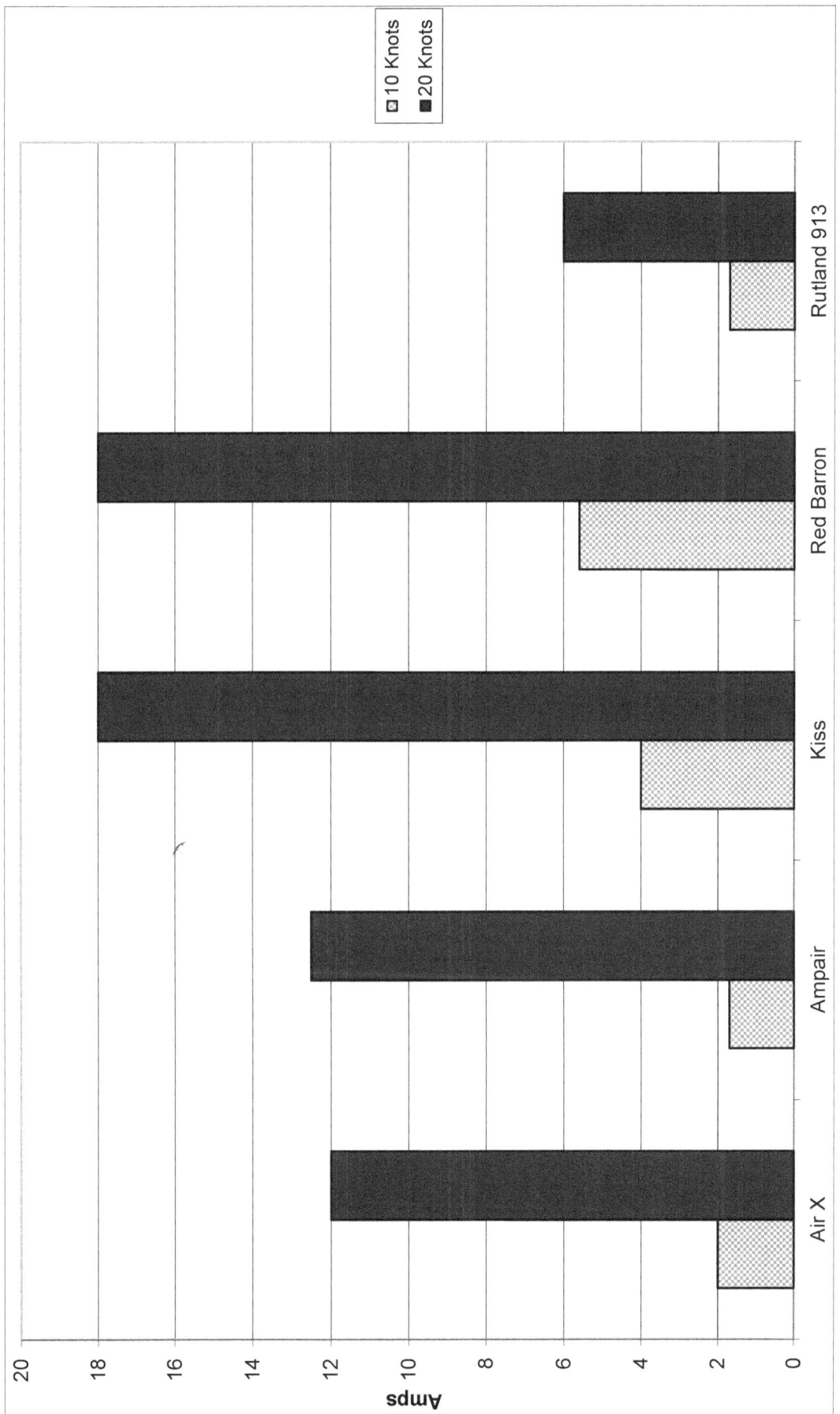

Wind Generator Output

This chart is based on approximations drawn from a variety of industry sources. Manufacturers generally publish complete power curves of the wind generator models they offer.

WIND GENERATORS • 57

This wind generator is strongly supported by two supports forming a triangular stainless steel structure with the mounting mast.

are charged, Verbeck simply hauls the turbine up on deck until the following day.

Essential to this system is an optional, three-phase, "smart" microprocessor-controlled regulator, which keeps the battery banks from frying. Verbeck devised a junction box on the engine compartment bulkhead immediately below the controller to house a diode preventing accidental discharge and a fuse protecting the wiring.

Marlec of U.K. offers the small yet popular Rutland 913, which produces roughly 1.7 amps at 10 knots of wind, 6 amps at 20 knots, yet whose blades cut only a 36-inch-wide footprint. A molded, six-blade rotor makes efficient use of the wind, ensuring what Marlec claims is the lowest wind start-up speed of any wind generator on the market—only 5 knots. Fiberglass-sealed magnets and stator coils protect the generator from the elements and eliminate AM radio interference, and "automatic thermostat protection" guards against damage to the generator in gale conditions. Particularly interesting is how the 913's blades and internal design combine to produce what Marlec calls "a high-inertia generator whose flywheel effect generates smooth, continuous power between gusts when other wind turbines have lost the power in the wind."

The 913's smaller, lower-priced sibling, the Rutland 503, was designed for sailing vessels under 30 feet LOA, in which battery charging demands are generally meager compared with those of larger yachts. Its diminutive turbine, measuring only 8.9 inches in diameter (smaller than the average frying pan), generates a trickle charge at a wind speed of 5 knots and a full 2 amps at 19 knots, more than what you can expect realistically from a 36-watt solar panel, even on a cloudless day at latitude zero. The Rutland 913 and 503 both incorporate a three-phase shunt voltage regulator coupled with a controller, ammeter, LED voltage level indicator, blocking diode, and fuse, all of which are housed in a white plastic box. The 913 control box also includes a selector switch for one or two battery banks.

Deck and Arch Mounting

The basic rule governing the positioning of a wind generator is simple: make sure there will be an uninterrupted flow of air from all directions to the turbine. Be careful to mount the unit as far as possible from obstructions, such as a mizzen mast, wind steering airvane, or equipment arch, to ensure proper air flow. If the boat is swinging at anchor without a stern anchor set, wind will nearly always come from within a few degrees of the bow. On the other hand, strong tidal flows may alter the direction of the apparent wind, causing the vessel to lie broadside and roll in a heavy chop. The wind turbine will be less efficient while rolling, but since it pivots 360 degrees on its pole mount, it can still remain directed into the oncoming airflow and continue to generate power.

A stroll through any cruiser marina will reveal a variety of mounting techniques for wind generators. One may be mounted atop a dedicated mast cut from aluminum or stainless steel tubing or galvanized pipe, while another might be suspended between the jib halyard and the foredeck, or mounted on a stern arch. Some vessels offer no alternative but to mount the unit to the mizzen mast head of a ketch or yawl rig. This approach seems workable as long as the extra weight aloft does not interfere excessively with the vessel's righting moment or the mast's standing rigging. Also, another more pragmatic concern looms over this installation: how easily can crew gain access to the generator, especially while offshore in unsettled weather, with a four-foot-long knife slicing the air?

The two most practical mounting strategies appear to be either on a vertical tube solidly affixed to the arch, or atop a dedicated, deck-mounted mast tube, the latter being by far the most common solution. The only potential problem with the arch installation is the difficulty in installing rubber mounts to absorb sound and vibration from the turbine at high speeds. Most of the wind generators available on the market today have undergone extensive redesign in recent years to alleviate excessive vibration, but at high wind speeds, especially above 30 knots, some turbines are still liable to scream from air cavitation. As long as crew can live with the possibility of vibration at high speeds on an older model, the arch provides a solid base, keeping the deck clear of extra mounting tubes.

For deck installation, you will need to acquire a properly sized length of aluminum or stainless tubing and mount it solidly in a corner of the stern, making sure to buttress the main mounting pole with at least two diagonal support tubes. The mast base and the connection between the diagonals and the main tube might need to be custom pieces in order to fit the large diameter of the mast, but the anchors for the diagonals will be standard hardware used to install spray dodgers and biminis. Assuming you are preparing for an offshore voyage, securing the mounting pole or diagonals with hose clamps is not advisable. Even the best-made hose clamps are bound to snap from constant twisting, vibrating, and crevice corrosion at some point during an extended cruise.

Verbeck used a pair of stainless U-bolts to secure his Red Baron to Beatitude's stern rail. He further secured the main mounting pole with a pair of highly polished stainless diagonal tubes connected to the side stern rails with swivel mounts. The finished installation is a glistening, attractive, unobtrusive complement to the overall rear deck layout.

For wind generators prone to a lot of vibration, particularly older models, some skippers install rubber sound-absorbing mounting pads between the mounting feet and the deck. A loud mechanical rumble reverberating through the hull is the last thing you want to hear while sipping cocktails and watching the sunset in some palm-fringed anchorage in your little corner of paradise.

Installation Kits

One way to demystify the deck installation process is to find a wind generator model that comes with an optional mounting kit. Boost Energy Systems of Berkshire, U.K., offers the Scanstrut stern mount kit for its Ampair 300 generator. Company spokesman David Sharman said the installation kit "is well suited to larger turbines and 'posher' vessels." Sharman added, "The Scanstrut consists of an 8-foot-long, 3-inch-diameter aluminum, white powder-coated pole which accepts the swivel of the generator. The base has a universal ball and socket for easy mounting to any deck angle on the stern of the yacht. Two adjustable stainless steel bracing struts clamp to the pole at their upper ends and mount to the deck at their lower ends. These resist the thrust and

Two wind generators mounted in tandem equate to double power; the starboard unit has been depowered to prevent over charging. The mounting structure also holds a GPS antenna, a VHF antenna, and two solar panels.

inertial loads of the wind turbine. A stainless steel guardrail bracing strut is also included."

The Air-X mounting system features a 9-foot powder coat aluminum pole with a tilting mast base, plus a pair of stabilizer poles and swivel clamps. Both the Ampair's and Air-X's main mounting poles may be disengaged from their diagonal struts and swung down to the deck to allow inspection and repair of the generator and turbine.

Other Considerations

An important point to keep in mind is that the more battery storage your vessel has, the more you will be able to take advantage of the charging power of a wind generator, particularly of the high-output variety. The choice should be directly related to the charging needs of the vessel and the specific features of the unit, not solely to price, much less to appearance, although some models are decidedly easier on the eyes—and ears—than others.

As a final note, the $1,000 to $2,000 you spend purchasing and installing a new wind generator can buy a lot of diesel fuel (500 to 700 gallons at current U.S. fuel dock prices), but a gallon of diesel still weighs approximately 7 pounds. This equates to over a third of a ton at 100 gallons, as opposed to an installed weight of less than 40 pounds for the typical marine wind generator. That should be reason enough to install not just solar panels and a wind generator, but as you will read in the next chapter, a hydro generator as well.

Chapter 8
Hydro Generators

MOST CRUISING SAILORS SEEM TO BE CONTENT WITH ONLY TWO alternative power sources: the sun and the wind. This conservative approach appears to make sense, at least at first glance. After all, with a pair of 50-watt panels and a wind generator averaging 8 amps in a fair breeze while at anchor, who needs anything else, right? But consider this: when you are sailing downwind, which means most of the time while you are in the trades, your vessel's downwind speed significantly reduces the apparent wind to the wind generator. So you have all this power behind you, but to what avail? This is where a water generator comes in. A hydro generator harnesses the power of the oncoming water current, producing far more current than a wind generator, given the same wind conditions while under sail.

Advantages of Water Power

Saltwater at its surface has an average density of about 64.1 pounds per cubic foot, as compared to the atmosphere at sea level, which has a density of just .08 pound per cubic foot. With saltwater having a density 800 times that of air, it should come to no surprise that a wind generator with a prop pattern diameter of four feet is still no match for a hydro generator blade with a pattern diameter of only one foot. Without even looking at the numbers, any sailor can appreciate intuitively the sheer force of water on a rotor pulled through the water at cruising speed. When anchored up a river with the tide going out, a small hydroelectric plant hanging from the transom provides all the power you need to keep you batteries topped off and your vessel's electrical systems up and running around the clock.

Just for grins, let's compare some numbers. Sailing downwind in the trades in a fresh breeze of 18 knots, a boat measuring 36 feet on the waterline (e.g. Sabre 426) can expect to maintain a theoretical hull speed of 9 knots, leaving 9 knots of apparent wind blowing forward over the transom. At 9 knots of wind speed, the Air X wind generator produces less than 2 amps. At the upper end of the scale, the Red Baron wind generator configuration produces about 5 amps. Assuming the same true wind speed of 18 knots while towing a submerged water generator turbine downwind, we now have a vessel speed of about 8 knots if we subtract a knot (could be less) for drag. At this speed, the Ferris WP200 in hydro generator mode whips out a scorching 20 amps of direct current, or 480 amp hours (5.76 kilowatts) per day. These are just hypothetical numbers, of course. In reality, the trade winds, depending on location and time of year, taper off somewhat at night, meaning significantly less charging power until mid-morning. Nonetheless, it should be clear that the daunting power of a hydro generator deserves serious consideration for inclusion in a robust, multi-source, alternative energy system.

A common concern among skippers regarding hydrofoils in general is the potential for drag. As much as we all love sailing, catching fresh blue fin tuna, and watching gorgeous sunsets, we also want to get to our destinations. So we take seriously any kind of potential hindrance to speed, be it a servo blade on a windvane steering system, a non-folding prop, a hydro generator rotor, or much worse, a bad case of zebra mussels. However, very little information in the form of solid, useful data exists for sailboat drag, and this also applies to hydro generators. Magazine articles and sailor blogs give anecdotal reports coalescing around a speed loss of less than 1 knot. As speed increases, so too does the rotational speed of the water generator's rotor, generating more drag. However, the rotor's drag on speed can be offset by vessel length, tonnage, sail area, and other factors. One 40-foot vessel with Brand X hydro generator might lose half a knot while another, more lightly built 40-footer might lose .75 knot. One skipper scrubs the hull once a month, and the other scrubs every two months. How do we account for these fine differences? We can't. However, we can all bank on one fact: because of the significantly greater power generated by water as compared to wind, the spinning of a rotor through the water can fulfill most vessels' daily charging needs in just four to six hours. For the remaining 18 to 20 hours, the vessel can fly along at full speed. Boats consuming in excess of 200 amp hours day after day to run a hydraulic autopilot, an air conditioner, a deep freeze, a radar, two radios, a multi-function chart plotter, and all the other bells and whistles may be the exceptions, more than likely having to depend on a diesel-powered genset to keep up with their bourgeois lifestyle on the water. But for the humble proletarian with a small fridge, paper charts, and a laptop computer with small-scale raster charts for navigating the occasional serpentine harbor entrance, being able to switch between wind power at anchor and water power while under sail guarantees energy solvency and almost complete freedom from the engine alternator.

Design and Construction

At the core of every water generator is a watertight, hydrodynamic compartment containing a brushless, permanent-magnet alternator like the one found in a wind generator. This simple design precludes the necessity of exciter voltage from the battery and the corresponding field wire, reducing size and complexity. Only two wires lead from the generator assembly to the selected battery bank via the vessel's alternative energy controller. Low-friction seals and internal construction are designed to minimize heat when the unit is mounted on the taffrail or transom. In models with submerged motors, the surrounding water provides consistently adequate cooling. Some homemade taffrail models have been crafted from automobile alternators, but these tend to generate very little power because they are designed to run at a higher range of RPM than that produced by a rotor at typical sailboat hull speeds. Figuring out how to waterproof a DIY unit is yet another source of frustration for home tinkers. Fabricating a properly sealed box to protect the alternator from the corrosive effects of salt water intrusion while managing the unit's temperature under the hot sun poses a challenging set of requirements for a dependable hydro generator.

A classic hydro generator, such as the Aqua4gen, is anchored to the taffrail on a gimbaled mount and has a long piece of double-braided rope attached to a rotor that spins while trailing the vessel. Nothing electric is submerged, only a rotor with a long axle extending from the forward end of the rotor and attached to the tow line. The design of the rotor and alternator is optimized for high output within the speed range of typical cruising vessels. Minimum speeds for charging range from 2 to 5

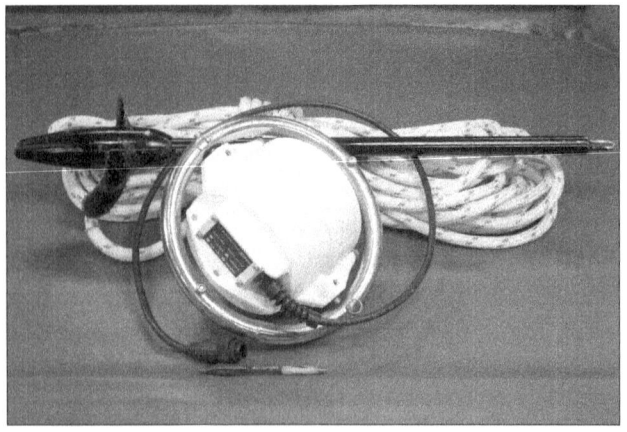

Photo courtesy of www.mahina.com

Ampair towed water generator with towline and rotor.

knots, with most manufacturers citing 3 knots as the threshold. A few hydro generator builders offer an optional 24-volt alternator for larger yachts, and a few offer two sizes of rotors, each tailored to a specific range of vessel size and average speed.

A few major problems, at least for some sailors, have made the whole business of towed hydro generators a bit of a challenge. The first is the difficulty in retrieving the tow line from the water. Anyone crazy enough to grab the taught, spinning piece of double-braided line is guaranteed to try this only once. It is difficult to imagine what a human hand would look like after such a stunt, and I hope I never witness such a tragedy. The proper method of retrieving the tow line is to place a funnel around the towline and let the funnel slide down the towline to cover the rotor like an umbrella so that it may be hauled up onto the deck. A funnel is generally supplied with each new unit. If you need to fabricate a funnel, especially in the case of a used hydro generator, the funnel should be of a strong plastic and wide enough to completely depower and stop the rotor. A large funnel used for collecting used engine oil would probably do the trick. A common way of deploying the funnel is to cut it open on one side, punch a few holes through either side of the cut, slip it onto the tow line, and lace it together with a strong, thin cord before sending it down to the rotor.

Another potential problem with these devices is the possibility of interference with servopendulum windvane self-steering systems. The arcing of some servo arms, particularly on narrow transoms, may cause the tow line to get tangled up in the steering lines extending from the swinging arm. I have seen an Aqua4gen mounted next to a Monitor windvane on a 30-foot sloop that sailed from New England to New Zealand with no trouble at all, so again, a successful, compatible installation of both devices depends on the model of each unit and planning on the part of the installer.

The last two complaints regarding hydro generator tow lines concern fishing, both intended and unintended. If you are like most cruisers and happen to love trolling for tuna and dorado, remember not to engage in this while trolling a hydro rotor. The potential for a major tangle is too great for taking a risk. On the bright side, trolling is best in the early morning, when the wind is relatively settled. Shortly after you have reeled in the day's catch, the wind will just be starting to kick up, and it will be time for the hydro generator. By mid or late afternoon, you will be dropping the funnel and hauling in the rotor and getting it ready for redeployment the following morning. The last concern regards the tendency for the rotor to become a lure for surface-feeding pelagic fish, most notably sharks. Reports of these occurrences are rare, but the possibility of this happening is always disconcerting, especially as the rotors are anything but cheap. If you opt for a towed-rotor system, you are well advised to pack a spare rotor.

Someone somewhere along the line got the notion that if we mount the hydro generator directly to the transom with a handle to pull it straight up out of the water, we can dispense with tow lines altogether. This is an immensely safer and easier way to operate a mini hydroelectric plant. This means no tangles with trolled fishing lines, no disturbance of the servopendulum self-steerer, and little likelihood of attracting sharks. If they liked hull-mounted props that much, they would first go after the shiny bronze one a few feet away. A rigid, transom-mounted system also eliminates the possibility of a rotor skipping out of the water and knotting up the tow line, an irksome problem that starts at about 7 knots. A strong, steady flow of water around the rotor blade equates to a faster, better, uninterrupted three-phase charging process for the battery banks.

Towed Water Turbine

The Aqua4gen, built in the U.K. by Jabsco, the well-known producer of marine plumbing parts, is one of the few models of water turbines offering one mode of deployment, a simple rope-mount system attached to the aft pulpit. Their affordability and no-frills ease of use contribute to their enduring popularity among cruisers, particularly on small boats with little room to spare on their transoms for a larger, bulkier charging apparatus. The operator mounts the Aqua4gen between the upper and lower tubes on the aft pulpit and then attaches the tow line to a stainless shackle hooked to the armature stem. The rope arrangement is a

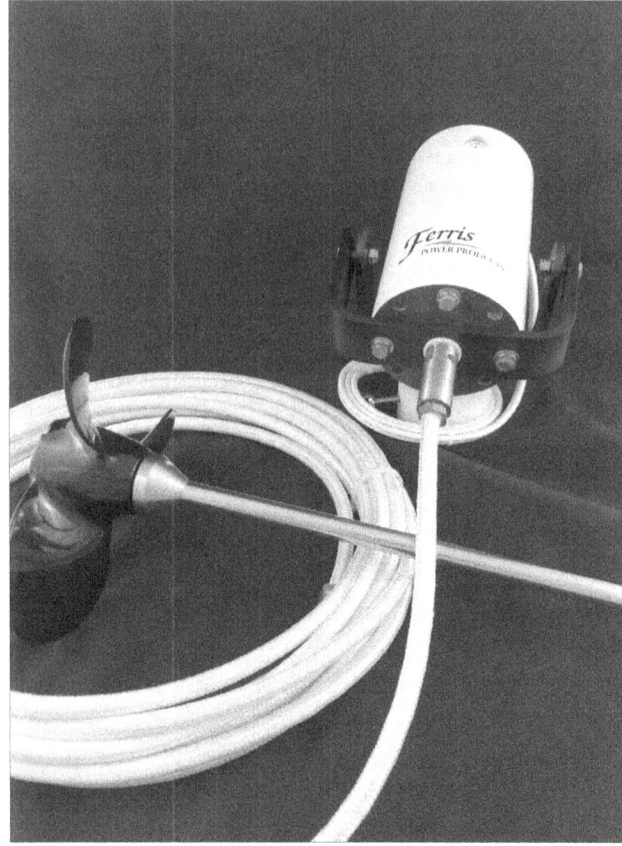

Photo courtesy of Hamilton Ferris

Hamilton Ferris water generator with taff rail mount, towline, and rotor.

strong, shock-absorbing, universally swiveling system that would be difficult to imitate with fancy engineering, metallurgy, or high-tech polymers. The rotor's unconventional appearance makes it look like a homemade spare, but if you look more closely, you will note the carefully engineered hydrodynamic blades screwed onto the rotor shaft. The Agua4gen's output is modest at lower speeds, generating 2 amps at 5 knots, but the curve rises sharply to an amp per knot from 7 to 10 knots.

Wind-Water Conversions

For cruisers who want the charging advantages of both a wind generator and a hydro generator but would rather not have to purchase and install two separate systems, there are numerous conversion systems on the market, an option that has gained in popularity steadily over the last couple of decades. A wind-water conversion system allows the user to take full advantage of the water's power while under sail, and of the wind while at anchor. At the center of a conversion system is a waterproof alternator that may be mounted atop a mast and fitted with a large, wind-driven rotor blade while the boat is at anchor, or fitted with a smaller water rotor and dropped from the transom while the vessel is under way. Even with the new towline-free options appearing on the market, some cruisers eschew extra equipment being bolted to their boats' transoms, preferring the traditional, uncluttered towline, which evolved from the old-fashioned towed knot logs that predate the modern through-hull knot log and the more recent GPS.

One popular conversion system is Ferris Waterpower's WP200 water generator, which switches to wind mode with a separately purchased kit. At 6 knots of vessel speed with the water generator, Ferris claims its unit produces a whopping 12 amps of power, or approximately 200 amp hours of power per day, more than most cruising vessels can expect to consume. The WP200 comes packed with a 30-amp multi-source regulator, an analog ammeter, a 75-foot torque line, and "a retrieval funnel to stop the unit underway." An 85-watt solar panel is also available to round out the go-anywhere alternative energy charging system. In wind generator mode, the WP200 may be mounted on a free-standing mast or slung from the rigging over the foredeck, whichever is better suited to the overall deck layout. Separately sold accessories include mounting poles and a rigging mount system for the wind generator configuration.

The Four Winds Red Baron wind-water conversion generator has been popular over the years for its high output and simplicity of installation and use but apparently is not in production anymore. As with many companies serving the sailing industry, Four Winds is, or was, a small operation catering to a niche market. If you can find a Red Baron charging system at a cruiser swap meet, you might find yourself a deal too good to pass up. Fellow Southern California cruiser Dick Verbeck of the 34-foot Bruce Roberts cutter Beatitude paid $60 for a used Red Baron wind generator at a cruiser swap meet (see Chapter 7). He ordered the water conversion kit from Four Winds, setting him back only $150, and now in water mode, the configuration covers all daily

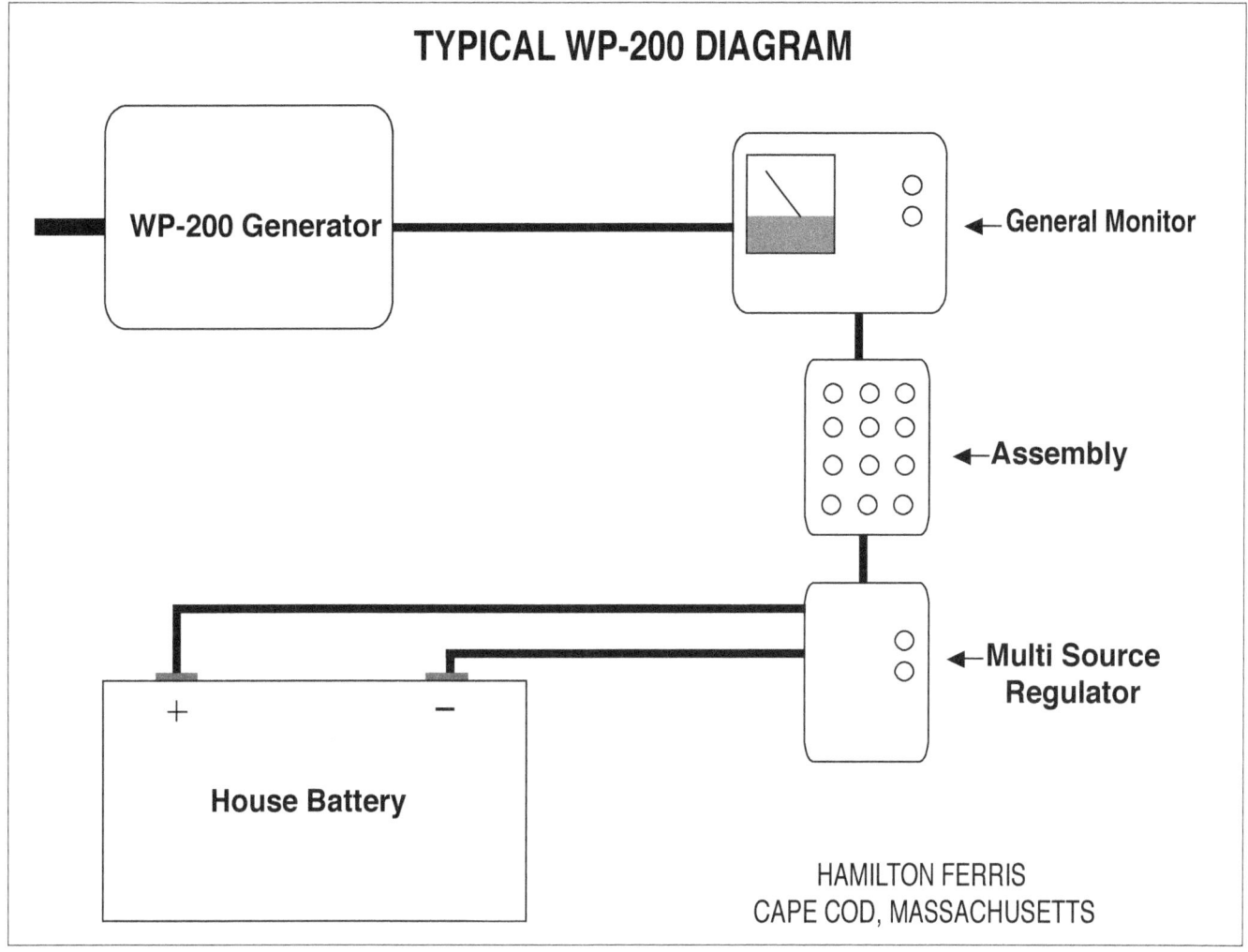

power requirements with only six hours of charging at a hull speed of 6 knots, at which the Red Baron cranks out an impressive 8 amps.

While wind-water generator conversions are popular for many cruisers, if it uses a towline, such a system requires the operator to reinstall the wind mount apparatus periodically, and this may or may not be a minor nuisance. Storing the mounting mast or the rigging mount while under way and then having to set it all up again every time you anchor could compel you to seek out a better way to continue enjoying the best of two worlds with less work. Fortunately, there is at least one new dual system amply capable of switching between both charging modes without the hassle of reinstalling the unit.

The DuoGen-3, manufactured by Eclectic Energy Limited in Nottinghamshire, U.K., is a hybrid wind-water system using no towline and requiring only a minor reconfiguration every time you switch between modes. The whole unit is mounted on the transom and stands upright with the air rotor installed in wind generator mode, where it is capable of producing 6 amps of current in a moderate breeze of 15 knots. For water mode, the operator removes the wind rotor, extends a carbon fiber arm to accept a water rotor, and then sets the unit in the water. In hydro mode, the DuoGen-3 generates 8 amps at 6 knots hull speed and an incredible 16 amps at 8 knots. Any fear of compromised performance in connection with a dual-mode generator will find no basis in these numbers. Cruising guru Jimmy Cornell has installed a DuoGen-3 on his aluminum-hull Garcia Exploration 45 *Aventura IV*, and numerous participants in Cornell's Atlantic Relay for Cruisers (ARC) have given highly favorable reports of the system's charging capacity in the sometimes grueling conditions of the North Atlantic.

Towline-Free Hydro Generators

The Watt & Sea hydro generator, built in La Rochelle, France, and distributed in North America by Hydrovane in British Colombia, is arguably the easiest of this type of generator to deploy among all of its competitors. And this is why every entrant in the 2012-2013 Vendée Globe non-stop, single-handed, round-the-world race was fitted with a simply designed, virtually bullet-proof Watt & Sea charging system. Mounted directly to the transom, the Watt & Sea dispenses with the towline, allowing easy manual retrieval in all kinds of weather. If the Watt & Sea has one limitation, it is the device's single purpose as a water generator instead of a combo wind-water system. However, for many offshore racers and cruisers, straightforward design and a dedicated purpose are Watt & Sea's greatest allure. Cruisers who want to harness wind power have the option of installing a separate, permanently mounted wind generator for their typically long periods at anchor.

Aside from its singularity of purpose, the Watt & Sea's 300-watt cruising version and 600-watt racing version both reflect a high order of ingenuity in reducing the process of deploying a water generator system to the fewest possible steps. Two short lengths of thin double-braided line are used to drop and retrieve the hinged unit, which is suspended from a stainless mounting bracket included with the system. Then a long stainless shaft is used to stabilize the unit when set in the water. The rotor remains permanently attached to the outboard end of the NACA foil leg, whether in or out of the water.

A great deal of attention to design and construction details is evident in the strong, simple lines of the Watt & Sea, which closely resembles a thin spade rudder. Hydrovane has engineered an optional deployment apparatus for the Watt & Sea, but the foil, rotor, and electronics remain the same. Hydrovane also has developed a mounting system that attaches the Watt & Sea directly to the Hydrovane self-steering gear's vertical mast, making a smaller overall footprint on the transom, which also equates to fewer holes drilled into the hull. The Watt & Sea comes with a watertight electrical control box complete with sealed cable ports and LED lights showing charging status. All rotors produced before September 2012 were made of marine-grade aluminum. All Watt & Sea rotors sold after that point are composed of tough, non-corrosive composite.

The Aquair is another well-designed, strongly built, transom-mount hydro generator, easily deployed on a long, narrow, sturdy framework that folds down from the transom and locks into place when the generator is submerged. At 14.5 inches in length and weighing 30 pounds, the Aquair's profile looks like a short, stubby self-propelled torpedo. The generator itself is a low-speed, high-output, permanent-magnet alternator housed in an oil-filled bulb originally designed to charge lighting batteries on barges in the North Sea. In addition to its duties at sea, the Aquair also serves as a mini hydroelectric plant for homes along river banks in remote areas.

Photo courtesy of Hydrovane

A Duogen air/water generator mounted to the mounting tube of a Hydrovane with a Bakelite spacer on the stern of a Tayana 37.

A Watt & Sea hydro generator mounted to a Hydrovane self-steering rudder tube on an Outbound 46.

Photo courtesy of Hydrovane

Available in three configurations—12 volt, 24 volt, and 48 volt—this versatile workhorse can handle unusually high speeds of water current, allowing it to produce correspondingly high levels of amperage. Although excessive amperage is more likely to be a challenge during a heavy rain storm on a river, Ampair does offer a 40-amp controller just in case your vessel is surfing at high speeds in strong winds and you have better things to do than lean over the transom in towering, breaking seas to pull the generator out of the water.

Before laying out funds for a permanently mounted hydro generator, consider first how and where exactly you plan to install the device. Consider what obstructions may compete for the same space, such as a swim step or a windvane self-steering system. If your vessel has a servopendulum, the arc of the pendulum shaft may cross the section to be occupied by the generator mounting frame. On a wide transom, this can probably be avoided. A Sailomat self-steerer is raked back, so there should be no problem with any Sailomat model. Likewise, a trim tab or a Hydrovane should easily accommodate either a separately mounted Watt & Sea or an Ampair.

Motorboat-style wooden swim steps are not that common on sailboats, but many cruising boats do have swim steps on a raked, or sugar scoop, transom, which will indeed render the installation of a water generator a major challenge. Such an installation would require a separate mounting structure with upper supports affixed to the taffrail and lower supports fastened to the sugar scoop or lowest level of the swim step. Then again, you will probably find it easier to install a towline system instead. In the case of a boomkin, unless there is some way to attach the hydro generator to the hull, perhaps between the boomkin's support tubes, here again you are probably better off with a towed system. In most cases, though, a transom-mounted hydro generator is easy to accommodate, and the least cumbersome method of mechanically generating electricity offshore.

Experimental Technology

As long as there are sailboats on the sea, there will be people experimenting with cleaner, easier, cheaper ways to generate electricity for offshore cruising vessels. And, of course, there are always those who are looking for that overlooked scientific theory or law of physics, which if brought to light could provide for our onboard energy needs. One innovation that could make generating electricity far easier was actually invented in 1868 by James B. Francis of Lowell, Massachusetts. The collects rushing water and forces it into a round tube, or scroll case, that narrows as it wraps around an impeller, which rotates and powers a generator. Water is released through a series of ports, each with equal pressure due to the narrowing scroll case. If you have ever seen a nautilus split in half, you have an idea of what a Francis turbine looks like. The Francis turbine is the standard technology for large-scale hydroelectric plants on all corners of the planet, including the world's highest-output hydroelectric plant, Three Gorges Dam on the Yangtze River in China.

Idle talk among cruisers suggests there are individuals experimenting with through-hull scoops, which would force water into a Francis turbine in the same manner as a large generating plant. In theory, such a system should be fairly straightforward to design. As a boat rushes through a body of water, a scoop near the keel receives the high-pressure current, and the Francis tube forces it through a rotating impeller, which powers a generator cranking out somewhere between 5 and 20 amps of DC current. That all sounds great, but the pessimist in me conjures up visions of barnacles, kelp, Sargasso weed, and other flora and fauna taking up residence within the scoop, Francis tube, and impeller blades, causing the whole thing to crunch to a halt until someone disassembles, cleans, reassembles, and reinstalls the little gizmo. And naturally, two weeks later, it will break down again and require another two hours' work to get the generator back up and running again. Is this technology possible? Probably, but ease of maintenance will be the number-one concern among offshore sailors if and when the Francis tube ever becomes a reality as the next big technological breakthrough in the field of marine electric power generating systems.

There is no "best" way to harness the power of water in order to charge our vessels' battery banks. The traditionalist will stick to the towline generator and deal with skipping and tangles as they come, developing skill in avoiding these problems over time. The sailor relishing the opportunity for a "twofer" will enjoy the benefits of a conversion system, whether it be a traditional towed turbine with an optional windvane configuration or the DuoGen-3, a unique transom-mount system that flips upward to be transformed into a wind generator. And finally, some sailors will want to take advantage of the dependability and ease of operation of a fixed transom-mount system while leaving the job of anchorage power production to a set of solar panels and a separate wind generator.

Chapter 9
Voltage Regulators and Controllers

A MULTI-SOURCE ELECTRICAL GENERATING ARRAY, SUCH AS THE configuration you may install on your sailing vessel, must be backed up by a charge control system that is up to the task. Often, each charging unit comes with its own optional smart charge controller, while your vessel's engine might still be controlled by a traditional mechanical voltage regulator. Overlapping all of these inputs can cause confusion, with each one sensing what we assume is battery charge rather than charge current coming from an external source, which could be a diesel generator set, a solar panel, wind generator, or hydro generator. Typically, no more than two charge inputs run simultaneously, so "confusion" may be a bit overstated here. Again, each of these can be configured to regulate its own output, but it does so not by arbitrarily setting a limit after X amount of time charging, but by constantly the charge level of the battery bank receiving the charge current. And with a multi-input charge controller, competing levels of current are managed by a microprocessor, alleviating our worries about over- or undercharging the battery banks.

In order to plan how we want to control and monitor our vessels' overall charging plan, we must have a working understanding of the components involved and how they interact in order to keep our onboard electrics working consistently. These systems may include a traditional engine "black box" voltage regulator, one or more single-purpose "smart controllers," a controller with multiple inputs, and one or more battery isolators. As you will see, the trend is toward centralizing the control and monitoring functions as much as possible to permit easier reading of the monitoring process, and to prevent the unnecessary and often detrimental overlapping of battery monitoring.

The specific methods and electrical components you use in coupling your wind generator, for example, to the vessel's charging array naturally will adhere to a combination of vessel needs and personal preference, but also must allow properly regulated input from other sources. This component may be integrated into a system that includes an extensive battery bank charged by two alternators, plus a combination of other charge sources. There are numerous ways to bring all of these devices together; as long as the charging scheme is safe and responsive to your charging requirements, your overall electrical complex should serve you well.

As always with marine electrical work, the best strategy is to leave the job to a qualified electrician

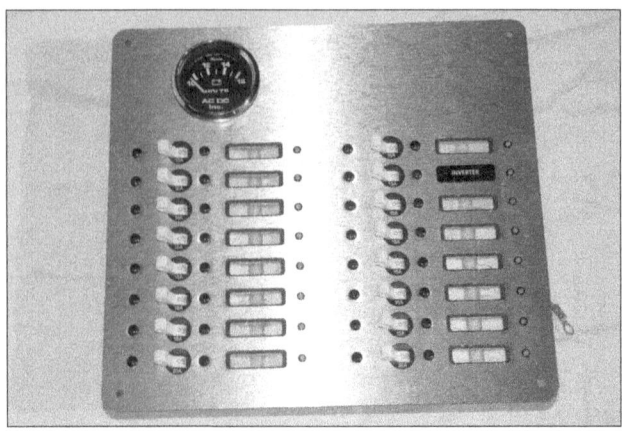
Variations of this panel are custom made to order by AC/DC Marine in Torrance, Calif.

who adheres to the relevant U.S. Coast Guard requirements and ABYC guidelines. If you intend to do the job yourself, be sure to follow manufacturers' instructions in connecting their products to your vessel's electrical matrix. The installation manual should include such details as recommended wire sizes and types of fuses and diodes to prevent fires and equipment failure.

Voltage Regulators

When it comes to charging and monitoring, an auxiliary engine on an offshore sailing vessel is in a separate class. It has, or should have, its own dedicated cranking battery and voltage regulator, and this self-contained system needs to have a switch to isolate it completely from the house banks. This will ensure that alternator current will not damage the windings in a wind generator or some other charge component.

Battery charging from older generators and alternators is controlled by an external, mechanical voltage regulator, usually mounted in or near the engine box. The regulator senses battery charge by the amount of electromagnetic tension working against a spring adjusted for a specific charge. As battery charge rises, a magnet activates a rheostat, or variable resistor, to trim the output current to the battery bank. A trained technician can adjust the maximum allowable battery charge by closely monitoring the charge with a multimeter and adjusting the rheostat with a screwdriver.

Mechanical regulators definitely still have their place on modern vessels, even if we are seeing fewer of these devices. A traditional regulator offers the benefits of highly precise voltage regulation, easy adjustment, high resistance to surges and overloads, high tolerance for extreme temperatures and humidity, and low cost. On the down side, black box regulators are slow to react to sudden changes in charge levels, such as from an outside charge

---

Installing Multiple Charging Controls

Six rules to keep in mind when installing one or more voltage regulators or microprocessor-based controllers in your alternative energy battery charging system:

1. Always disconnect the batteries before conducting work on any part of the vessel's electrical circuitry.
2. Before measuring electrical current or making other tests of "live" electrical equipment or wiring, remove your wristwatch and all jewelry to prevent shock.
3. The combined maximum rated output of all power inputs passing through a given controller or regulator should never surpass the maximum capacity of the regulating device.
4. Watch for "pre-regulation," or the premature slowing of the wind turbine due to another source voltage being read as battery charge. Though harmless to the controller and other components, pre-regulation can lead to less-than-optimum charging.
5. Install switches, fuses, and protective diodes to prevent the destruction of controllers from electrical surges, particularly from the engine alternator.
6. Always follow U.S. Coast Guard and American Boat and Yacht Council (ABYC) guidelines for wire and fuse sizes when installing electrical components.

This new, solid-state replacement for an old-style voltage regulator consists of a Zener diode, a thyristor, and a couple of resistors in place of a sensing coil, spring, and rheostat.

source, and their mechanical components require occasional inspection and maintenance to ensure they are free from water intrusion and rust. An occasional dose of WD-40 will help to keep moving parts adequately lubricated and operating properly. Another downside of regulators is the possibility of sparking from the rheostat and contacts, although any palpable danger from this is probably minimal or non-existent. If gasoline fumes, which are not to be found in a diesel engine compartment, are concentrated enough to pose a danger, the fumes can be ignited by sparks from carbon brushes in a traditional engine generator, or by stray electricity somewhere else in the engine box. Since voltage regulators are sealed fairly well from the surrounding atmosphere, the chances of an explosion from voltage regulator spark are extremely minimal.

While your charging matrix may be controlled by a modern transistorized regulator or digital controller, you may have an old Westerbeke or Cummins genset that still uses mechanical governors to control rpm and a mechanical regulator mounted on a circuit board inside a large box mounted on the side of the genset. A large box houses a wiring buss and screw-in rectifier diodes to ensure accurate 12-volt or 24-volt charge current from the generator side. Acquaint yourself well with the technology used in your genset and find out if it uses a mechanical regulator or a smart controller. Being well-acquainted with the ins and outs of your generator and regulator will help you to ensure safe operation of the unit and to accommodate its charging characteristics within your vessel's whole multi-charging setup.

Many, not all, of today's auto and marine engine alternators are equipped with internal regulators to provide consistent current and voltage, bypassing the need for an external regulator. Internal regulators use diodes to rectify current from AC to DC and transistors to control voltage, taking the place of the old-fashioned spring and rheostat. Since modern components are internally mounted and thus difficult for the home mechanic to repair, the cause of any malfunction in the alternator is likely to remain unknown to the operator. This leaves us two options: get the alternator repaired by a trained technician, or as is often the case, purchase a whole new unit.

An elevated level of current coming into the battery banks from a high-output source can fry the batteries if the current has no other place to go. A "shunt" regulator, which may be mechanical or transistorized, redirects excess current to some other target, such as a water heater, or a heat dissipater, to protect the battery. Regulating the current of charge sources can be done separately or combined in one multi-input regulator/controller. A number of manufacturers offer multi-input shunt controllers for surprisingly affordable prices, an added boon when we consider the alternative of having to replace hundreds of dollars' worth of battery banks or potentially thousands of dollars in charging equipment from harmful reverse voltage.

SES Flexcharge of Charlevoix, Michigan, produces the Flexcharge 7-amp PV7D shunt regulator, which is designed for small solar panel installations but is capable of charging two battery banks. The diminutive controller fits in the palm of your hand and can be used on flooded, gel, and AGM batteries. The Flexcharge Model NC25A Controller is capable of many times the amperage of the PV7D in a package only slightly larger. Roughly the size of a single-patty cheeseburger, the NC25A combines 0.1 amp to 25 amps of alternative energy charge current from one or two charge sources and is expandable to 35, 60, or 100 amps. Flexcharge claims an incredible 99.9 percent efficiency rate for the NC25A. Rather than shifting through bulk, taper, and float charge levels, the NC25A is a sliding controller, adjusting itself gradually by sensing the precise charge of the single or dual battery banks. The NC25A's "Charge

A Sunsei Sm25000 microprocessed solar charge controller keeps Saltaire's *house battery topped off while extending the life of the battery.*

The Nature Power 8-amp charge controller is safe for use on a solar panel array of up to 130 amps.

Jet Propulsion Laboratory, and NASA, regulating power from solar panels and wind generators for equipment measuring tectonic deformation in the West Antarctic Rift System.

Some of these charge controllers may be purchased as part of a package with the various alternative energy products available on the market. The Ampair wind generator may be purchased with Boost Energy's "configurable" regulator, which combines the Ampair's input with a solar panel array and is adaptable to a 12- or 24-volt battery bank. Similar to the Flexcharge controllers, the Boost Energy controller also has two output ports allowing you to distribute power to separate battery banks. The Rutland 913 Windcharger, a wind generator built by Marlec Engineering of Corby Northants, U.K., may be coupled with a solar panel of up to 50 watts with Marlec's optional SR200 controller. The SR200 is a shunt-type regulator housed with an ammeter, dual battery voltage LEDs, fuses, and a switch for charging one or two isolated battery banks. Though the SR2000 still enjoys a popular following, Marlec has recently started offering its HRDi smart controller as another option for regulating multiple charge inputs.

Divert" feature routes excess charging energy to other tasks, such as refrigeration or a water heater, or back to a permanent magnet charging source, such as a wind generator, in order to dissipate energy and in this case to reduce turbine speed in high wind conditions. Charge Divert activates only after the battery banks have reached their full charge.

As a side note, the Flexcharge family of controllers has played a vital role in seismic and geological research, an industry that demands instruments of high precision and close-tolerance calibration. On A22A, an iceberg the size of Delaware in Antarctica, Flexcharge controllers regulate charging networks employed to power GPS tracking equipment. The company's charge controllers are also at work on a joint project among the University of California,

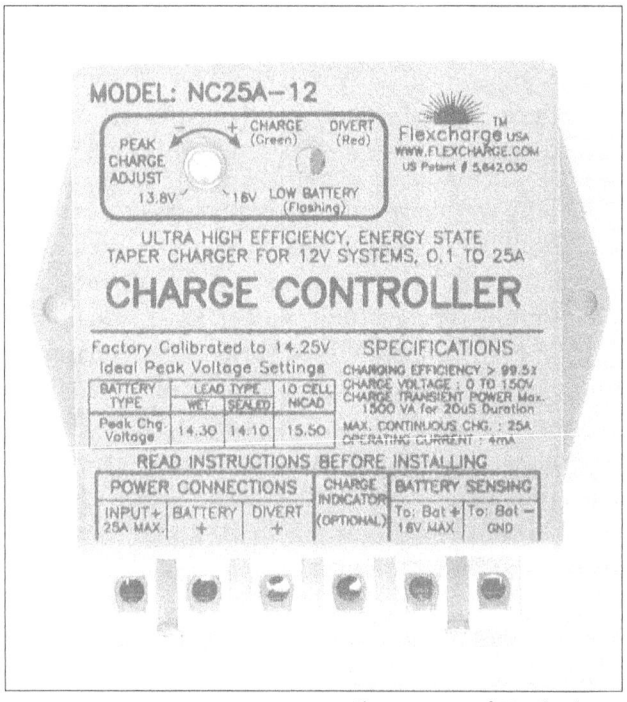

Photo courtesy of SES Flexcharge

The NC25A Charge Controller handles up to two charge inputs totaling 25 amps and is expandable to 100 amps.

Smart Controllers

Traditional charge regulators/controllers have done a great job of protecting batteries for motorists, cruising sailors, and motor boaters, but technology has moved on to the smart controller, which is a smaller, faster, more efficient method of regulating charge current.

Fortunately, the companies producing many of the widely marketed engine alternators, wind and hydro generators, and solar panels also offer controllers designed specifically for their units, and virtually all of the late-generation controllers are microprocessor-based smart controllers that follow either a three-phase charging pattern or a graduated "taper" charge cycle. A few still offer a choice between a traditional shunt regulator, which uses heat dissipation to discard excess charging amperage, and a smart controller, but the dependability and ease of use of this newest technology will probably replace the older devices within a few short years. Whereas a traditional regulator controls charge current through a sensing coil, a smart controller uses a logic circuit to calculate instantly the battery charge level, input amperage, and battery temperature in order to apportion the optimum levels of current and voltage needed by the battery. Marine smart controllers are small, light, waterproof, and maintenance-free, and many of them can be coupled with a monitoring device.

A key component of Balmar's line of marine alternators is its Max Charge line of three-phase, external smart chargers. The small size of these controllers belies their ability to manage high levels of amperage produced by Balmar alternators, up to 220 amps. The operator first programs the controller with a magnetic stylus, selecting the best combination of charging variables for the battery in question. To make things easy, the Max Charge is pre-programmed along the whole list of possible settings, an arrangement that will work for most batteries. To program the controller for a specific battery, one indicates several settings, including the battery make, size, cut-off voltage, cut-off amperage, and temperature. Each Max Charge also features a digital readout of a list of codes indicating the installation and charging conditions detected by the unit. If you have used an OBD II diagnostic monitor on a late-generation automobile, you should have an idea of how this kind of code protocol works.

ElectroMaax's E-Maax takes the science of smart, multi-stage charge controlling to another level with its easy, push-button programmability. This product line boasts a list of unique features, including alternator RPM detection, PC interface, P-type and N-type alternator compatibility, solar panel and wind generator control capability, and a healthy list of sensors not found in other comparable products.

Aside from engine alternator regulators, a number of controllers exist solely for the purpose of regulating current from alternative sources. If your wind generator does not come with its own internal regulator or controller, you will need to select a control device in order to prevent battery overcharging and further damage to your vessel's electrical system. In the case of an off-the-shelf controller or regulator, make sure it is matched for the maximum output of the wind generator, lest you fry the controller. Some controllers, such as those available from Sunsei, are designed strictly for solar panels, which generally produce less amperage and do not impose the powerful surges produced by wind generators.

The Sunsei Solar Monitor Sm25000 is a small, microprocessed, 12-volt solar panel controller with a digital charge readout, and the best part is that it costs less than 40 bucks. The Sunsei on *Saltaire* has been controlling the charge from a 38-watt Siemens panel to the same Group 31 battery for over six years, and the battery is still in top shape. The Mastervolt ChargeMaster, available in either 20 amps or 40 amps, is reported to give similar results, with the added benefits of a PC interface and adaptability to flooded, AGM, or gel batteries. The ChargeMaster controllers are much more highly priced than the unassuming Sunsei, but their extra features are a near-guarantee of state-of-the-art performance in protecting your batteries from excessive charge current.

A rather unique item among charge controllers is Victron Energy's Battery Balancer, which does exactly as the name suggests: it senses and equalizes two or more batteries connected in series or parallel. Acting like an electric Robin Hood, if it detects an unequal charge in a group of batteries, it will draw up to 1 amp from the battery with the highest charge until the lowest battery is brought up to par. The small but effective Battery Balancer has LED lights indicating the banks with high and low voltage, plus an alarm to make this system complete.

A major problem to watch for when using a multiple-input controller is pre-regulating a wind generator that uses electronic self-braking technology, such as that found in the Air-X, formerly manufactured by Southwest Windpower and now produced by XZERES Wind in Wilsonville, Oregon. The Air-X's internal controller is pre-set to dampen the turbine to a slow spin when the battery has reached its full charge or when wind speeds reach light gale force, around 35 knots. If the battery is receiving a charge from more than one source simultaneously, the Air-X may read the other input current as battery charge and prematurely drop to a slow spin, having been "pre-regulated" by the interfering charge. Incidentally, this causes no harm to the Air-X's internal wiring or controller. In its advertising literature, the company cautions the user to "test the possible interference by disconnecting the other charge sources to determine the possible interference source." Realistically, the only other charge source likely to be interfering is the engine alternator or hydro generator, since solar panels produce only a small fraction of the amperage of an alternator. If you need to run your engine to top off the cranking battery, just make sure the battery selector switch is set for that bank, not ALL, in order to allow uninterrupted charging of the house bank by the solar panels and by either the wind generator or hydro generator.

A rare but possible danger to your charging complex is a powerful surge emanating from the engine alternator and sizzling any controller or regulator not rated for the alternator's output. Small, unprotected controllers for alternative charging devices have been known to burn quickly, spewing noxious smoke while the engine is starting. A switch, fuse, or protective diode—or better yet, all three—between the battery and the control device will safeguard the device from harm.

Switches, Isolators, and Solenoids

Battery switches, isolators, and solenoids are not controllers per se, but an awareness of their function and versatility is essential to understanding the whole battery control and gate-keeping process, from charge source to battery bank. Switches have evolved a long way from Perko's classic, red, 2-ALL-1-OFF switch, which many of us still use on our vessels. These are durable, well-designed devices and they perform their job well, allowing us the option of charging or drawing from two banks hooked up in parallel. The one problem with using this as a stand-alone switch is the gradual discharging of one battery to the other, even with the switch off. To prevent this from happening, some skippers prefer to separate the two batteries with an isolator, a device that prevents discharge from one bank to the other, whether the battery selector switch is on or off. While the engine is running, the positive (red) lead from the alternator sends current directly to the isolator, which splits the charge current between the positive terminals on the two banks. Both banks are being charged simultaneously, but a solid-state diode in the isolator prevents current from flowing from one bank to the other. With the isolator in place, the operator still has the option of selecting ALL in order to draw from both banks simultaneously. Again, it is highly recommendable that the cranking battery be electrically isolated from the house bank; if the cranking battery has been depleted from charging a dead house bank and there is no time to wait for alternative charging systems to recharge either bank, the only thing left is the boat's sails.

Carrying a variety of fuses and fuse holders is cheap insurance against electrical calamity during a long voyage.

One problem found with some battery isolators is a charge voltage drop of half a volt or more at the diode between the two battery lead posts. The voltage loss also produces heat, which is why isolators often have cooling fins. Sterling Power of Eliot, Maine, claims to have found a way to eliminate voltage loss and heating in its ProSplit-R Zero Voltage Drop Isolator. The marine-grade, waterproof unit is available in a variety of battery and voltage configurations and features an LED display of charging status along with "alarm status information." The ProSplit-R also shoulders one critically important function of a controller: if either the alternator or regulator malfunctions, the ProSplit-R disconnects charge input to prevent batteries from overcharging.

Several isolators are available from Blue Sea Systems, the various models scaled in size and complexity depending on total combined amp hours. Their entry-level 65-amp and mid-range 120-amp Automatic Charging Relay with Starting Isolation (ACR) have automatic switches that connect a charge source with a battery when the ACR senses a low battery charge. Once the battery is full charged, the ACR cuts off the charge current. Either of the small ACRs can also be purchased as part of Blue Sea Systems' Add a Battery kit, which includes a battery selector switch.

Blue Sea Systems accommodates higher-amperage alternators with their ML-ACR 7620, rated for 500 amps of continuous current. This charging relay would easily accommodate a large, 200-amp alternator and battery banks in excess of 600 amp hours. The ML-ACR 7620 is designed to accept two ML-RBS remote battery switches and a pair of link busses, rather than cables, to connect the three units into a single integrated isolator-switch device. ML-Series remote switches, one with lock-out protection, the other without, allow easy control of Blue Sea Systems' ML-Series charging relay and switches, which may be mounted to a bulkhead in an inconspicuous area close to the battery banks.

By strategically placing extra switches and solenoids between the house banks and large or exposed loads, you add an extra layer of protection against short circuits and fires. First, on large yachts with highly complex electrical networks, a battery charge panel with a pair of circuit breakers for the house and cranking banks allows you to manage the automatic charging relays from the nav station instead of the engine compartment. Next, you might want to consider adding heavy-duty switches for large loads, particularly an electric windlass (a high-amperage appliance notorious for causing fires) and an AC inverter, which may be rated in excess of 1000 watts. Perko, Blue Sea Systems, and Marinco offer a variety of heavy-duty on-off switches, some included with electrical panels, others fitted with key locks or removable switch handles, and one designed specifically for an electric windlass.

Another way to handle remote, high-amperage loads, such as an electric windlass or a davit motor, is to install a solenoid with a remote switch, allowing you access to large amounts of amperage without having to turn a switch mounted on the thick red cable itself, which is probably routed

Water-resistant circuit breaker boxes make good sense, particularly in areas of the cabin or cockpit prone to spray or dampness.

An assortment of various types and sizes of marine circuit breakers.

through deep recesses along the hull. A solenoid is a switch activated by an electromagnetic coil and may be designed for either intermittent duty, as for an engine starter motor, or continuous duty, as for an anchor windlass. Cole Hersee, based in Boston, produces a long list of intermittent and continuous-duty solenoids for marine use. Each solenoid has 5/16" threaded copper studs, along with washers and hex nuts, and silver internal contacts. The solenoids are available in 12, 24, 36, and 48 volts. You make hook up any kind of 24-volt switch you desire to the smaller pair of posts on the solenoid to give you remote control. A small toggle switch or, as is becoming vogue, a switching device with a wireless remote wand, may be used to activate the solenoid from any point on the vessel, enabling you to drop anchor or raise the dinghy with the push of a button. This old sailor is sticking with his manual anchor windlass, but by all means, help yourself to the red, ergonomic, wireless rubber button.

As a final note on isolator-combiner relays, simultaneous charging of multiple banks is a rather slow means of topping off large-capacity banks. With an aggressive alternative charging scheme drawing power from solar panels, a wind generator, and possibly a hydro generator, the primary role of the engine alternator is to keep the cranking battery charged. On the other hand, when alternative power is not available for whatever reason, it is comforting to know you can start the engine, top off the cranking battery for 20 minutes, and then manually set the switch for the house bank, totally bypassing an automatic switch. As with virtually everything on your vessel, the choices are not always cut and dried. You are the final judge of what works best for your boat.

Even the most humble of offshore sailing vessels these days have at least some rudimentary electrical circuitry installed in their cabins. And since batteries running these systems need to have charging sources, these inputs must be reined in by adequate voltage regulators, or even better, by the latest in microprocessor charge controllers. As with every other electrical and mechanical apparatus onboard, it is advisable to pack a spare for every key item that may break down, including an extra multi-input charge controller for the solar panel, wind generator, and/or hydro generator. Small charge controllers are inexpensive and easily stowed in a drawer, and you can forget about finding a new one in the Marquesas. A spare regulator for the engine alternator is also wise to have along, but frankly, voltage regulators last a long time and rarely pose problems. Each vessel, even of the same make, model, and year, is outfitted uniquely, according to the tastes and needs of each skipper. By planning your electrical system carefully and safely, according to your own requirements, you will prevent calamity and add a considerable measure of comfort to your ocean voyage.

Chapter 10
Monitoring Systems

A CRITICALLY IMPORTANT ASPECT OF MINDING OUR VESSEL'S VARIOUS energy inputs and electrical storage is a monitoring system that gives us quick, ongoing, specific readings of the main components in the electrical matrix, including the engine and alternator, renewable energy sources, and battery banks. There are analog and digital meters for monitoring battery voltage and amperage, alternators with LCD readouts, and small, microprocessor-controlled, multi-input controllers with displays showing multi-phased charging. At this juncture, though, unless we are talking about a large commercial vessel, such as a cruise ship or container ship, there appears to be nothing available on the market to give you a complete, integrated, visual readout of your vessel's charge sources and battery banks on one screen, be it on a panel or on a PC. There are systems that cover portions of this, but not the whole operation. Wouldn't it be nice to look at one, big NMEA 2000-networked screen and see everything that is going on with our electrical setup, enabling us to make strategic decisions about starting up or shutting down certain charging sources? For now, we leave it to automatic controllers to make those decisions for us as they sense battery charge levels and direct charge current to different battery banks according to need. We place our trust in these automatic sensors and relays, blithely assuming they will never malfunction, or worse, destroy our battery banks. Beyond that, the best we can do is keep an eye on the battery charging monitors, frequently check the engine control panel while the engine is running, and most importantly, maintain a vessel energy plan to make sure the whole system is configured to get the best guarantee of available battery power for the least amount of money spent on diesel.

Vessel Energy Plan

The place to embark on a vessel energy plan is the total load, or current draw in amp hours, for a given time period. A period of 24 hours sounds right, except when we consider the engine alternator, which on a small boat may not be run for several days, assuming the vessel is fitted with a healthy array of alternative energy sources. Lengthening our planning period to a whole cycle of discharging and charging, perhaps a week to include at least two or three runs of the engine alternator, might be more reasonable. On larger yachts with a genset being used on a daily basis to keep up with a much greater daily amp hour demand, a 24-hour cycle is probably going to give us a fairly accurate, consistent picture of amp hour usage. For planning purposes, do not include an electric windlass because this is used only on occasion, and virtually always while the main engine is running, both to enable navigation in tight quarters and to supply sufficient amperage for the high current draw of the windlass motor. For better accuracy, you should have one plan for when you are at anchor and the other for under way. Navigation systems are only for passagemaking, save for the GPS anchor alarm, and the VHF radio will probably get a lot more use in an anchorage than on open water, where the single-sideband is the primary means of communication. And remember, a 100-watt SSB uses four times the amperage of a typical VHF base-mount radio when transmitting. However, many crews leave the VHF on 24-seven as long as they are on board, and the SSB is on usually only when checking in with cruiser nets.

Be realistic in listing all the possible draws on the house battery. For starters, you may refer to the "Energy Planning Chart" to give you an idea of how to put together a spreadsheet. You can take the time to enter all of this onto an Excel spreadsheet, or you can download an auto-calculating chart for free from the Internet. Multiply the number of amps of each load by the estimated number of hours of usage per day, and then add up the totals to give you an estimate of how much battery power your vessel is consuming on a daily basis. Hopefully, your battery consumption is staying within this rule of thumb: total daily electrical consumption should not surpass one-fourth of the total rated amp hours of the house bank.

Assuming you are making minimal use of the engine alternator, no more than an hour or two per day, and drawing power from at least two renewable sources, your vessel's batteries should always be above their critical marks, which vary depending on type of battery and manufacturer. Just to make sure, list all the charging sources with the number of amps normally contributed by each. To calculate amp hours, multiply solar output by 10, wind power by 24, and the hydro generator by the number of hours you determine is adequate. These figures, of course, depend on average wind speed, availability of sunshine, or vessel speed while under way with a hydro generator. Each day is slightly different, so you are trying to establish a conservative average for planning purposes. Also, add up the amount of time you plan to run the engine. This will vary, since you will be running your engine selectively to fill in during those periods where the alternative sources may have fallen short. Add up your total amp hours and compare this figure to the final total on the Energy Planning Chart. A deficit will require extra engine running time, which in turn converts into gallons per day. That can add up faster than you think if you are not keeping daily records of battery charge and usage. The more you skimp on engine usage and rely on renewable energy, the greater the chances of your reaching your destination with fuel left in the tank.

Analog and Digital Monitoring

The two hemispheres of the world of electrical monitoring, analog and digital, offer distinct benefits and for this reason often live side-by-side on an electrical control panel. The trend toward all-digital monitoring is undeniable and understandable in light of the extra options, memory, and automaticity it offers. However, there are still applications where analog systems make good sense: their weather resistance and readability from a distance make them ideal in the cockpit in inclement conditions.

Analog and digital meters provide identical information, but they process the data in different ways. For example, an analog ammeter uses a sensing coil to read amperage while a digital meter employs a shunt resistor to detect amperage. The needle in the analog meter moves depending on

Custom engine panels like this one from AC/DC Marine can spruce up a cockpit on an aging boat.

Energy Planning Chart

Load	Amps	Hours per day	Ah per day
Lights			
Running lights			
Anchor light			
Cabin lights			
Plumbing			
Electric head pump			
Bilge pump			
Pressurized water			
Water desalinator			
Navigation			
GPS			
Autopilot			
Depth sounder			
Weather fax			
Display console			
Laptop computer			
Communication			
VHF			
SSB			
Refrigeration			
Refrigerator/freezer			
Air conditioner			
Entertainment			
Stereo			
Flat screen monitor			
DVD player			
		Total Ah/day	
To calculate total amp hours, multiply the amperage of each item by the number of hours used each day, and then add up the total Ah/day.			

Saltaire's Beta Marine engine panel has survived a complete circumnavigation of the earth, its analog gauges still give dependable readings.

This beautifully rendered recessed gauge panel by AC/DC Marine features a tachometer, oil pressure gauge, temperature gauge, and ignition keyway.

the level of magnetism induced by the current. With a digital ammeter, we are reading amperage as detected through voltage, which is the pressure of the amperage passing through the shunt resistor. To review Ohm's Law for a moment, voltage equals amperage divided by resistance, or $E = I/R$. Therefore, assuming a fixed value for resistance, any change in amperage running through the resistor results in a corresponding change in voltage. In practical terms, the differences we see are in how we read analog and digital meters. An analog meter presents the voltage or amperage with a black dial swinging across a white, circular, numbered face, and a digital meter displays the data numerically on a gray LCD screen.

An analog meter offers a number of distinct advantages. First, it can be seen at a greater distance than an LCD. Even if you cannot read the numbers on, say, an engine thermometer from eight feet away, you can tell at a glance whether it is rising, falling, or holding steady. Next, if a dial is exposed to a bit of dampness, it will probably continue working, at least until it corrodes and finally stops after decades of abuse. If moisture enters an LCD face, a portion of the numbers may be blotted out, or it may be completely destroyed. Some captains say analog meters last longer than digital systems with LCDs, although I have seen no solid evidence of this. Analog systems run on solid-state circuits, which may sound sturdier, but perhaps not after a capacitor, resistor, transistor, or diode blows out.

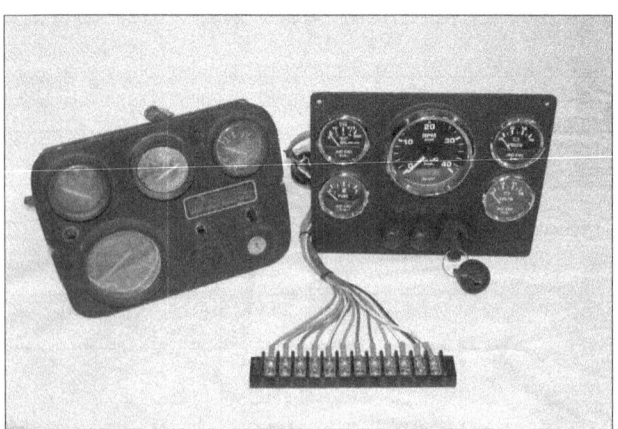

An original Volvo-Penta engine panel and its after-market replacement by AC/DC Marine.

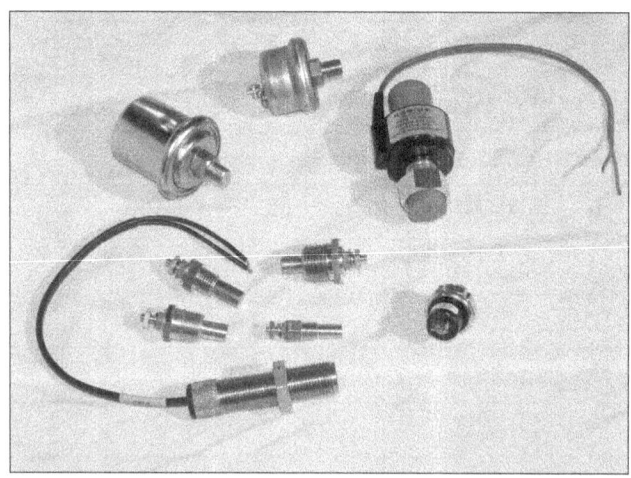

Maintaining a store of extra sending units for oil pressure, tachometer, engine temperature, and transmission oil pressure may be going a bit overboard, but it could save time and money later on during your voyage.

Lower cost is one of the driving factors behind digital electronics, but not the only one. To be sure, a silicon chip on a tiny, printed circuit board is far less expensive to produce than a big, meticulously crafted board covered with shiny wires and solder, tiny tin can transistors, and "Chicklet" capacitors. However, a tiny board with a silicon chip microprocessor, if packaged in a waterproof package, is also likely to last longer because there is nothing to burn out or break. A set of logic algorithms now supplants all those colorful things on the old-fashioned circuit board. Instead of having a mechanical dial that might flick back and forth erratically from partial oxidation, a faulty coil, or a loose wire, an LCD display has no moving parts, so it can last indefinitely in the cabin or out on deck as long as it is completely sealed off from moisture. The LCD on *Saltaire's* Signet depth sounder has survived direct sunlight, humidity, and ocean spray for over 15 years and still works as well as the day I installed it.

Other big plusses with digital microprocessors are memory, programmability, and the ability to process information and present it instantly. In the old days, we measured battery charge exclusively with an analog multimeter, measuring each bank separately after turning the selector switch to the correct voltage or amperage range and hopefully not turning the switch to ohms, which could cause the nine-volt multimeter battery to explode. Now we have digital logic systems that not only read both banks simultaneously, but also direct charge current to the battery in greater need until both batteries are equally charged. And what's more, these devices are surprisingly inexpensive and so small they just do not look big enough to perform all that work. Data links between your laptop or tablet on one side and the engine and charging components on the other bring at least some of these functions together in one place and make the job of monitoring and managing these systems much easier.

Engine Monitoring

Regardless of the type of digital monitoring apparatus you wish to install, your engine will already have a control panel installed. If you are purchasing a new engine, make sure you order

This older-generation Heart Interface 2000 battery monitor faithfully gives precise readings of current battery charge.

the best, highest-priced control panel available, not the cheap one with "idiot" lights. The panel should have needle gauges for the tachometer, oil pressure, coolant temperature, and alternator, plus an odometer-like engine hour counter. In addition to these standard features, the panel may include alarms and, yes, idiot lights for low oil pressure and excessive temperature. Oil pressure in the U.S. is measured in pounds per square inch (PSI), and the alarm is set by the manufacturer at the minimum allowable oil pressure for that specific model. Maximum engine temperatures also vary among diesel engines, but they all tend to lie just below the boiling point of water, which is 212°F.

If your vessel does not have needle gauges for the engine, you can purchase marine gauges a la carte in a variety of attractive styles from Faria, Sierra, Stewart Warner, and Teleflex (makers of Morse engine and transmission controls). These gauges are waterproof and, since they are sold separately, offer you the advantage of being able to install them in whatever manner you wish, which could be a panel of your own design, tailored to fit the exact spot you have in mind.

Garmin, Lowrance, Raymarine, and other manufacturers of marine electronic controls offer virtual engine panels, each one with a set of graphic meters that are probably easier to read than the gauges currently installed on your boat. The bright, colorful gauges are set against a dark background, making them easy to read at night. You can access the virtual panel on your GPS chart plotter at the helm or through a remote display at the nav station. Remote panels, such as the Garmin Remote Input Device (GRID), allow you full access to all the functions on the main panel, a feature you will certainly appreciate in the middle of a sustained full gale. Take time to keep yourself informed of the rapidly advancing technology in marine integrated GPS monitors, as this industry is constantly streamlining and expanding the capabilities of these products. The latest, top-of-the-line technology integrates an incredibly diverse array of systems aboard a modern sailing vessel, including depth sounder/fish finder, radar, weather, iPod and iPhone menus, Sirius SM Satellite Radio, DVD player, stereo speaker controls, and various memory functions in addition to the standard GPS and engine panel displays.

Battery Monitoring

Battery charge is one critically important function that appears to have been left out of the race to integrate monitoring on today's pleasure craft. We can assume that is a whole different story aboard the USS Nimitz or the Majesty of the Seas cruise ship. In time this will change, but for now we must continue to assess battery status through a separate set of devices. The old standard for giving a quick reading on battery health, and still popular with many sailors, is a separate analog voltmeter gauge for each bank, commonly mounted on the switch panel. The switches themselves may wear out from time to time, but the needle gauge voltmeter is likely to outlive the crew. The problem with needle gauges in general, though, is precision. After a while, you acquire a "feel" for what the meter is saying, knowing that when the gauge reads 14 volts, your digital multimeter could be reading perhaps 13.8 volts. Sometimes the needle is just a tad less precise than the digital voltmeter. That is generally not a problem until you measure your cranking battery after an hour of charging with the engine alternator and the needle gauge voltmeter battery shows a charge of 12.2 volts—right on the edge of retirement. The vessel is fueled up and stocked with booze, food, and water, and you have a perfect weather window for the five-day cruise to the next island. Do you waste a precious day and buy a battery now, or wait until the next big town somewhere down the line? Reluctantly, not wanting to accept fate, you place the digital multimeter's leads on the battery posts, and you get a reading of 11.9 volts. Bye-bye, battery. A low house bank charge is something we expect after many hours of use without a charge, as it can accept 200 full cycles or more before dying completely. But the starting bank is a different story. The cranking battery has a very low tolerance for deep cycling, so we need to be able to measure voltage as precisely as possible.

If you do not have a multimeter, a quick and dirty way to get a reading on battery charge is to turn the ignition key to the "on" position for a moment before cranking the engine. Since the only voltage to be read at that moment is from the starter bank, you can see the battery charge level at a glance. With a full charge, the battery will read only about 10 volts on an analog engine panel volt meter. By turning the battery selector key to the house bank, you can get a rough reading of that charge, too. For a precise reading, you will need to measure the battery at its positive and negative terminals with a proper voltage measuring device, but the analog engine panel meter is better than nothing at all.

To keep up on every measurable aspect of a battery's status, we can take advantage of the most recent battery monitoring technology. Some systems are small, stand-alone devices offering a surprising level of comprehensive data on a battery, and some may be configured for two banks. At the most basic level is the humble Nasa Clipper BM-2 Battery Monitor from the U.K. This small monitor features an LCD screen showing volts and amps discharged with a bar scale of current charge level. The device is limited to one battery bank, so at least two will be needed for both the cranking and house banks. Also, the BM-2 is designed for use only on flooded lead acid batteries, which covers a lot of smaller cruising vessels. The BM-2 measures up to 16 volts DC and a maximum current of 199 amps on its 200-amp shunt.

The Xantrex LinkPRO and LinkLITE LED monitors indicate battery charge for a dual battery bank, letting you "read your battery bank like a fuel gauge." The LinkPRO, the direct replacement for the old Xantrex XBM battery monitor, handles up to 10,000 amps DC and monitors two battery charges simultaneously. The lower-priced LinkLITE is rated at 1,000 amps. Both monitors display voltage, amperage, consumed amp hours, remaining charge, and time remaining in the battery bank. The two units also feature a 500-amp shunt, enabling them to measure a high range of amperage. Unlike the larger, rectangular footprint of the Xantrex Link 2000, each of the new monitors is encased in a round bezel.

Xantrex has expanded the utility of its LinkPRO with its Pro Battery Monitor Communications Interface, intended for use with a laptop computer. The separately sold monitor system consists of an interface box, a proprietary serial cable, and Windows-compatible software on a CD-ROM. Before ordering this interface, it is advisable to phone Xantrex and ask a technician about the latest developments regarding software compatibility.

Victron markets a comparable gauge, also with a round bezel roughly the same size as the Xantrex pair. The Victron BMV 700 measures a voltage range of 6.5 to 95 volts and has a shunt selection capacity of up to 10,000 amps through its 500-amp quick-connect shunt. A big advantage offered by Victron is its BMV 702 Color Control unit, which brings together charge monitoring data from up to four BMV 700 monitors through CANbus (NMEA 2000), Ethernet cable, or USB. Bluetooth capability allows you to receive real-time charging data through your smart phone or tablet computer. For additional communication ability, you can add a Victron Global Remote, a modem that sends updates and alarms to your cell phone via text messages.

Monitoring Charge Sources

Keeping tabs on the battery banks is only half the equation in the overall management of the vessel's electrical matrix. That being said, most cruising skippers are content with just reading the battery voltage levels and trusting all of the charge sources to do their job. Yet it is also wise to keep an eye on how much electrical energy is being deposited into the vessel's electrical storage and how much current is coming from each source. The constant minding of the engine alternator, genset, hydro generator, wind generator, and solar panel array requires a robust monitoring system to prevent overcharging and to alert us in the event of an underperforming or defunct piece of charging equipment. We covered the essentials of controlling charge inputs in Chapter 9, so the monitoring function dovetails directly into that discussion, and you will recognize some of the manufacturers, except this time from the monitoring side.

Just as with battery charge, our first step in assessing alternator output is volts DC. A typical analog DC voltmeter scaled from 8 to 18 volts, or 10 to 16 volts, is commonly included on the control panel of every new boat engine. Ideally, the needle should read 14.1 to 14.5 volts while the engine is running.

Measuring current is also key to assessing the alternator's health. An ammeter for the alternator is a common sight on many sailing vessels. Often placed on the engine control panel alongside the other gauges, including the voltmeter, the ammeter tells us whether the alternator is charging within its normal range of current for a given engine speed. If we have a 50 amp alternator on an engine running at top speed, say 3000 RPM, we want to be sure the alternator is producing close to 50 amps. If your engine's panel lacks an ammeter, you can purchase a high-quality, marine-grade analog gauge for anywhere from $30 to $200. Blue Sea Systems and Paneltronics carry digital ammeters towards the upper end of this price spectrum. Install the device in a convenient place as conveniently close to the voltmeter as possible, whether on the engine panel or inside the cabin next to the switch panel.

For alternative power applications, a variety of ammeters and voltage meters are available, sometimes combined in the same control panel, and usually as part of a charge controller. An example of a single-source regulator is Nature Power's 28-amp Solar Charge Controller, which includes an LCD readout of the charge source voltage and amperage being handled by the unit. This particular model can manage up to 450 watts at 12 or 24 volts DC, and the digital LCD screen shows batteries, amperage, and battery voltage in five-second intervals. The unit also features adjustable voltage settings; to play it safe, stay within the maximum rated charge recommended on each battery.

Mastervolt's MPPT Solar ChargeMaster 25 is another single-purpose device with an LCD display of battery charge in volts, charge current, wattage, and load as measured in watts. The unit features a temperature sensor, several alarms, a serial interface, and a separately purchased interface adaptor for use with a personal computer. The ChargeMaster 25 may be used to charge flooded, AGM, gel, or Mastervolt-brand 12- and 24-volt lithium ion batteries.

If you want to read the charging status of two sources through one regulator, Marlec's HRSi charge controller accepts up to 160 watts of solar panel input along with its Rutland 504 Windcharger and also features a tri-color LCD charge indicator. This is not quite a full-featured control monitor but is notable in that it is designed for more than one type of charge source and for two battery banks.

Additional Monitoring Devices

Besides monitoring engine status, battery health, and various charging systems, numerous

The bilge counter from AC/DC Marine keeps track of how many times the bilge pump has switched on in a given time frame, alerting crew of a potentially loose packing gland or faulty through-hull fitting.

other devices on a cruising vessel need constant gauging. These include refrigerator temperature, cabin temperature, fuel and water tank levels, bilge counter for keeping track of bilge pump activity, wind speed and direction, and barometric pressure. All of these require sending units and either analog or digital gauges; some, such as engine temperature, also may be linked through NMEA 2000 to your laptop computer or multi-function display. The main components of these gauges, except perhaps for the aneroid or digital barometer, may eventually malfunction and cease to provide usable data. Decide which of these functions are most critical

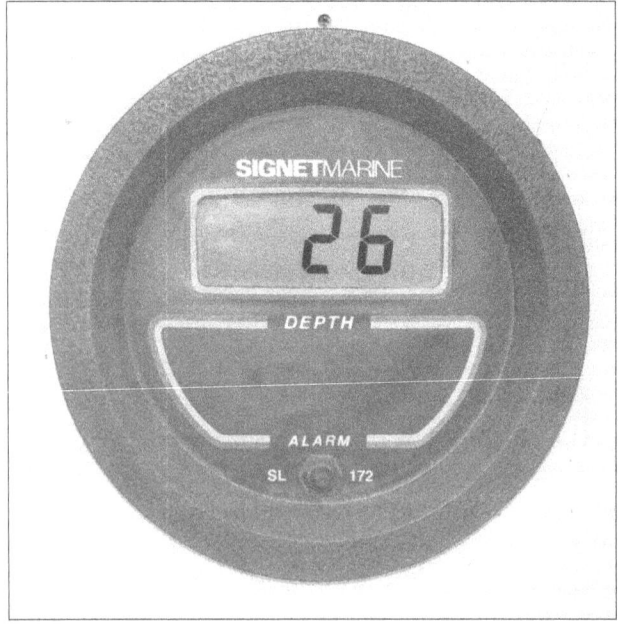

Saltaire's Signet depth sounder was recently rebuilt by Signet of Torrance, Calif., after 15 years of service and will probably last another 15 years before its next rebuild.

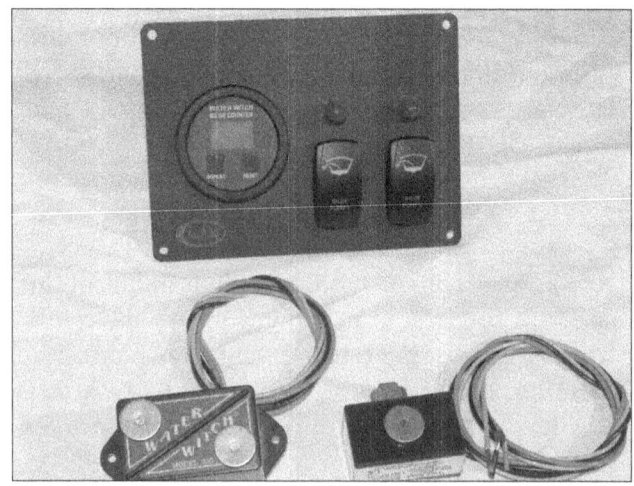

The bilge counter panel gives readings from Water Witch sending units.

and consider purchasing a spare for each of these devices. The most likely to malfunction are the fuel and freshwater gauges, so it would be wise to pack, at the very least, a spare sending unit for each of these.

It is a safe bet that the marine electrical industry will continue to integrate battery and charge monitoring systems into comprehensive, stand-alone packages, making it easy for us to see every aspect of our vessel's charging array and other functions at a glance. Ideally, a comprehensive electrical monitoring system will track the charges and total loads on all battery banks, along with the charging volts and amps of every solar panel, the hydro generator, the wind generator, and two alternators if necessary to put together one highly complex, yet easy-to-read picture of the vessel's electrical status. For now, we enjoy the benefits of the state of technology as it is and fill in the blanks with our engine controls, single-purpose voltmeters and ammeters, and hand-held multimeters. As long as we are living within our vessel energy plans and being diligent in keeping all of our monitoring systems in good repair, we can survive successfully for many years on the cruising circuit.

Chapter 11
Lighting, Navigation, and Communication

MANY ELECTRICAL LOADS DRAW FROM YOUR BOAT'S HOUSE BATTERY bank over a 24-hour period. Instead of trying to cover all of them in this chapter, you will find them narrowed down to three categories of essential systems: lighting, navigation, and communication. Cabin lighting is essential at night for charting and making log entries, and either the running lights or anchor light is necessary for safety. For navigation, we need at the very minimum a GPS running around the clock, and for vessels with radar and full GPS mapping on multi-function displays, that equates to a significantly larger dose of current. Radios do not draw much amperage over time, but they do need to be supported by a dependable supply of juice for brief contacts and for peace of mind in an emergency. These three broad categories combined, depending on the vessel and skipper, can draw anywhere from a miserly 20 amps to a princely 200 amp hours per day; such is the range of cruising platforms and styles on the world's oceans.

Navigation Lights

Sailors differ in their opinions regarding the use of navigation nights at night, whether they are sailing along the coast or on open ocean. When sailing close to shore where there are other vessels present, it is prudent to let your presence and heading be known. If there is any question about this, U.S. Coast Guard regulations leave no room for doubt: all waterborne vessels must carry an approved combination of lights, given the vessel and its purpose on the water, even at anchor. I will confess that when my vessel is beyond a day's sail from land, I generally shut off all lights until I wake up in the middle of the night and spot the running lights of another vessel. At that instant, I flip on the running lights and VHF and hail the other vessel in order to share our speed and heading so that we may avoid collision. Once the two vessels have moved safely away from each other, I turn off everything but the old Garmin 128 GPS and crash back into my berth. Yes, I know, I'm supposed to be awake and on watch 24 hours a day, but I'm only human.

Over the last three decades, the boating industry has gone from incandescent bulbs, to halogens, and now to LED (light-emitting diode) lights, including LED replacements for just about every type of bulb imaginable on a modern cruising boat. The LED replacements, available with single-pin, double-pin, bayonet, or festoon mounts, come at jaw-dropping prices, but on the positive side, they last a very long time. On smaller vessels with limited battery capacity, LEDs, which use only a small fraction of the amperage of an incandescent of the same size, make it possible to run navigation lights all night long. For example, a double-contact, bayonet-mount incandescent or halogen bulb for a cabin coaming running light draws roughly an amp, while the LED replacement draws less than a tenth of an amp. But there are two sticking points, the first of which is price. The short-lived incandescent costs less than $5.00, the halogen close to $10, but the LED will set you back about $30. Even if price is not a problem, the larger LED cluster might not fit inside some of the older light fixtures. Owners of older yachts with classic bronze and glass light fixtures may wish to preserve the original appearance of their vessels. But the amp hour savings are indisputable: three incandescent running lights consume a combined 30 amp hours over a 10-hour period, while three LEDs use roughly 2.4 amp hours—almost nothing. If your boat has a single-bulb mast-head trilight, an LED should fit with no trouble. Now you are down to .8 amp hour per night, which *is* nothing. When we factor in the longevity of LEDs, over 50,000 hours, or about 14 years of use at 10 hours per night, and how much money we would spend on incandescents or halogens over the same period, the LEDs are essentially free. You just have to make them fit inside the lenses, that's all. As for the festoon-mount steaming light on the forward side of the mast, there is an LED that should fit perfectly, but since the light is on only when the engine and alternator are running, what's the point? That extra 30 bucks will buy a half-case of tequila in Puerto Vallarta.

Cabin Lights

Even in this day of creative, energy-saving lighting options for the cabin, some traditionalists love the glow of a brass kerosene lamp over the saloon table. In an old wooden schooner or Tahiti ketch with its big brass lamp and voluptuous glass flu, you half expect to see old Blackbeard himself lumbering down the steps to join you for a wee dram of grog. In reality, though, a kerosene lantern is first of all a health risk with its black smoke and carbon monoxide giving you a piercing headache. And then you have to contend with the constant swinging and squeaking of the lamp and the banging against your head in rough weather, and storing enough of the flammable liquid to keep the smelly

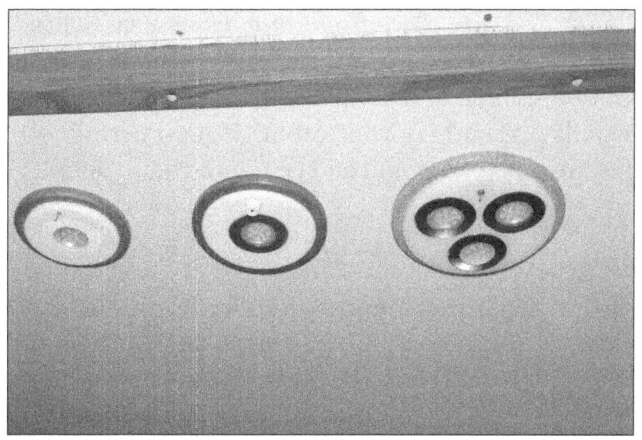

Custom LED lighting by AC-DC.

thing operating. And when it is lit, it provides just barely enough light to read a chart, and that's only if you have a strong magnifying glass. But boy does that lamp look cool.

As with navigation lights, all of your electric cabin lights can and should be converted to LEDs. A typical 35-foot sailing vessel can have over a dozen cabin lights: two or three around the saloon table, two in the galley, one or two at the nav station, one or two in the head, two in the vee berth, and one in each quarter berth. A dozen incandescent bulbs all on at the same time comes to 120 amp hours per night, more than half the storage of a deep-cycle, 12-volt, AGM 8D battery. With LEDs, that drops to 12 amp hours, easily handled by a Group 24 battery. No boat will have all those lights on for the entire night, but all the same, there is an undeniable savings in amperage and increased battery life with LEDs. And because few if any of these cabin fixtures have lenses, they should be easy to fit with the slightly larger profile of LEDs.

Adding new light fixtures to replace rusty or worn-out fixtures should not be a problem as long the original wiring is still intact and in serviceable condition. If not, you will have to run new wire. The original wiring, as you undoubtedly know, was laid in places where you have no access: behind the cabin or roof liner, between the hull and cabin molds, or between layers of marine plywood. Your only recourse is to run wire behind settees, around tanks, through the bilge, or the worst of all fears, right out in the open across beautifully varnished bulkheads. A table saw and a router can produce attractive wire cover molding from ash, white oak, teak, or mahogany, all stable woods which can be stained and varnished to blend in with the woods presently in your cabin. A good wiring job requires planning and an eye for aesthetic detail.

Navigation

For navigation, except for the traditionalists, the world has moved beyond the lead line, knot log, and sextant. As back-ups just in case of battery loss, though, having these three items onboard is still a good idea. Boiling lead in a tin cup mold and drilling a hole down the middle for the cordage will provide you with a depth sounder, but a handheld digital sounder is much easier to use. You will find on the Internet numerous handheld sounders and fish finders measuring depths of up to 200 feet, and most are priced between $90 and $150. Old, bronze mechanical knot logs are still to be found on some yachts, and they are a great back-up if the batteries fail. As for navigation, many sailors still keep up the art of celestial navigation with a sextant. However, with handheld GPS and even programmable GPS wristwatches with LED displays available at affordable prices, as long as the geostationary satellites are operating properly, there is no need for the knot log or sextant.

Permanent-mount GPS and chart plotting systems are available in so many sizes, capabilities, combinations, and levels of power consumption that there is a package for every vessel, no matter how humble or ambitious your needs may be. The particular models and their capabilities are evolving constantly, and you are well advised to stay abreast of this technology before committing to a navigation system that you could be using for the next 20 years.

Our main focus, for purposes of this discussion, is to keep power usage as low as possible while ensuring many years of safe voyaging. Your choices will take into account your preferences and, for reasons that remain unclear to me, vessel size. I suppose a larger vessel reflects a bigger bank roll and hence the perceived need for a bigger, fancier multi-function nav station. I have been using the same, simple Garmin 128 GPS for 15 years and have seen the same unit on a 50-foot ketch doing the exact same job. Both skippers use paper charts with dividers, a triangle, and a pencil, and we succeed equally well at making the same ocean crossings. Some cruisers prefer a handheld GPS, enjoying the benefit of always having the vessel's position and trajectory available anywhere on the boat. You can find a full-function, waterproof, handheld GPS starting at about $100 online or in just about any sporting goods shop or chandlery.

The biggest, most expensive, and most battery-guzzling electronic navigation arrays are found on large motor vessels, particularly fishing boats. Two large diesel engines, each fitted with two 220-amp alternators (21.12 kilowatt hours per day) could power up a whole fishing village.

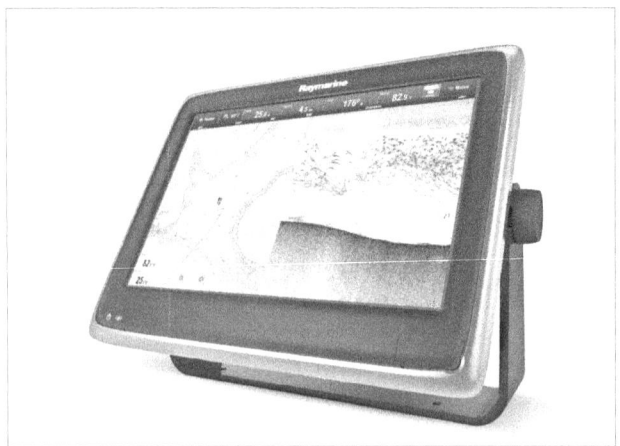

Photo courtesy of Raymarine

The Raymarine a128 multifunction touch screen, split-chart display offers the latest in chartplotting and autopilot control technology, powered by Raymarine's LightHouse III user interface.

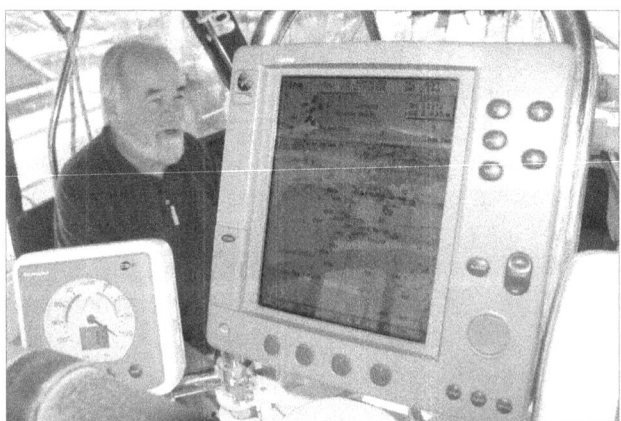

This legacy Raymarine Pathfinder RL80C chart plotter endured a 15-year circumnavigation aboard Greg and Deborah Claesson's Hunter Passage 450 Sonrisa.

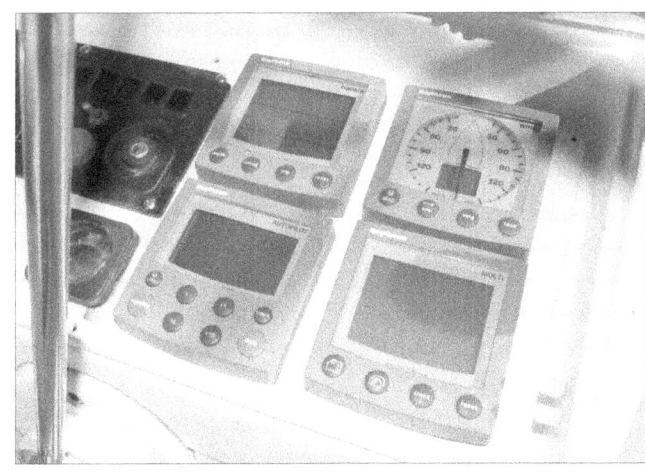

Clockwise from top left: the Raytheon/Raymarine ST60 depth sounder/speed indicator, ST60 wind direction indicator, ST60 multi (includes apparent wind direction and speed), and ST6000+ autopilot control.

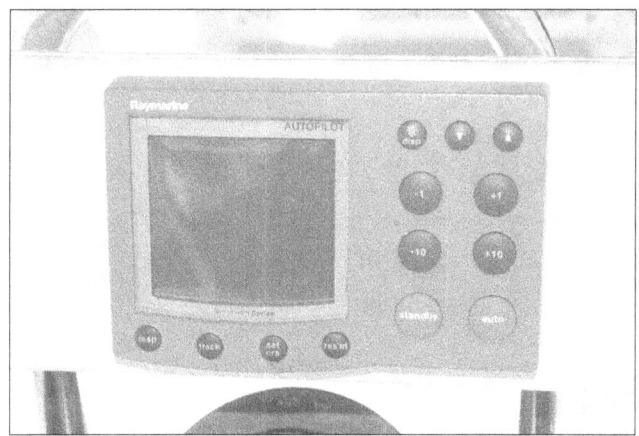

This Raymarine ST7001+ SmartPilot, installed on a Hunter 43, can communicate with a chart plotter and an autopilot using SeaTalk or NMEA data.

Cruising trawlers, which are continually gaining in popularity, also produce high levels of power though not at the level of large sport fishers. Larger sailing vessels, producing only a tiny fraction of that amount, a few hundred amp hours per day, still have enough for a comprehensive, fully networked array of electronics, including an open-array radar, graphic sonar, a multi-function color monitor, and radios, and that does not include the autopilot, the hydraulic steering drive unit, or other assorted equipment. The navigation devices with the largest amperage draw are likely to be the radar (1.3-12 amps), charting sonar (4 amps), and chart plotter (1-3 amps) for a total range of roughly 6 to 19 amps, or 144 to 456 amp hours per day. Even at the low end, that is a lot of amperage for the average cruising vessel, and we have not included all of the navigation systems here.

Realistically, most cruising sailors budget for a much leaner amperage diet in their navigation equipment. They install a low-powered radar, and many use it only at night. At 4 amps, that's 40 amp hours instead of 96 amp hours. An alternative to radar and consuming less than half the amperage is the latest Automatic identification system technology (AIS). AIS, installed in some higher-end VHF radios, such as the ICOM MA500TR permanent-mount VHF transceiver, allows you to track the name, GPS position, heading, and speed of nearby vessels and to share your information with them as well. You can share data with any vessel within the transmitting distance of your VHF antenna and track other vessels on your chart plotter, using it like a radar screen. The best news is that the ICOM VHF with AIS consumes only .7 amp in receive mode and 1.5 amps in transmit, which is roughly the same for all base-mount VHF radios. AIS is useful only when other vessels are equipped with the same capability, meaning a small powerboat zooming your way in a coastal fog will be unaware of your presence. Offshore, though, you can expect most large commercial vessels to be using AIS. Caveat: AIS does not completely replace a radar system, the only sure means of identifying other vessels or other obstructions in your vicinity.

For measuring depth, the typical sailing vessel is equipped with a standard depth sounder instead of a charting sonar, and a sounder is generally used only on approach to an anchorage or marina, when the engine is likely to be running. In an area riddled with shoals, such as Biscayne Bay, Nadi Waters in Fiji, and portions of the north coast of Crete, you will need to keep the sounder on for a much longer period, perhaps an entire day until reaching your destination. But don't worry. The transducer and LED screen of a standard, no-frills sailboat depth sounder consume about a third of an amp, or 8 amp hours per day.

Charting

Charting is another facet of navigation likely to continue undergoing profound changes for decades to come. For now, as in the past, the most

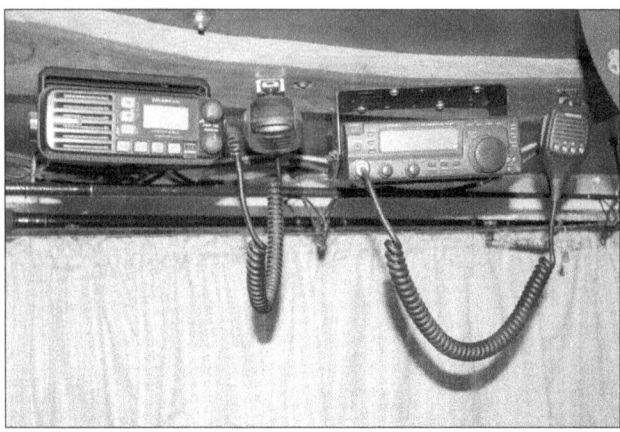

A VHF base mount radio with DSC and either a marine SSB or a ham HF transceiver are the minimum communications equipment you should carry onboard an offshore cruising vessel.

dependable way to keep track of where you are is by using up-to-date paper charts published by NOAA, the British Admiralty, or some other government-run geological or oceanic mapping authority. Charts are no longer printed by NOAA but are printed and sold "on demand" by chart agents. Paper charts give you the advantage of seeing the "big picture," giving you the perspective you need in order to plan and document an ocean voyage. NOAA charts give you the best accuracy, and once you chart your position, the only thing likely to compromise the data entry is a spilled cup of coffee.

Since all U.S. Government publications are in the public domain, you can download NOAA raster charts as PDF files and print them on a large printer, or refer to them on your laptop while underway. A number of free, downloadable chart plotters are available online, an example of which is Sea Clear, which can be used with your GPS, as long as it has a USB port and NMEA 0183 or 2000 capability. With a Garmin GPS 152, you can buy a USB data cable for about $25 and have virtually the same GPS plotting capability as you would have with a $6,000 chart plotter, not including the Navionics or C-Map charts, each of which costs more than the Garmin 152 itself.

Communications

The essential function of a VHF radio is to enable communication within a short radius of your vessel. A five-watt handheld VHF radio gives you a range of five to eight miles, and a base-mount, 25-watt VHF radio with a mast head antenna gives you about 20 miles. Make sure your handheld VHF is rated as waterproof and has a DC charger with a cigarette lighter adapter. The base-mount VHF must have DSC (digital selective calling) capability and a connection to your GPS to access the DSC emergency locator system. Some skippers expect the red DSC button on the VHF to lead the Coast Guard to their precise positions, but there is no way the coasties know your exact position without a latitude and longitude from the GPS. If all they have is a radio signal, they have to revert back to the RDF (radio direction finder) of the old days.

The absolute worst means of communication for reporting an emergency on the ocean is a cell phone, virtually useless for summoning help aboard a boat. Nonetheless, this is probably the most commonly used emergency communication device on coastal waters. Imagine looking for a sinking vessel while trying to follow, "We turned left after the big, white lighthouse like, um, two hours ago." (Frantic voices in background). "Huh? Oh yeah, I mean three hours ago. I can see a gray tower on a green hill. Can't you see us? We're right here, damn it! Glug, glug, glug..." A digital cell phone signal communicates with a cell tower, not directly with another cell phone, so it cannot be singled out among the thousands of other cell signals by an RDF. If you know your precise GPS coordinates and are able to pass that information on to the Coast Guard via cell phone, then you can summon help. More than ten miles offshore, though, a flashy cell phone with a lead ball and a treble hook makes a great trolling lure.

Serious cruisers have depended on amateur ham single-sideband radio (SSB) since at least as far back as the early 1960s. Imagine sailing in the middle of the Pacific and talking to a guy drinking beer in a cottage in England, or to a senior government official in an African republic. This is the power of ham radio. Your primary duty as a sailor, though, is to maintain contact with other sailing vessels in your group or region and to share crucial information regarding weather, sailing conditions, and the most up-to-date information regarding checking-in procedures at various ports.

Upper-sideband marine radio on 40 meters is normally enabled through a dedicated marine band HF (high frequency) radio transceiver, such as the 150-watt ICOM M802. However, it is also common practice to modify a standard ham radio rig, such as the legacy Kenwood TS-50 ham transceiver, to receive and transmit on marine SSB channels. The FCC and similar government agencies around the world forbid ham sets from transmitting on marine SSB frequencies, but this is standard procedure among sailing amateur radio operators. The exception to this law is when there is danger to human life. Information regarding severe weather conditions, sea state, obstructions, and piracy is meant to save human lives, and those are the issues you are discussing routinely. If you happen to throw in a recipe for tuna casserole during one of your contacts regarding a gale near Socotra Island while crossing the Arabian Sea, believe me, no one cares. Do your best to keep your conversations focused on topics involving safety, but don't lose any sleep over the legality of using a ham set on marine frequencies.

The use of ham and marine SSB radios requires licensure by the Federal Communications Commission (FCC), although there are significant differences in what the two licenses cover and in the process for securing the licenses. The application procedure for an FCC Ship Radio License is a simple affair requiring you to fill out a form and pay a one-time fee of $60. An FCC Amateur Radio (ham) License permitting communication on many radio frequency bands, including 40 meters where the marine SSB channels are, requires you to pass the General Class amateur radio test. To qualify for a ham radio license, you must understand basic electronics, radio reception and transmission, antenna propagation theory, and the laws governing amateur radio transmission, all of which will help you use your ham set and associated equipment for best service. If you are a serious cruiser, you owe it to yourself to pass the Technician and General ham tests, the two levels of FCC tests required for your General Class ham radio license. If you enjoy math and want to study additional antenna theory, you can study for the Extra Class test. Most of the chatter on ham radio, though, is on the General Class portions of the ham frequency bands. If you have only a marine station license, your license and your marine SSB are limited to exactly that, marine SSB. No licensed ham operator in any country will respond to an unlicensed ham radio operator (easily verified online), except in a life-threatening emergency. With a General Class ham license, you have access to more frequency bands, allowing you far more flexibility in how you communicate. Ham includes not only SSB but also FM, AM, and continuous wave (CW), which involves using Morse Code.

Besides being able to chat with other cruisers and ham operators on your SSB, your ham radio can be linked to your laptop computer via a Pactor modem to enable communication through Sail Mail. For a small annual fee, cruisers who want world-wide email access can join this non-profit organization in order to send and receive email from any point on the planet. Other than the annual fee, there is no further charge to send or receive an unlimited number of emails through Sail Mail via SSB, or through Inmarsat or Iridium satellites. Sail Mail will provide you with an updated list of SSB frequencies in their network so that you are always capable of contacting a Sail Mail station.

A ham radio installation on your vessel will take some time to plan properly. You will need not only a transceiver, but an automatic tuner, too. A long length of copper foil connecting the radio and tuner ground terminals to a couple of bronze through-hull fittings will provide the counterpoise you need for a solid signal capable of reaching amateur stations thousands of miles away. In addition, your rig will need a dependable random-wire antenna coupled with the automatic tuner. The most commonly used wire for this purpose on a sailing vessel is an isolated backstay. You may have noticed two cylindrical couplers, one near the top and one near the bottom of a backstay, on some sailboats. Those are ceramic isolators, like the dark brown disks on power poles, protecting radio transmissions from being absorbed by the mast or the ocean. Other antenna options are a shroud wire or whip antenna, but the long backstay antenna is generally the easiest and most effective random wire installation.

The secret to having the best transmitting capability in your cruising fleet is maintaining a really good ground/counterpoise. That means carrying plenty of extra Gordon West copper foil and inspecting the counterpoise at least once a month. If the copper is turning reddish brown and crispy from exposure to saltwater, cut out the affected section and splice in a new piece by crimping the ends together and, if necessary, stapling the foil joints to keep them from pulling apart. In a cruiser anchorage, the alpha skipper is the one with the tallest mast. Offshore, it's the skipper with the strongest signal.

In terms of power consumption, the compact Kenwood TS-50 and other radios in this class use slightly over 8 amps for transmitting, but the receiver uses considerably less, about 1.5 amps. Since our cruiser net sessions usually last no more than half an hour, with my talking for only a few minutes, the ham radio consumes a negligible amount of power over a typical 24-hour period.

One of the best things about cruising is not having to answer the telephone, respond to text messages, or "like" somebody's chicken cacciatore on Facebook. That is, until someone shames you into buying a satellite telephone. There are at present three types of sat phones on the market: text-only, voice and text, and voice and text with full Internet capability. The handheld texting device and monthly service fee are so reasonable these days that I must admit it is hard to find a reason why not to enjoy this simple communication capability. The hard-core cruisers will stick to their Sail Mail, which gives them email access to the entire world. Nonetheless, the texting device, as an adjunct to ham radio, is an easy way to communicate with folks back in the U.S., and you do not need a Pactor modem to run it.

A true global phone will cost a bit more to purchase, but it will still be fairly affordable. This type of device will permit all of the functions of a simple, land-based cellular phone: texting, calling, and voice mail. A global phone works with a U.S. service provider, allowing calls only to other U.S.-based telephone numbers. The third option, a fully functional satellite phone, provides all the services of a land-based smart phone: voice, text, voice mail, and Internet access with download speeds of 2 megabits per second. As you might expect, this type of phone system, along with the dome antenna, will set you back a daunting sum. As of this writing, that comes to roughly fifteen grand, more than the price of some very fine cruising boats. And that doesn't include the monthly service fee. The rich and pampered never seem to go without, even if the greatest joy of cruising is going without.

AC Appliances

Most of us carry high-power AC lighting along with a smorgasbord of AC electrical tools and appliances aboard our vessels. An AC lamp for carrying out emergency repairs at night, plus a drill motor, jig saw, electric soldering iron, random orbital sander, and maybe even a portable ice maker or curling iron, are liable to find their way onto a cruising vessel. And the way we power up these devices is with a DC-to-AC inverter connected to the house battery. When shopping for an inverter, make sure it is rated for marine use and is capable of providing more than enough AC power for the combination of appliances you anticipate using simultaneously at any given moment. The standard minimum is 1000 watts, which equates to 9 amps at 110 volts AC. That's not a huge amount of power, but generally sufficient for limited

A Samlex 1500-watt modified sine wave inverter provides current for high-powered AC lighting, small power tools, and other appliances.

duty in order to operate one or two AC devices at once. While using power tools or other high-amperage devices, you will need to run the engine so as not to deplete the house bank. Larger yachts with permanently installed AC appliances, such as a front-opening refrigerator or washer and dryer, require a generator set running round the clock to supply adequate power. Xantrex, Samlex, and Heart manufacture various sizes of marine inverters, and all have well-established reputations for quality and longevity. Mid-range inverters in the 1000-watt to 2000-watt range usually produce modified sine wave current, which works satisfactorily with most small appliances, including laptop computers.

As you map out all the systems you want to include in your vessel's electronics array, keep a tally of amperage consumed by each device and the number of hours it will be used each day to get an idea of how much battery power you will need. Again, if battery storage equals four times your daily usage, and the engine alternator amperage is one-fourth of the battery storage, a good rule would be, total daily amp hour consumption equals one hour of the engine alternator's maximum output. Maintaining the critical balance between charging and battery usage will be a key contributor to the success of your voyage.

We can all agree that having adequate lighting, navigation capability, and electronic communications contributes immeasurably to the overall success of a voyage. A simple lifestyle is fine, but we still need to know where we are, and we need to be able to communicate when necessary with the world beyond our vessel, particularly in emergency situations. With the availability of competitively priced lighting fixtures and electronic systems, even the most humble of aspiring cruising sailors can avail themselves of these technologies. As you will read in the remaining chapters, there are yet more ways to save energy while enjoying a safe, comfortable passage under sail.

Chapter 12
Refrigeration

REFRIGERATION IS ONE OF THOSE THINGS THAT ADD A CIVILIZED feeling to an otherwise minimalist lifestyle aboard an ocean-going sailing vessel. Sipping an ice-cold soft drink or cocktail while watching stunning sunsets a thousand miles from the nearest shore enhances the magic and romance of an ocean crossing and makes those warm tropical nights feel just a little cooler. Of course, from a technical point of view, an efficiently functioning, permanently installed refrigeration system drawing a conservative amount of amperage from the house bank takes a great deal of planning and attention to detail in the installation process. Sometimes such an installation on a small to mid-size yacht, particularly while cruising in the tropics, comes short of fully satisfying the crew's needs for dependable refrigeration. Many refrigeration installations have a difficult time keeping up with the excessive heat and humidity, running their condenser motors constantly without achieving the target temperature. However, if properly planned and installed, a refrigerator can keep food fairly cool within a manageable range of amperage draw.

As you read through the options for refrigeration, bear in mind that a permanently installed refrigerator may or may not be what you really need—or should I say, want. After all is said and done, a refrigerator on a boat carrying an abundance of fishing tackle and large stores of canned and dry food is essentially a luxury. For some crew members, though, certain luxuries, like ice cubes and cold beverages, provide just enough psychological comfort to keep the spirits up on a long passage. A permanently installed refrigerator is one option, but there are also other ways to provide refrigeration on an as-needed basis. We must keep an open mind in our quest for cold.

Assessing Refrigeration Needs

Findings ways to conserve battery power while the refrigerator is running is not only about making a smaller footprint on the places we sail to. Using as little amperage as possible for the refrigerator is also about guaranteeing enough reserve amperage for the essential systems aboard: autopilot, chart plotter, radar, running lights, and radios. In the tropics, a refrigerator can consume more than 40 percent of the house battery's storage, sometimes necessitating full cycling several times a week and thereby greatly shortening the battery's life. This is why it is necessary to conduct an honest needs assessment of both crew and cabin to determine what type of refrigeration is needed and to figure out where and how the unit will be installed, wired, cooled, and insulated. A large freezer-refrigerator combination unit will require much more electrical current than a smaller refrigerator without a freezer. On the typical sailing vessel, you will want to stick with the smallest size that meets your needs, not the largest you can fit into a given space. A smaller cooled space equates to more space for insulation, netting a colder fridge temperature with less draw on the house battery. Generating battery charging current for your fridge should be a manageable process instead of a constant headache.

If your vessel has a refrigerator that requires replacement, or an ice box that can be converted into a refrigerator, you will have an easier job of it than if you had to carve out the space. After removing the old fridge, you should be able to house the compressor-condenser unit in the same compartment as the old one. And with all the options in evaporators available, you should be able to mount this component in the cold box easily. If your vessel has an air-cooled system designed for the temperate zone, you will need to make some additional alterations before aiming the bow toward the tropics. As you must see by now, there is no such thing as an "easy" refrigerator installation.

Before investing in a refrigerator, freezer, or combination unit, first determine what level of cooling you will require. Where will you spend most of your time cruising, in the fjords of Scandinavia or the islands of Polynesia? In cooler climes, you have a greater chance of getting full use of a refrigerator and a small freezer in a small package. In the tropics, you are probably limited to a refrigerator, and even that will be tough to keep cold, given the warm, humid air and warm water. If you intend to keep meat and ice cream frozen long term, you will be better off with a trawler or a very large sailing yacht equipped with several large house batteries and a generator that cranks on automatically whenever the battery charge level dips below a prescribed level. On the typical 35-foot cruising sailboat, this is science fiction, plain and simple. So we need to be realistic about what we really need in a refrigeration unit.

Either a dedicated refrigerator or a small freezer will require fewer amp hours of energy to operate than a combination unit but will still be a challenge in the tropics. Nonetheless, on most cruising

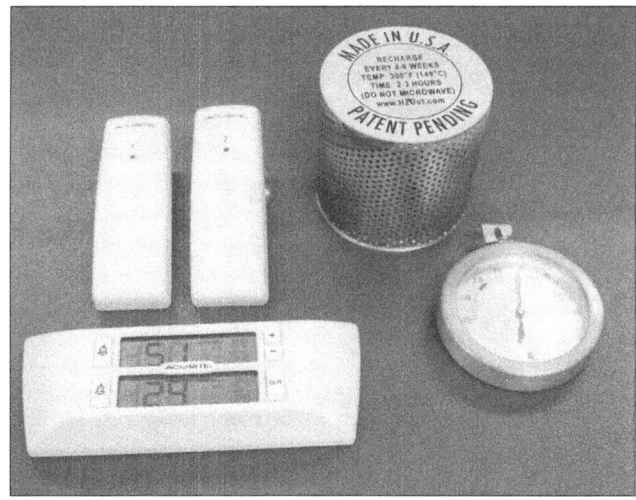

Photo courtesy of www.mahina.com

Mahina Tiare III's *crew keep their fridge cold and dry with Accurite base-mount and remote controls, plus a canister of silica gel and a thermometer.*

yachts, a consistently cold space for storing such items as cheese, milk, and other beverages is achievable. On the other hand, many items that we are accustomed to refrigerating actually do not require such care. Eggs, especially if they are bought fresh and not previously refrigerated, may be kept at room temperature for up to two weeks. Most items preserved with either vinegar or ascorbic acid, such as mayonnaise, catsup, mustard, pickles, steak sauce, and hot sauce, will keep indefinitely after they are opened. I have opened jars of mayonnaise, which contain whipped eggs, and left them unrefrigerated for months in the South Pacific without ever getting sick. Thank goodness for vinegar, the poor man's refrigerator. Smoked fish, beef jerky, cabbage, and some cheeses can be stored at ambient temperature if they are kept in a dry, well-ventilated place away from direct sunlight. While in Tahiti, stock up on lots of La Vache Qui Rit (Laughing Cow) cheese wheels and stow them with your boxed wine, affectionately known to cruisers as Chateau Carton.

An ice maker will be found in a top-of-the-line, front-opening refrigerator on a monster yacht, but ice can also be produced by a portable ice maker. If all you truly desire is cold beer and margaritas, or some way to keep fish fresh overnight, a portable ice maker may be just the solution you seek. There are a couple of ways to make ice, so we will look at this option later in this chapter.

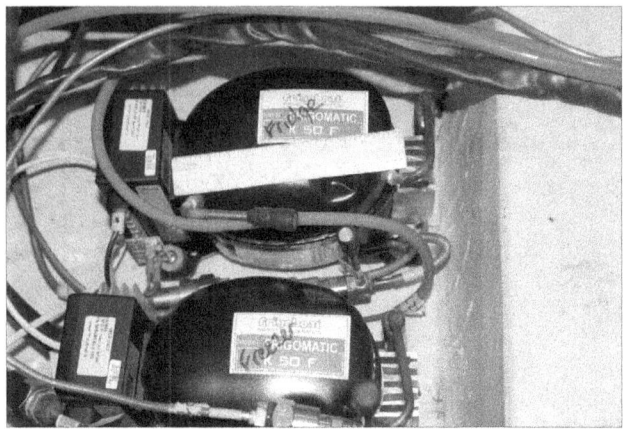

These dual compressors keep a fridge and a separate freezer operating around the clock.

Finally, air conditioning under sail is about as bourgeois as it gets, but a small percentage of vessels in the 40- to 50-foot range, and occasionally smaller, are equipped with this luxury. If you are interested in AC for your cabin, for a few thousand bucks you can achieve that dream. The hard part, of course, is figuring out how to keep it running 24/7. It is inconceivable how this can occur without constant use of a genset backed by a massive store of diesel or gasoline to feed the beast. Unless you are running a floating hospital, proposing a "green option" for air conditioning on a cruising vessel is beyond the bounds of reason. However, if that is what you seek, there are several makes of marine air conditioning systems and numerous online sources to inform you of the options. When I get too hot, I dump a bucket of sea water on my head—quite refreshing!

How Refrigeration Works

Most refrigeration systems operate by the same principles of compression, condensation, and evaporation. Propane refrigerators and ammonia systems are a bit different, and both have been used in sailboats as ways to save battery power. Nonetheless, the obvious dangers in a propane-burning refrigerator and the chances of a leak in an ammonia unit are the reasons you will probably never see either of these on a cruising vessel.

In a standard cold system, a motor-driven compressor pushes liquid refrigerant through a long condenser tube, where heat absorbed on the cold side of the unit escapes into the surrounding air or water mass. At the opposite side of the condenser, the liquid squeezes through an expansion valve, basically a Venturi tube, where it emerges as a cold gas and enters the evaporator tubing, drawing heat from the external surface. Depending on the size of the evaporator and how it is configured, it may be employed to freeze a small space, refrigerate a larger space, or cool the air of a whole room or building. A thermocouple senses the temperature of the enclosed space and signals the compressor-condenser to begin cycling until the thermocouple senses that the temperature has dropped to the operator-selected level.

Until the late 1980s with the international passage of the Montreal Protocol to protect the ozone layer, the DuPont chlorofluorocarbon Freon, or R-12, was the standard coolant used in refrigeration units worldwide. Freon has not been sold in the U.S. in nearly 30 years, yet many older refrigeration units still contain this substance and continue to provide service to this today. All newer systems use the refrigerant R-134a, which causes no harm to Earth's ozone layer. If you purchase an old, used refrigerator for your boat, there is a good chance it still contains Freon. Instead of attempting to service the unit yourself, take it to a licensed refrigeration technician to empty the old Freon properly and recharge it with R-134a after modifying the unit to accept the new substance. Or better yet, buy a new refrigerator and leave that hassle to someone else.

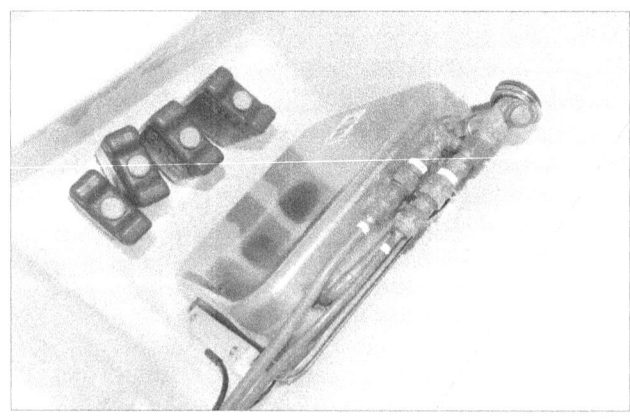

The Technautics holding plate stores cold in a frozen fluid jacket around evaporative coils, maintaining target fridge temperature while saving amperage on compressor cycling.

Refrigeration and Climate

The refrigeration systems we use in our homes and boats were designed for use in temperate climates, meaning low relative humidity, daytime temperatures ranging from 60 to 85 degrees F, and water temperatures averaging 50 to 75 degrees F. In this setting, the hull remains cool and the cabin air livable. When the boat is left unattended with the refrigerator operating in a closed cabin, solar-powered vents can keep the cabin air cool enough to permit adequate cooling of the condenser and a manageable draw on the house bank.

In the tropics, the average temperature of both air and water conspire to keep the temperature surrounding the evaporator high both day and night, forcing the compressor motor to cycle up to 50 percent of the time; in the worst scenario, with the cabin closed up, cutting off all air circulation, the unit will cycle almost constantly, completely draining the house battery on short order. Solar-powered vents give little relief when the outside temperature is 90 degrees F with 95 percent relative humidity and the water is 80 degrees F. Some cruisers in the tropics resort to using the fridge only on weekends, or only for the occasional deck party. Others turn the unit off periodically throughout the day, keeping the unit at about 60 degrees, just cool enough to keep the lettuce crisp, the cheese firm, and the beverages drinkable.

Air-Cooled Systems

In the temperate zone, a standard, air-cooled, 4-cubic-foot, top-loading sailboat refrigerator should stay at or below 40 degrees F, safe enough to store milk and raw meat, while cycling roughly 10 minutes out of every hour. At an average 5 amps during cycling, that comes to 20 amp hours per day. A single 50-watt solar panel generating half its rated power over a 10-hour period produces 21 amp hours, just enough to power the refrigerator for a 24-hour period.

But when we get well inside 23 degrees, 26 minutes north or south of the equator, with the fridge cycling 45 minutes out of every hour, the draw jumps to 90 amp hours per day, half the reserve amp hours of a 4D battery and over a third that of an 8D. At anchor with a few days of heavy cloud cover and calm air, reducing amperage from the solar panels and wind generator to a trickle, means running the engine and 100-amp alternator for at least an hour a day—or learning to enjoy warm beer.

One way to reduce cycling and maintain a more constant level of cooling is to install a cold plate, or holding plate, which is a thin, flat compartment with an evaporator tube in a bath of coolant that freezes at a point below the freezing point of water. When the coolant rises to a certain temperature, the automatically kicks on to freeze the solution again. Even in a warm, tropical climate, a cold plate can keep the fridge cold while cycling only a few hours a day, which is a huge advantage over fridges with standard evaporators. If there is a drawback to the cold plate, it is the greater amount of amperage used while cycling. Over a 24-hour period, though, you can expect to cut total fridge amperage by half. Technautics of Escondido, California, claims their CoolBlue holding plate system can chill a 7-cubic-foot freezer-refrigerator at 24 amp hours per day, significantly less than conventional refrigeration. With the holding plate installed in the typical sailboat fridge measuring 3 or 4 cubic feet, we can expect even greater amperage savings.

Water-Cooled Systems

One alternative to the standard-issue, air-cooled fridge that comes stock in many new yachts is a water-cooled system, which is more efficient at removing heat from the condenser tubes. Like the radiator on an automobile engine, applying a comparatively cool liquid to a hot surface draws out heat far faster than air. A water-cooled system involves the installation of a water pump, a raw water filter, input and discharge hoses, an above-waterline discharge through-hull fitting, various plumbing parts, and a 12-volt switch. The pump is usually quite small, using only an amp or so of power, but the overall savings in daily amperage can be in excess of 25 percent, more than offsetting its meager amperage draw and offering a significant advantage over a conventional air-cooled boat fridge. Reducing the 90 amp hours of the air-cooled system by 25 percent gives us roughly 68 amp hours per day, a savings of 22 amp hours. Let's not kid ourselves, though. A diet of 68 amp hours per day is still a huge demand on the typical cruising boat's reserve power, far greater than that of any other single system on the vessel.

Keel-Cooled Refrigeration

An even more efficient water-cooled fridge may be achieved through a keel-cooled system, which is also used for some engine installations. Keel cooling uses fresh water to cool the condenser coils in the same manner as a standard water-cooled system, except that coolant passes through a heat exchanger attached to the outer side of the hull. It is called a "keel" cooler because of its location close to the keel to guarantee constant submersion. Frigoboat and Isotherm both offer keel-cooled refrigerator kits with hydrodynamically shaped heat exchangers to reduce drag. A self-contained fresh water cooling system eliminates the need for a strainer, since no seawater passes through the hull. One downside to a keel cooler is the need to inspect and replace zincs regularly on the bronze heat exchangers. Also, while sitting in an anchorage without a constant current of water running under the hull, the water immediately surrounding the heat exchanger can heat up and reduce its cooling capacity. However, owners of keel-cooled fridges are generally quite pleased with the superior cooling of this straightforward system, even in tropical anchorages. Another potential problem is the growth of barnacles and algae on the bronze heat exchanger, and some cruisers claim that external heat exchangers cannot be painted with

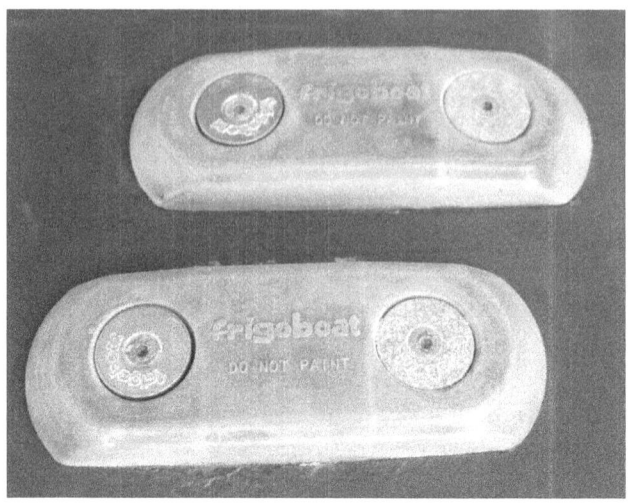

Photo courtesy of www.mahina.com

Coolant passes through these two hull-mounted heat exchangers, one for the fridge and one for the freezer, providing a steady source of coolant without the need of a pump to draw cooling water into the vessel.

antifouling. However, Rob Warren of Coastal Climate Control in Annapolis, the main U.S. distributor of Frigoboat, pointed out, "You will lose a little refrigeration performance by painting [a heat exchanger], but not enough that you will notice. I made some tests several years ago, and I found that it was better to have one painted than for it to be really heavily fouled."

Photo courtesy of www.mahina.com

A closed-cell foam cover over the fridge, like this one aboard the Hallber-Rassy 46 Mahina Tiare III, significantly cuts fridge cycling time.

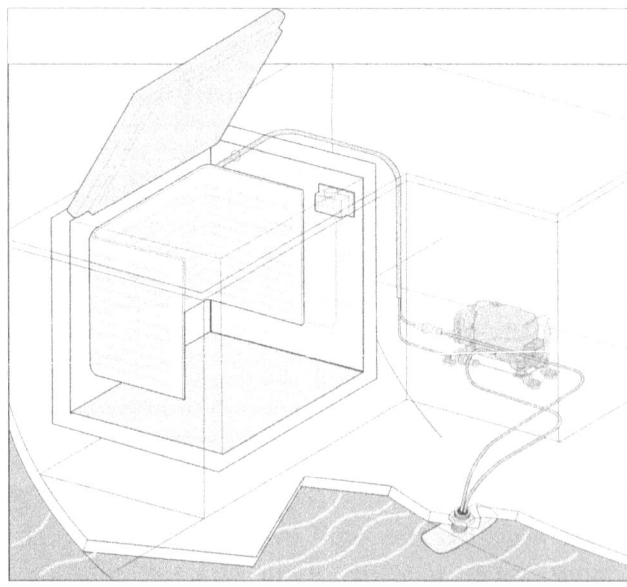

Courtesy of Frigoboat

Frigoboat's keel cooler absorbs heat from the condenser and pumps the coolant through a heat exchanger under the hull to maintain the desired fridge temperature.

Cruiser Options

At this point it should be fairly obvious that maintaining a maximum refrigerator temperature of 40 degrees F on a 35-foot sailing vessel around the clock in Pago Pago Harbor is feasible, but it will not be easy. Offshore in a fair breeze with a water-cooled or, even better, a keel-cooled fridge and a hydro generator cranking out the amps, you can have all the snow cones, margaritas, and ice-cold beer you want. But since we spend most of our time at anchor, if we really need a fridge, we need to compromise, enjoying some of the benefits of refrigeration while not killing the house bank.

If your vessel currently has only an icebox, you can turn the compartment into a fridge by installing a conversion kit. A standard air-cooled kit with condenser, evaporator, compressor motor, and fittings can be purchased for well under $1,000. A top-of-the-line, keel-cooled fridge with a holding plate will cost appreciably more. You will need to identify what space is available for the compressor unit, which may need to be installed several feet away from the fridge. Allow a path for the copper tubing between the fridge and the compressor, making sure the tubing is safe from impact and sharp objects; copper is a very soft metal and easily cut.

The number-one variable in the success of a refrigerator installation is the type and thickness of insulation surrounding the entire ice box, including the underside of the lid. A three-inch to four-inch thickness of urethane foam encasing the installation is the basic minimum for keeping the fridge cold. Sailors also experiment with spray insulation foam, vinyl mats on top of the lid, and reflectors outside the hull where the fridge is located in order to achieve the lowest possible temperature and amperage draw. A dark hull under the tropical sun makes the fridge's job extremely difficult. Switch to a white hull and you will sleep better and save on amperage. Talk to experienced cruisers to get the best advice on keeping the fridge cold in a warm climate.

In the interest of thoroughness, I must mention self-contained, drop-in refrigeration units, even if they are generally for large power boats, not sailboats. If you have a large sailing vessel with a boxy hull, you might want to consider this easy approach because it will save you time and effort installing the compressor unit and running copper tubing. Additionally, you may need to install a water pump if the model uses this type of cooling configuration. Such systems generally have minimal insulation, as they are intended for boats running either the main engine or a genset constantly.

If you want to circumvent everything you have read here up to this point on refrigeration, you can opt for a portable 12-volt DC or 110-volt AC fridge and use it as circumstances dictate. The smallest units from Dometic consume about 3 amps at 12 volts DC, making them ideal for special occasions or for long stays in marinas where 110 volts AC is available. When switching to 220 volts AC, you will need a transformer, but remember the electrical current outside the Americas will be at 50 Hz, not 60 Hz. The lower frequency will probably mean just a slower compressor motor and poorer cooling, but first verify with the manufacturer whether any damage could be incurred by the motor.

The more I read about portable ice makers, the more I am tempted to buy one for *Saltaire*. Imagine plugging a machine into the AC inverter and drawing less than 3 amps to produce 2.5 pounds of ice in less than 15 minutes—in the middle of the ocean. As long as the ambient temperature is below 90 degrees F, you can make enough ice to chill several cans or bottles of liquid in the Igloo.

The current standard portable ice maker is manufactured in China and sold through such brand names as Dometic, Emerson, Magic Chef, NewAir, EdgeStar, and MaxiMatic. The singular difference of this ice maker among all these brand names is the price, which is generally under $200. The unit measures 9.5 inches by 12.9 inches by 14.1 inches and its net weight is 18.3 pounds; filled with water it weighs 27 pounds. It consumes a maximum of 2 amps at 115 volts AC, half that of a typical boat fridge. You will want to secure this device properly with straps, leaving the right side unobstructed to allow the cooling fan to function properly. The ice maker should be used only in settled conditions or while at anchor to keep it as level as possible. Also, avoid using an extension cord, which can overheat and cause a fire.

Finally, there is a little-known trick for quickly producing very cold ice that we all grew up learning about but probably never dared to try. Carbon dioxide at room temperature is in gaseous form and is completely harmless. Plants break down carbon dioxide gas, absorbing the carbon and releasing oxygen into the atmosphere. In solid form, CO_2 may be poured into fire extinguishers and used to fight a variety of fires. When sprayed out of a fire extinguisher's nozzle, CO_2 demonstrates the Joule-Kelvin effect, instantly dropping from ambient temperature to a point below -109.3 degrees F and converting into what we call "dry ice." Instead of melting into liquid form, frozen carbon dioxide "sublimates" directly back into a gas. A CO_2 fire extinguisher puts out fires by freezing the burning surface and starving the fire of its oxygen through sublimation.

If you want a quick way to make ice and happen to have a CO_2 fire extinguisher aboard, grab a pillow case, blast the CO_2 fire extinguisher into it for about three seconds, and then collect the dry ice with a spoon while wearing gloves to protect yourself from frostbite. Place the dry ice in a small bowl, pack it down tightly with your spoon, and place it in the bottom of the Igloo with your food or beverage. You can also experiment with a small bowl of water placed on top of the dry ice to freeze a chunk of ice, which you can break up and use as ice cubes.

For many cruisers, refrigeration is the prime benchmark dividing the civilized from the Philistines. Having circled the globe on little *Saltaire* with no such luxury, I could not agree more. One day near the equator in the middle of the Indian Ocean, the last few potatoes rotted, the one remaining egg became green and smelly, the onions turned to mush, and the Chateau Carton went down as hot as a fresh pot of coffee. I would have sold my very soul for a single ice cube, which I could have mixed with water and a teaspoon of Tang to deliver me, if only for a fleeting moment, from the torment of my surroundings.

A luxury such as refrigeration or simply a quick source of ice has the power to restore faith and optimism in a crew stuck in the Doldrums for weeks, not knowing when or where the wind

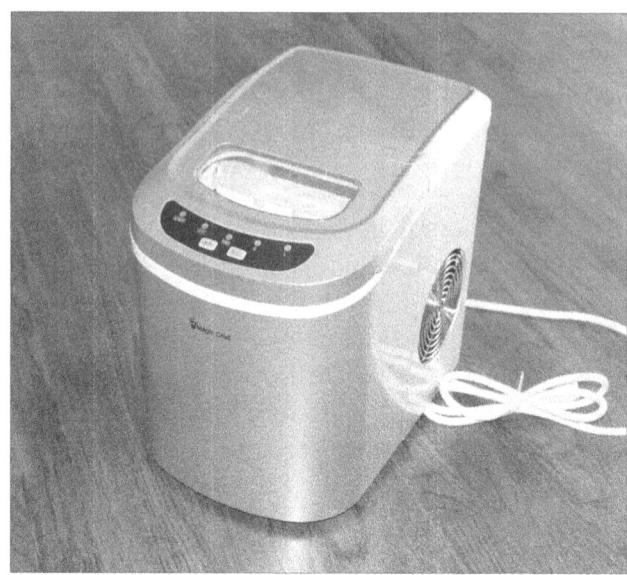

The Magic Chef portable ice maker, also sold under numerous other brand names, is a quick, energy-saving means of making ice aboard a sailing vessel.

will return. A shot of rum over a couple of ice cubes can assuage despondency and summon the gods of hope and vitality. Take time to weigh the options for refrigeration, and keep in mind that whether you need 24-hour access to refrigeration regardless of your climatic surroundings, or just a bowl of ice to throw into the blender to concoct your favorite smoothie or inebriant, there is an energy-efficient system that will fit your budget, your vessel, and your waterborne lifestyle.

Chapter 13
Windvane Self-Steering

SEASONED OFFSHORE SAILORS WHO HAVE EXPERIENCED FREAK WAVES, knockdowns, and serious equipment failures generally agree there is one piece of equipment without which they could not imagine leaving port: a windvane self-steering system. The story is all too familiar. A retired couple with little or no offshore sailing experience sets off on an ocean crossing, and 800 miles offshore they are hit by a freak wave that swamps the vessel and wipes out all the electronics except for the handheld GPS and VHF radio. They finally clear the cabin of water, and they are still able to sail, but the autopilot no longer has a power source. Reluctantly, they resign themselves to alternating three-hour stints at the helm until they reach the next port 1,200 miles away. More commonly, it is the autopilot itself that breaks down a few thousand miles into a cruise, requiring parts and technical expertise rarely found outside the developed world. Imagine the time, expense, and headache they could have saved by installing a well-designed, solidly built windvane system on their transom. Windvanes routinely survive knockdowns and even capsizes with nothing worse than a broken plywood airvane, easily replaced in under two minutes while under way.

When considering windvane self-steering, some cruisers worry about lines across the deck, or their boat's suitability for self-steering, or the thought of an "ugly" machine on their vessels' transoms, or not truly being able to believe that a non-electronic apparatus can safely steer a boat in anything from a light breeze to a full, sustained gale through a full circumnavigation of the earth without breaking down. But don't worry, no matter what type of sail rig or transom configuration your boat has, if your boat's LOA measures between 20 and 65 feet, there is a windvane solution for your sailing vessel. Vessels with canoe sterns or boomkins may require a bit more creative engineering to design a mounting system, but most windvane manufacturers have installation plans ready for virtually every production boat in the world's cruising fleet. And for those skippers who are obsessed with aesthetics, some windvane models are so sleek and unobtrusive, you would hardly notice them.

Windvane Versus Autopilots

Besides being totally mechanical rather than electronic, there is one other underlying difference between windvanes and autopilots: a windvane follows the angle to the wind that the operator selects, while an electronic autopilot follows a compass course. The disadvantage with a windvane is that if you are asleep and the wind turns, so too does the boat, which means someone needs to be checking the compass or GPS every couple of hours and adjusting the airvane on the vane gear to ensure the proper heading. One limitation of an autopilot is that the watch needs to adjust the sails whenever they start flopping because of a change in wind direction. However, the greatest downside of an electronic autopilot is far more ominous: it is not a matter of if it will break down, but when.

Autopilots (see Chapter 14) can take the form of an above-decks tiller pilot, or at the other extreme, a highly sophisticated, integrated system controlling a wheel steering quadrant with a hydraulic ram controlled by a microprocessed sensor. If the sensor blows a circuit board, or the ram bends and freezes up below decks, or some little plastic part in the tiller pilot cracks in the middle of a storm, the autopilot must be disconnected from the steering quadrant or tiller to allow for manual steering. While an autopilot does have its place on a cruising vessel, it functions best as a back-up to a mechanical windvane self-steerer.

Servopendulums

Before settling on a particular type of windvane, or "vane gear," you first need to have a basic understanding of what types of systems are available on the market. The most common is the servopendulum. This machine uses a thin, flat, vertical piece of plywood or plastic to transmit changes in the apparent wind via a push rod and bevel gears to a submerged servo blade. The servo blade responds by swinging sideways in the oncoming water and controlling the helm with a pair of steering lines.

Photo courtesy of Bob Johnson

A Monitor windvane mounted to the canoe stern of a Tayana 37.

The author's 1966 Cal 30 Saltaire circled the globe with this Fleming 301 Global servopendulum vane gear minding the helm.

Photo courtesy of Scanmar

At anchor, the Monitor servopendulum mounted on a SwingGate opens to allow easy access to the swim ladder on this Catalina 34.

There are numerous advantages to installing a servopendulum. First and foremost is the pendulum's capacity to generate hundreds of pounds of force through the servo blade, overpowering the strongest helmsman when the boat really gets moving. Another plus is the pendulum's anti-yawing tendency. When running before the wind under headsail or spinnaker alone, the wind's force is on the bow, while the immense force of the following seas is on the stern. As the vessel slides down a wave, the elevated stern tries to overtake the bow, which digs into the back of the previous wave, causing the hull to fishtail, or yaw. With a servopendulum, as the hull shifts to one side, the servo blade catches the water and automatically pulls the helm back on course.

Another key feature of servopendulums is that their blades can easily be folded up out of the water or removed when not in use. This is an important consideration when motoring in reverse or maneuvering near submerged fish nets and mooring lines. Most pendulum shafts have shear pins, breakaway connectors, or collapsible tubes protecting the servo blade and the rest of the servopendulum apparatus from collision damage.

I offer my own vessel and vane gear as an example of the attributes of the servopendulum. A Fleming Global 301 servopendulum steered 30-foot *Saltaire* 30,000 nautical miles around the earth without a single repair, except for a couple of broken airvanes during a severe storm in the Tongan Triangle of the South Pacific and in the northern Red Sea. To this day, *Saltaire* still does not carry an electronic autopilot, although a tiller pilot would be handy for motoring through calms.

The Monitor, built by Scanmar in Point Richmond, California, is one of the world's most popular servopendulum windvane systems. Constructed of 316 stainless steel, save for the bronze pinion gears, the unit is relatively light and highly responsive to wind changes in all kinds of weather. Scanmar offers a generous warranty and is known for going out of its way to send parts to some of the most far-flung places on earth. Although the company offers a complete parts list on the Internet, along with instructions for online ordering, its chief engineer and office staff also advise customers by telephone, referring to warranty installation photos in order to help owners troubleshoot and repair their vane gears.

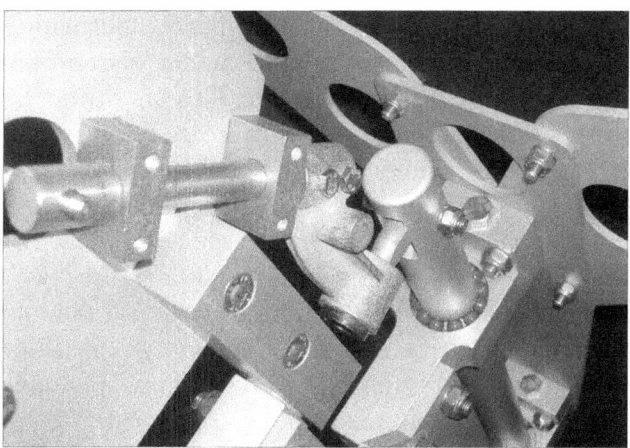
Photo courtesy of Sailomat

Beautiful in its simplicity, the Sailomat 760's patented spherical-joint technology, anodized aluminum alloys, and long-lasting Torlan bearings are even more appealing when put into action.

Another highly popular servopendulum is the Sailomat, which continues to evolve into newer models every few years. The Sailomat 3040, with its familiar "double-rudder" system, was a familiar sight on American cruising vessels back in the 1970s and 1980s, and can still be seen in cruiser anchorages around the world. Dr. Stellan Knöös, inventor of the 3040, originally had wanted to offer a single servopendulum model to cover every conceivable type of sailing yacht, beyond the standard rear-cockpit sloop with tiller steering. He aimed to accommodate yachts with hydraulic steering, a center cockpit, or some other combination of features that prevented a standard servopendulum installation. To meet the wide variety of boat and main steering configurations, Dr. Knöös designed the Sailomat 3040 to be a completely self-contained steering system comprised of both a servo blade and an auxiliary rudder, which together steered the vessel with the main steering trimmed and locked. The latest-generation Sailomat 800 is a servo blade-only servopendulum, although it preserves Sailomat's signature anodized aluminum construction, raked servo shaft, and "patented spherical joint system" in place of the standard bevel gears to transmit impulses from the airvane to the servo blade.

Peter Förthmann of Hamburg, Germany, incorporates a similar "double-rudder" system in the Windpilot Pacific Plus and Plus II, although the gearing system consists of standard bevel gears. As with the Sailomat 3040, the Windpilot Plus models are self-contained auxiliary rudder systems completely capable of steering a sailing vessel with the helm lashed. Windpilot also manufactures two sizes of standard servopendulum, the Windpilot Pacific and Pacific Light. Other highly reputable builders of traditional servopendulums include Aries Denmark, Fleming, and Cape Horn.

Cape Horn, the brainchild of Yves Gélinas of Quebec, is unique in its use of a "Z" rod rather than bevel gears or ball joints. The Z rod, lying inside a horizontal mounting tube near the base of the transom, rotates with impulses from the airvane and drives the servopendulum, which in the below-decks models turns a quadrant located inside the lazarette. Double-braided lines run from the quadrant through blocks in the lazarette to jam cleats in the cockpit for instant connect/disconnect and trim. In the outboard model, the servopendulum drives a steering arm connected to the tiller via control lines. The operator installs the mounting tube by cutting a hole through the transom and bonds the two with epoxy and fiberglass. The horizontal portion of the tube, through which the Z rod passes, is supported by a pair of stainless steel struts bolted to the transom. At anchor with the airvane removed, the Cape Horn is a barely noticeable, short, shiny, vertical mast, a flagless flagstaff.

Trim Tabs

Another type of self-steering system is the trim tab, the best known of which is the Auto-Helm, built by Scanmar and not to be confused with Autohelm autopilots. The trim tab, similar to an airplane aileron, is hinged to the trailing edge of an auxiliary rudder so that the two operate together in lieu of the vessel's main steering. The helmsman trims the system's airvane parallel to the apparent wind in the same manner as with a servopendulum. The Auto-Helm offers some unique advantages. First, the airvane mast is connected to the auxiliary rudder by a cable similar to the one used for bicycle brakes, allowing the mast to be mounted at a remote location, such as on the arch or wherever else it has direct access to the wind. Second, the Auto-Helm is generally far more sensitive to light airs than servopendulums. When sailing downwind in a light breeze, the apparent wind over the transom is sometimes too light to provide enough power for a servopendulum to lift its blade up from the vertical position.

Servopendulums: Pros and Cons

Pros

- Steering force increases with wind speed and vessel speed.
- Servopendulum shafts may be folded out of water, or servo blades may be removed when not in use.
- Works directly on main steering.
- With a simple coupling device, servopendulum amplifies tiller pilot response, greatly reducing amperage draw and tiller pilot wear.

Cons

- Conventional systems require steering lines to cockpit.
- Conversion required on most—not all—systems for use as emergency rudder.
- Generally heavier than trim tabs, the buoyant auxiliary rudders of which usually make the final installation much lighter than that of servopendulums.

Trim Tabs: Pros and Cons

Pros

- More sensitive than servopendulums in light airs.
- Smoother, quieter steering.
- Good alternative for center cockpits and hydraulic or stiff steering.
- Completely self-contained; no conversion necessary for use as emergency rudder.

Cons

- Minimum anti-yaw protection
- Less steering power than servopendulum.
- If used with auxiliary rudder, remains permanently installed and vulnerable to collision.
- Auxiliary rudder may affect steering when motoring in reverse or when maneuvering in a marina.

The airvane dips, but the servo blade just hangs unresponsively from the lack of sufficient water flow. Unlike a servopendulum, the light, thin foil of a trim tab system will shift at the slightest hint of a breeze, turning the rudder until the airvane stands vertically, as long as there is enough wind to fill the sails. Third, rather than keeping the trim tab mounted to the stock Auto-Helm rudder, the trim tab can be installed on an existing transom-mounted rudder, saving a considerable amount of money. And finally, the Auto-Helm, as with all trim tab vane gears, is a self-contained auxiliary rudder system.

Wind-Powered Auxiliary Rudder

Another type of self-steering system is what we may call an "airvane-controlled auxiliary rudder," known as the Hydrovane, manufactured in Nottingham, England. The Hydrovane converts wind impulses from a very large airvane directly into steering power through reduction gears. The operator chooses the reduction force with a selector knob, and has the option of disconnecting the airvane and steering the vessel with a short tiller connected to the reduction gearing in the case of loss of main steering. Tom Bridgman of the Pierre Garroff-designed 40-foot, center-cockpit ketch *Axe Calibre* (Axmouth, England) told me that on one occasion when the boat was at anchor, he jumped into the water and tried to turn the auxiliary rudder manually with the airvane set in about 10 knots of wind. With his arms bear-hugging the rudder and one foot pushing against the transom, he tried with all his might but could not budge the rudder; such was the force as amplified by the reduction linkage. In a manner somewhat like the Cape Horn, when the airvane is removed from the Hydrovane, you have to look twice to notice there is an apparatus installed on the transom. It is little more than a vertical mast with a small control box at the top, a barely noticeable feature in the yacht's appearance.

Matching Windvane to Boat

Finding the best match of windvane steering system for your vessel takes careful consideration. The main variables you must take into account are your boat's main steering, cockpit location, transom profile, and LOA. The easiest vessel to

Photo courtesy of Hydrovane
A Hydrovane steers an Ovni 385 under sail.

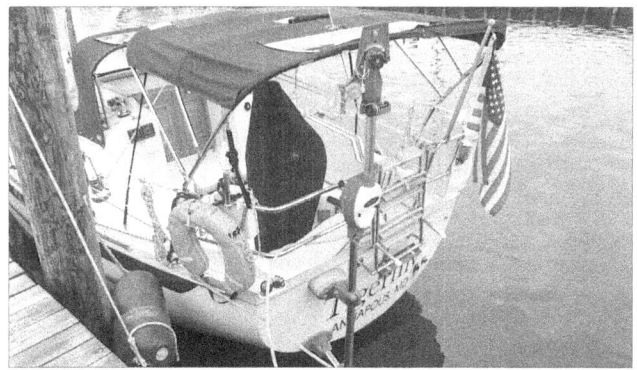
Photo courtesy of Hydrovane
A Hydrovane mounted off-center to allow room for a swim step on a Pacific Seacraft 31.

accommodate with vane gear steering is a 35-foot sloop with tiller steering, an aft cockpit, and a vertical or slightly raked transom. This conservative vessel design can accept every type of vane gear available on the market, including a Hydrovane, which would be a bit large for a boat measuring less than 30 feet LOA.

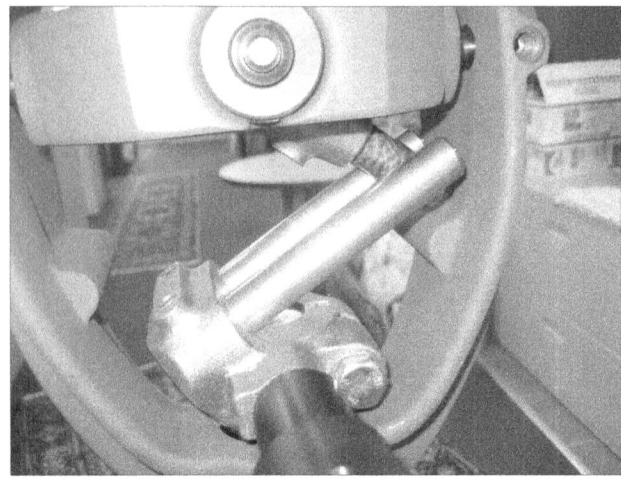

Photo courtesy of Hydrovane

Reduction gearing in the Hydrovane performs a powerful job for the minimal space it occupies.

A more difficult challenge would be a vessel of 50 feet or more with a canoe stern and hydraulic steering. Forget about a servopendulum in this case. Consider instead the Hydrovane or perhaps the Windpilot Pacific Plus II, each one very different from the other but equally useful where you must totally bypass the main steering in favor of a self-contained auxiliary rudder.

Scanmar's Saye's Rig, although very rarely seen, is a hybrid servopendulum-trim tab system custom-built for yachts in excess of 50 feet LOA. The entire Saye's Rig unit is installed directly to the rudder and controlled by a large, wedge-shaped cloth vane, or wind sensor, on a vertical axis.

Other options exist for situations where traditional servopendulums are impractical. The Cape Horn, because it may be configured to operate directly on the steering quadrant, is but one possibility for boats with center cockpits. Another option is the Auto-Helm trim tab, available in two different packages. The more popular option is the complete auxiliary rudder system. For those who want to save money on the auxiliary rudder and trim tab, there is the option of purchasing only the airvane mast base and then building the two hydrofoils at home, incorporating—we would hope—appropriate NACA foil shapes for reduced drag and optimal steering response. NACA, incidentally, stands for National Advisory Committee for Aeronautics, which was replaced by NASA, the National Aeronautical and Space Administration, in 1958.

In the case of a transom-mounted main rudder, a home-built trim tab connected to the main rudder's trailing edge and controlled through cables by a remote Auto-Helm airvane head is the obvious choice where a trim tab is desired. If your vessel has an arch over the stern, install the Auto-Helm head in the middle of the arch between the solar panels or among your array of antennas, taking care to allow enough lateral swing room for the airvane.

For owners of vessels with canoe sterns, boomkins, or transom ladders who prefer the power of a traditional servopendulum, fear not: as long as you have an aft cockpit and either a tiller or a wheel with cable or bevel gear linkage, there is a way to couple your choice of vane gear to your vessel's transom.

Aris, Fleming, and Monitor all use mounting tubes in their installation. Therefore, for mounting to a canoe stern, it is simply a matter of extending the tubes far enough to accommodate the elongated stern. The closer the lower mounting tubes come to the waterline, the more weight-bearing and torsion-resisting capacity they have. A

Photo courtesy of Hydrovane

A Hydrovane side-mounted to the swim step transom of a Najad 460.

> **MATCHING VANE GEAR TO VESSEL**
>
> **Main Steering**
>
> - Tiller: any vane gear system serves well; conventional servopendulum most preferred.
> - Cable or rack and pinion: any vane gear system; servopendulum most preferred, except with center cockpit.
> - Hydraulic: auxiliary rudder system, such as trim tab (e.g., Auto-Helm), Hydrovane or Windpilot Pacific Plus.
>
> **Cockpit**
>
> - Aft: any vane gear system; auxiliary rudder system in case of hydraulic steering
> - Center: trim tab, Cape Horn (inboard), Hydrovane or Windpilot Pacific Plus.
>
> **Transom**
>
> - All transoms accept all systems; in case of canoe stern or boomkin, customized bracing will be required for all vane gear designs.
>
> **Vessel Size**
>
> - Under 30 feet LOA: numerous designs work well, but the Fleming 201 and Windpilot Pacific Light are specifically designed for smaller boats.
> - 30-50 feet LOA: encompasses the vast majority of cruising yachts; vane gear depends on considerations listed above.
> - Over 50 feet LOA: a number of vane gears will work satisfactorily, but the Fleming 601 and Windpilot Pacific Plus II are specifically designed for yachts up to roughly 65 feet.

boomkin may appear to be forbidden territory for a vane gear, but don't be fooled. Adaptors crafted from stainless steel plate and tubing can be custom-built to accept almost any vane gear design. You can expect to lay out a few extra bucks for an unusual installation, but windvane manufacturers are highly competitive and innovative in their zeal to please clients with solid mounting designs.

One of the most creative mounting concepts to come along in recent years is Scanmar's SwingGate, which Scanmar has carefully engineered to couple a Monitor with a swim ladder over a sugar scoop transom. The Monitor becomes a gate that may be swung open while at anchor to enable use of the swim ladder. Sound impossible? Tony and Mitsuyo Williams, whose insistence on a gate-mounted vane gear design led to the invention of the SwingGate, sailed out of San Francisco Bay on a Catalina 42 fitted with the original prototype and crossed the Pacific to New Zealand with nary a hitch. The SwingGate definitely lets you "have your cake and eat it too."

Installing the appropriate design of windvane self-steering system on your vessel is not only an efficient way of steering your vessel without using battery power. A vane gear is also cheap insurance when you consider what can happen if and when your vessel ever loses its main steering. A well-built vane gear system can be expected to outperform and outlast most, if not all, electronic autopilots.

For motoring in calms, most vane gear systems can be coupled with a tiller pilot, allowing you to save battery power and wear and tear on the electronic system while still enjoying the benefits of your servopendulum, trim tab, or Hydrovane vane gear system.

Installation Tips

Installing a new or reconditioned vane gear system will take some planning and a few hours of work. First inspect the transom and rear deck area to get a general picture of how you want to install the system. The job will go a lot faster and easier if you have an idea of how the unit and its steering lines, if any, will interact with obstructions near the vane gear. If you draft out an installation plan on paper, try drawing it to scale with measurements calculated as close as you can get them. Do not start cutting mounting tubes and drilling into the transom until you know precisely how the unit will fit into place.

If there is an overhead arch, make sure there will be at least a foot of clearance between the bottom of the arch and the top of the airvane in order to ensure proper airflow. A vortex of wildly buckling air develops downwind of obstructions, adversely influencing the windvane's performance while sailing to weather.

If you have purchased a new unit designed to fit your boat, the builder will have already designed a mounting system to accommodate whatever obstructions are present on the deck or transom. If you have a used unit, you will need to design or modify the mounting system yourself. Place the lower mounting tubes as low as possible on the transom, yet safely above the waterline, to give the whole installation adequate support for the compression load. The upper tubes work best if installed on the transom on a wider pattern than on the vane gear, providing ample lateral support. A critical part of installation is making sure the servo blade clears the water's surface as close as possible to the manufacturer's specification. A servo blade set too deep means too much force; too shallow means inadequate steering force. The installation photos you send to the builder will determine whether you have installed the unit correctly, and whether your warranty will be honored.

On a vertical or slightly raked transom, installing a vane gear is a fairly straightforward process. The ultimate challenge is a canoe stern with a boomkin and a transom rudder, such as you would find on a Westsail 32. If you are attempting the latter installation, ask the builder for either an installation plan or for photos of similar installations. On a canoe stern, the lower mounting tubes are quite long, reaching far enough along the sides of the hull to provide lateral and vertical support.

A sugar scoop transom will pose the opposite problem, although it is easier to deal with because you attach the lower part of the vane gear to the scoop extension and the upper tubes to the transom. This is precisely what Monitor's SwingGate was designed to overcome. For other makes of vane gears, unless you can come up with a design similar to the SwingGate, you will have to live with stepping around the vane gear to make use of the swim step.

In the case of conventional servopendulums, careful selection of blocks and steering, or control, lines will reduce friction and wear in these components and promote a more direct connection between the airvane's steering impulses and the helm. Low-stretch, double-braided polyester line, either 5/16-inch or 3/8-inch, is most often recommended. Spectra is a good choice but very expensive; Sta-Set from New England Rope or a similar product will provide many thousands of miles of consistent service. Remember to cut the control lines about three feet longer than needed. This will allow you to advance the line through the swivel blocks periodically in order to extend the life of the braided line. When the lines start to show some wear, turn them to end to end and reinstall them to put the wear on new points along the lines. Even with these precautions, steering lines will eventually fail and part, so make sure to have one or two pairs of steering lines pre-cut and ready to deploy at a moment's notice.

Blocks need to be light and strong with low-friction bearings. The best blocks for self-steering have Delrin sheaves and ball bearings between anodized aluminum sheaves, such as those available from Harken and Ronstan. These blocks need no maintenance, save for an occasional rinse in fresh water to cleanse them of salt and grit. Avoid older blocks with stainless bearings, which require occasional lubrication. The added friction they impose will dampen a servopendulum's steering impulses in light airs.

Emergency Rudder Capability

Another major advantage of vane gear steering mechanisms is their ability to double as emergency rudders. Every cruising skipper lives with the constant fear of losing main steerage, whether it be from a lost rudder, a broken rudder post, or failure of the steering cable or hydraulics. In the event your vessel incurs loss of, or damage to, the main rudder, a vane gear can provide the steering power you need to reach your next port. If your vessel is fitted with an Auto-Helm trim tab, Windpilot Pacific Plus, Hydrovane, or legacy Sailomat 3040, no adaptations are needed to use the system in place of your vessel's main steering while under sail. Simply lash the helm or steering quadrant, set the airvane for the desired heading, and let the auxiliary rudder steer the vessel. For motoring, each of these systems may be adapted easily for manual steering.

Most of the standard servopendulums, including Fleming, Monitor, and Sailomat, may be modified at sea with an optional kit to act as emergency rudders, but because they are not self-contained systems, they must be operated manually or with the aid of an electronic tiller pilot. When Hans Bernwall, founder of Scanmar International, was asked about the initial stages of designing an emergency rudder for the Monitor, he recalled, "Our challenge was to be able to convert the Monitor aboard a 50-foot BOC boat, in the roaring forties, into a true emergency rudder." The result of his design staff's toil was the MRUD, or Monitor Emergency Rudder, a large, stainless, high-lift NACA foil that the operator latches onto the Monitor's standard servo blade. On the MRUD's leading edge are four eyebolts, two on each side, where double-braided lines are attached to keep the rudder vertically stationary. The same type of connecting device found at the top of the servo blade shaft is located on the emergency rudder post. Only Monitors built since 1991 can accept the MRUD assembly; previous versions must be retrofitted with a "strutguard" between the windvane's two lateral legs. Installation of the MRUD requires the operator to affix a special brace to the strutguard in order to stabilize the Monitor's upper pendulum shaft.

The Fleming Optional Emergency Rudder (FOER) was designed by engineer and company founder Kevin Fleming as a bolt-on extension to the servopendulum blade, except without the hydrodynamic NACA foil shape of the Sailomat BEST (Blade Extension for Emergency Steering) or Monitor MRUD. Fleming's new management team has discontinued the emergency rudder system, but second-hand kits are undoubtedly available online and in marina surplus stores. If you acquire one of these kits at a cruiser swap meet, you will see that the FOER consists of an epoxy-coated steel brace, which is bolted to the servo blade along with two stainless steel bracing tubes.

To install the Fleming emergency rudder, the operator removes the two bolts on the servo blade arm connector, bolts the emergency rudder extension into place, and then reinstalls the servo arm before letting the blade swing back into the water. After securing the top of the servo arm

Photo courtesy of Scanmar

A Monitor SOS rudder raised from its lower mounts on a Wylie 39.

by lashing the steering lines, which are normally attached to the wheel or tiller, the operator steers with a small tiller, or handle, attached to the airvane mount. Suffice to say, anyone using this system in rough weather will have to keep an eye on the various parts involved during assembly. I have never used this emergency rudder on my own Fleming vane gear, but the system appears to be well designed and up to the task.

Sailomat's BEST is a wing-like foil doubling the area of the servo blade. According to Dr. Knöös, who has designed all of Sailomat's vane gear systems since the late 1960s, the BEST has been qualified as an emergency rudder in a number of ocean racing events where this valuable piece of safety equipment is required for entry.

The underlying principle behind converting a servopendulum into an emergency rudder is fairly simple. First, install the modified or substituted foil to the servo blade shaft. Then stabilize the main shaft so that it does not swing laterally. Generally, this involves nothing more than tying the steering lines to a pair of cleats. However, it is advisable to secure the servo arm with extra lines for additional support. Depending on the model, attach a handle, a pair of steering lines, or a tiller pilot to the swiveling airvane base at the top of the vane gear mast, and your emergency rudder is ready to steer.

Incidentally, Scanmar manufactures a separately installed, self-contained SOS Rudder, which is in a class all its own. The SOS appeals to the skipper who either does not have a windvane for easy conversion to an emergency rudder, or whose windvane for some reason does not readily lend itself for use as an auxiliary rudder. Entirely constructed of 316L stainless steel, the SOS Rudder has a mounting tube structure custom-designed to fit the individual vessel. The rudder is similar in shape to the MRUD, concentrating most of the effort at the top of the hydrofoil for less strain on the assembly. Totally self-contained, the package is complete with its own tiller and four mounting brackets, which are to be mounted permanently on the transom before the vessel leaves port. The SOS Rudder is designed to steer a boat up to 50 feet LOA, though the foam-filled rudder and hardware ensemble weigh only 16 kilograms, or 35 pounds. You can store the SOS Rudder, along with its mounting tubes and other hardware, in its big orange bag, emblazoned with the letters "SOS."

If you purchase this unit, allow for a space of 48 x 18 x 6 inches for storage. That may sound rather large, but let's face it: any emergency rudder you carry on your boat is going to occupy a lot of space. In the event of loss of steerage, that large spare rudder will save not only your vessel, but conceivably your life as well.

Independence from electronic steering systems and possession of an emergency rudder both contribute greatly to our self-sufficiency on open ocean. Windvane self-steering gives us the capacity to deal with all kinds of weather by harnessing the power of the wind rather than fighting it. An emergency rudder gives us an almost 100 percent chance of seeing land again after losing our main steering. And to repeat a major theme of this book, the less electricity we use to navigate the world's oceans, the less likely we are to depend on the main engine or genset to charge the battery banks, and the smaller a footprint we leave on the oceans we cross.

Chapter 14
Autopilots

ELECTRONIC AUTOPILOTS OFFER DISTINCT ADVANTAGES ON VESSELS where there is enough battery and charging power to run them. Easy push-button control over a yacht's trajectory under sail or motor power saves the crew from the irksome chore of hand-steering, particularly in hard weather conditions. Most die-hard ocean sailors still adamantly insist, of course, that wind-powered self-steering systems must be our first choice. But alas, sometimes the wind does not blow, and we still need to put miles behind us. Staying ahead of an impending storm or having to yaw across a fast-moving cross-current could mean spending many long hours at the helm while motoring if there is no autopilot to take over. If you are single-handed, as I was through two-thirds of a circumnavigation with only windvane steering, you need to avoid the dangerously long stints of sleep deprivation while motoring through a calm, sometimes two or three days at a stretch, in the absence of some form of electronic self-steering. An autopilot gives you a bit of room for some shut-eye, helping you to think more clearly while making critical observations and decisions about weather conditions, sail changes, course adjustments, waypoints, and vessel identification.

Operating Theory

Electronic autopilots consist of four essential components: course sensor, microprocessor, drive unit, and rudder reference indicator. The sensor may be limited to a fluxgate compass to transmit direction to the computer but also may include a GPS receiver to help keep the vessel on course. A fluxgate is a compass that indicates direction via electrical impulses rather than a rotating magnet and card. In an autopilot, as the compass rotates with the vessel, sensors read the minute changes in magnetism and relay the data to the computer, which in turn compares analog impulses from the rudder indicator to the heading sensed by the fluxgate. The computer then commands the drive unit to correct the rudder. In settled conditions, the fluxgate can tilt gently while continuing to provide accurate course feedback. But when exposed to excessive movement, ferrous materials, or electromagnetic interference from SSB radio transmissions or the alternator, the fluxgate may misread compass directions and send the boat off course. A GPS interface, which follows a course based on geosynchronous satellites, contributes added corrective data to the computer, where the GPS data are integrated with fluxgate impulses for finer course control. Wind sensing and chart plotting are optional interfaces added to more sophisticated autopilots, enabling them to steer more independently while responding to multiple changes in the sailing environment.

There are six main classes of autopilot systems built on the same core components. The three above-deck autopilot systems—tiller pilots, tiller rams, and wheel pilots—are designed for yachts of small to medium length and tonnage, and commonly serve as back-ups to windvane self-steering systems. The three most common below-deck systems, with their added power and amperage draw, are generally for mid-size to larger vessels, roughly 40 feet or longer. These are mechanical linear drive, hydraulic linear drive, and rotary drive, which commonly, though not always, provide the boat's main steering power on long ocean crossings.

Above-Deck Systems

Vessels up to roughly 6.5 tons displacement, or about 33 feet LOA, with tiller steering can take advantage of a completely self-contained tiller pilot, avoiding the hassle of installing all the components, brackets, data cables, and software involved with the other, more sophisticated types of autopilots. Weighing 5 to 8 pounds and occupying very little storage space, a tiller pilot operates on a fluxgate sensing system, and the direct connection to the tiller enables direct rudder sensing. The least expensive, most basic tiller pilots are completely self-contained, having no capability to be linked into a GPS system or larger navigation network. The helmsman sets the tiller pilot course by first getting the boat sailing on the desired course and then pushing a button to activate the automatic steering action. Fine adjustments in compass course may be made by pushing a port button or a starboard button. A tacking button pushes the tiller hard over 90 degrees to bring the vessel about, and then resumes course sensing and correcting in the same manner. More sophisticated tiller pilots, such as the Simrad TP22 and TP23, allow an interface with a wind sensor, an external fluxgate compass, and GPS via an NMEA 0183 interface cable. Being able to choose between GPS and wind references for course control gives the helmsman much of the same flexibility enjoyed with more highly complex below-decks autopilots but with less space consumed and less trouble with installation.

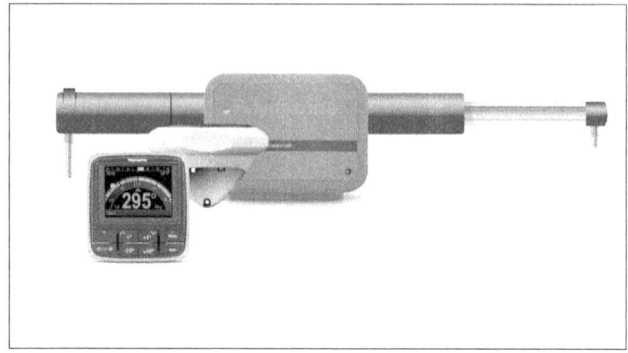

Photo courtesy of Raymarine

Raymarine's EV-100 Tiller autopilot provides more power than a stand-alone tiller pilot, along with complex sensing of the sailing environment and added steering power.

A unique capability of a tiller pilot is its ability to be combined with windvane self-steering in order to save battery power and prevent excessive wear and tear to the tiller pilot. Depending on the location of the vane gear, the backstay, and other details in the rear deck layout, you can fashion a steering connection to either the airvane yoke or, in the case of a Hydrovane, the unit's manual steering rudder. For all wind steering applications, be it Hydrovane, trim tab, or servopendulum, you will need first to construct a stainless, aluminum, or wooden mounting bracket for the main body of the tiller pilot. Then, in the case of a trim tab or servopendulum, you must fashion a stainless coupler to connect the tiller pilot ram tip to a small, vertical piece of plywood to be inserted into the windvane yoke. The coupler amounts to a bolt with a vertical swivel piece to accept the pin from the tiller pilot steering shaft. With the coupler set a few inches above the edge of the yoke on the

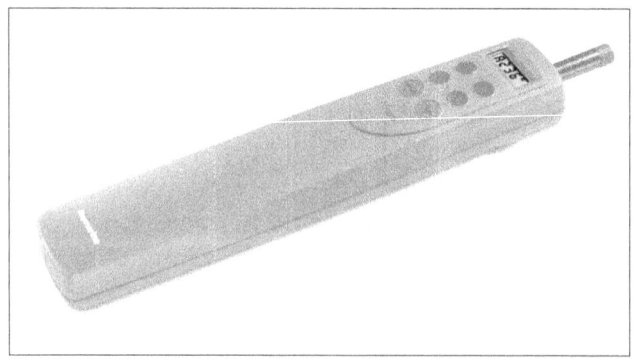

Photo courtesy of Raymarine

The ST2000 Tiller Pilot from Raymarine, suitable for vessels displacing up to 10,000 pounds, may be used alone or networked with SeaTalk / NMEA GPS.

windvane mast, the tiller pilot will have enough leverage to manipulate the windvane's steering action while using only a fraction of the amperage of its normal operation on the tiller.

Some inexperienced shoestring cruisers forgo a windvane self-steerer and opt instead for a less expensive tiller pilot, placing complete trust in the little box with its plastic gears and delicate electronics to steer flawlessly 30,000-plus nautical miles around the planet through gale-force storms and hair-raising seas topping 20 feet. Please understand that these devices are meant for coastal daysailing and taking over at the helm during calms—and nothing more. The tiller pilot capable of crossing the entire Pacific Ocean, much less circling the entire planet, without breaking down simply does not exist. And even if you can replace the tiller pilot repeatedly throughout the warranty period every few thousand miles, you will spend a good portion of your cruising career waiting on the mail and customs, which will probably entail a VAT (value added tax) and a maddening amount of time-consuming paperwork for the imported item. For the sake of the vessel and the safety and sanity of the crew, your main steering power on a small to midsize sailing vessel on an ocean crossing should be a windvane self-steering device (see Chapter 12).

The next step up from a tiller pilot is a tiller-mounted ram controlled by a separately installed fluxgate sensor, CPU, and control monitor. In the same manner as a tiller pilot, a tiller ram serves as a rudder indicator, eliminating the necessity of installing that extra piece of equipment to the steering system. The helmsman makes course adjustments to the tiller ram, along with tacking commands, on a monitor/control unit. A tiller ram is used on boats that are too large for a tiller pilot yet still have a tiller for their main steering. There are plenty of sailing yachts in the 33-foot to 40 foot range out there using tillers, and to provide adequate steering power and dependability for those ocean-going yachts, a tiller ram is preferable to a tiller pilot. Tiller rams tend to be more heavily built than tiller pilots, and if the ram fails during a passage, it can easily be replaced by a spare, which certainly beats waiting for warranty repairs on a tiller pilot. A tiller ram typically has about the same steering thrust as the top-rated tiller pilots but offers the advantage of external control, saving the helmsman from having to step out from under the spray dodger to make course corrections.

An above-deck mechanical wheel pilot is designed for use with mechanical main steering, not hydraulic. Mechanical steering refers to any main steering system using bevel gears, chain, or cable linkage to transfer steering action from the wheel to the rudder. An above-deck wheel pilot operates with a motor and belt-drive wheel adapter, along with a separate control/monitor unit, fluxgate sensor, and CPU. The Raymarine EV-100 Wheel features a Smart Rudder Sense system, eliminating the need for a separately installed rudder position transducer. To operate an above-deck wheel pilot, the helmsman sets the helm on the desired course, engages the wheel adapter and belt, and then activates the autopilot motor via the control unit.

The mechanical wheel pilot is probably the most common type of autopilot to be seen on the cruising circuit. Most mid-sized boats are fitted with mechanical steering, and their owners usually opt for some type of windvane self-steering to do the grunt work of steering across oceans while leaving the wheel pilot for close island-hopping

Photo courtesy of Raymarine

The Raymarine EV-100 Wheel autopilot uses the same course-sensing technology as the EV-100 Tiller but transmits steering impulses via motor and belt drive to a wheel adaptor.

and motoring through calms. You can easily tell whether a boat's autopilot is above or below decks: a conspicuous, large-diameter wheel adapter on the helm indicates a wheel pilot, and no adapter on a yacht over 40 feet in length, with or without a windvane, is a near-guarantee of a below-decks autopilot.

Below-Deck Systems

Larger yachts, those measuring over approximately 40 feet on deck and weighing in excess of 10 tons, are better served by a below-deck system, be it mechanical linear drive, hydraulic ram, or rotary drive. All three of these systems act directly on the rudder shaft or steering quadrant, unlike above-deck devices, which operate on the helm. A mechanical linear drive system installed below deck is a larger, more heavily built version of the above-deck linear drive, and its ram joins the rudder shaft via an auxiliary tiller arm, which provides leverage in lieu of a steering quadrant. One major disadvantage with a tiller arm is that in the event of failure, the shaft can freeze, leaving the rudder locked in one position until someone goes down below to disconnect the tiller arm from the rudder post. Depending on how cluttered the path is to the rudder post, this could take a bit of time to resolve, not something we want to face when the vessel is broaching in towering seas and threatening to capsize.

Hydraulic autopilots are capable of providing a huge amount of steering power and are therefore the choice for the largest yachts, measuring anywhere from 40 feet to over 60 feet LOA. There are two very distinct types of hydraulic autopilots. One uses a hydraulic ram, which is connected directly to the steering quadrant, as with chain- or cable-drive mechanical steering. A big benefit of this arrangement is that in the event of failure of the main steering, the hydraulic ram can continue to steer the boat. Likewise, if the hydraulic ram or the autopilot controls fail, the vessel's main steering is left intact. At worst, if the ram seals freeze up, or if the ram itself is bent (I actually have witnessed this), the ram can be disconnected from the quadrant to permit manual steering, although this could take a while.

The other type of hydraulic autopilot is an in-line device that integrates the hydraulic pump directly into a vessel's main hydraulic steering system. Tying the dual systems together requires two sets of bypass, or "check," valves, one pair for the main hydraulic line, the other for the hydraulic steering pump. This set-up allows the use of one steering pump (either manual or autopilot-controlled) while hydraulic fluid flows undisturbed through the other pump. Check valves in hydraulic main steering are meant to cushion a blow to the rudder, caused by either a side collision with a solid object or by a strong wave imposing a large amount of lateral force on the rudder. With two sets of check valves, the autopilot hydraulic pump is also protected from such blunt force. When selecting an in-line hydraulic system, verify that the pump capacity matches the hydraulic pump on your vessel. An exception to this rule is the Garmin GHP Reactor Hydraulic Corepack with SmartPump, an in-line pump capable of matching a boat's hydraulic steering fluid volume by automatically adjusting its flow rate from 0 to 2.4 liters per minute, covering most sailboat hydraulic steering configurations. Another handy advantage of the Garmin GHP Reactor is its patented Shadow Drive technology, a unique feature

Photo courtesy of Garmin

The GHP Reactor Hydraulic Corepack with SmartPump is a powerful autopilot package adaptable to most hydraulic steering systems, offering patented Shadow Drive technology to keep the boat on course the moment you let go of the wheel.

directing the unit to disengage automatically when you take over at the helm. After you trim the helm and hold the wheel steady for a moment, you let go and the Garmin GHP Reactor with Shadow Drive capability resumes steering.

Installing in-line hydraulic self-steering generally requires the services of a trained technician who knows how to lay out hydraulic tubing and ensure that the autopilot's hydraulic reservoir capacity properly matches that of the main hydraulic steering pump. If you damage the hydraulic pump of the autopilot or main steering through a negligent installation, you run the risk of voiding the warranty of one or both of the systems, either of which will set you back another several thousand dollars. As sailors, we love to be self-sufficient, but sometimes it is best to leave the more esoteric work to a professional.

Another caveat with hydraulic main steering is its inability to work with any form of windvane self-steering designed to work directly on the helm. The check valves can cause misalignment between the windvane system and the rudder position, rendering the windvane steering completely incapable of keeping the vessel on course. While an in-line hydraulic autopilot is certainly effective while the engine is running, remember that either a Hydrovane or an Auto-Helm trim tab self-steering rig offers completely self-contained, wind-powered steering capability without spending a single amp hour of your vessel's precious battery banks.

For boats with chain or cable steering, the appropriate below-deck autopilot is a rotary drive system. Instead of using a hydraulic pump or a worm gear to convert steering impulses, a rotary motor controls a chain sprocket or cable pulley along the path between the helm and the steering quadrant. The obvious limitation here is that in the event of failure of either the main steering or autopilot, steering is eliminated completely until the chain or cable can be shortened or replaced in order to bypass the defective component. If we assume the much greater likelihood of the autopilot motor freezing up, the skipper needs to have a plan in place for bypassing the autopilot rotary motor before leaving port. One solution is to install two steering quadrants, one on either side of the steering quadrant, with each steering system having its own blocks and cable. If either the main steering or the autopilot fails, one cable can be removed from its quadrant to allow use of the side still functioning properly.

Sailing With an Autopilot

Using an autopilot skillfully and strategically will reduce amperage draw and add to the life of the house bank while keeping your vessel on course. Of course, skill and strategy take practice and planning, and the best way to master all of this is by taking short coastal trips to put yourself and the vessel through the hoops before setting out on an offshore voyage. If the autopilot is integrated into a chart plotter, sail 20 or 30 miles with a few safe waypoints thrown in just to see how the autopilot and vessel handle the programmed turns. Do this safely offshore and make sure someone is on watch at all times to trim the sails properly during the automatic course adjustments. Your crew may find that some course adjustments simply cannot be carried out as programmed on the chart plotter. If a turn puts you straight into the wind, new waypoints will have to be entered to allow for tacking.

As you may have concluded by now, on a major ocean passage, steering a boat via a set of GPS waypoints on a chart plotter is not recommended unless you are motoring. The chances of your resetting the sails while tacking at the very moment the vessel changes course are slim. Imagine sailing slightly to windward in a full gale, climbing the oncoming seas to keep the vessel stable, and then suddenly seeing the boat turn away from the head seas and attempt to head straight down wind in response to a programmed course change at some waypoint on the chart plotter. That kind of maneuver under such conditions could cause the vessel to broach and capsize, or worse, to pitchpole stern over bow, a calamity from which few sailors have ever survived. Some skippers regard a chart plotter with the same detachment as they would a video game. But no matter how high-tech our navigation systems evolve over time, sailing will always be a rough, visceral undertaking, relying first and foremost on our eyes, ears, and hands in responding to rapid changes in wind and sea state with just the right canvas deployment and rudder control. Therefore, while under sail, particularly in rough conditions, chart plotting should be limited to telling us when to change course rather than being permitted to alter course automatically.

For best battery economy, effective sailing with an autopilot requires us to have a balanced rig at all times. Here again, we cannot simply delegate our responsibilities as sailors to an electronic gadget. Maintaining a balanced rig means keeping the sails perfectly trimmed for the best use of the air in the lightest of winds, and reefing the sails as soon as white caps appear on the sea and we hear the autopilot struggling to keep the boat on course. For both windvane and autopilot steering, it is wise to reef earlier than you would if you were steering by hand. Straining your arms against weather helm under full sail in coastal sailing to add half a knot of speed is not how we cruise offshore. We want to make the job of keeping the boat on course as easy as possible for ourselves and for the automatic steering of our choice.

In light conditions, some autopilots may tend to over-correct heading variance, causing the vessel to steer in an S formation. On the other hand, in storm conditions, some autopilots may be slow to respond to rapid shifts in the vessel's heading as waves pummel the hull and hard winds try to pull the bow into the wind. Wind sensors aid the autopilot's CPU in making course corrections and keeping the vessel on a given angle to the wind current. But in the very worst of conditions, absent a windvane self-steerer, the helmsman has no recourse but to disengage the autopilot and take over at the helm. Having sailed downwind with a servopendulum self-steering system in full gales with monstrous seas while sipping coffee in the comfort of the cabin, my heart goes out to those skippers who are forced to take manual control of the helm in the middle of a raging storm for days on end until it is safe to reassign the helm to the autopilot.

Using an autopilot on cruising boats has become a well-established means of crossing oceans. Dependable above- and below-decks systems offer ease of use and the ability to be integrated with GPS and chart plotters, as long as there is an adequate house battery and a robust means of keeping it charged. While windvane self-steering remains a far more dependable form of steering on offshore sailing vessels, some skippers prefer the push-button ease of an electronic autopilot. Whatever self-steering strategy you elect for your home on the water, always have a back-up plan—either heaving-to or switching steering systems—when things go awry. And most importantly, always respect your own personal need for sleep and peace of mind, no matter what happens on the high seas.

Chapter 15
Manual Windlasses

IF ANY SINGLE OBJECT ON A CRUISING VESSEL SCREAMS ENERGY independence more than anything else, it is ye olde manual windlass. Strong and dependable, it is emblematic of the rugged, die-hard individualist cruising sailor who insists on being in constant physical control of his ship, viscerally in tune with his watery, off-grid environs. You can just hear the exotic Mexican beer commercial: "His tuna lures are wild caught. He is the most interesting skipper in the world."

Despite what you may have heard about manual windlasses, operating one does not require superhuman powers. Quite to the contrary, a manual windlass is designed to make the job of raising the anchor easy, eliminating the strain you would otherwise endure by pulling up the hook and chain with your bare hands. The object of these machines is to offer a good measure of mechanical advantage, which means lots of cranking and a nice little workout, but well within the physical limits of an adult of average strength. And when compared to electric windlasses, the manual device can claim full allegiance to the green cause: it uses not a single milliamp to operate.

Major chandlery chains and online catalogs in North America now sell electric windlasses exclusively, but this does not necessarily signal the demise of the mechanical windlass. A handful of American and European manufacturers still produce fine manual windlasses, which are generally lighter, more compact, and less expensive than their electric counterparts. If we factor in the much greater durability of mechanical windlasses, plus their zero drain on the battery banks, one wonders why anyone would consider the electric appliance over the tried and true mechanical device. Not only are new mechanical windlasses selling well, but there is a brisk market in used and reconditioned mechanical units as well.

Overview of Manual Windlasses

The primary advantage of a manual windlass is, of course, that it uses no electricity. However, a sailboat's auxiliary engine is generally running as a precaution while retrieving the anchor, irrespective of the type of windlass being used. If a sudden gust swings the vessel dangerously close to shore or to other anchored vessels, the helmsman needs to be able to put the engine in gear immediately and take evasive action. There are times, though, when the vessel is anchored alone in a wide area, allowing crew to weigh anchor, raise the sails, and get underway without listening to the engine grumble, or breathing diesel fumes, or worrying about depleting a dwindling fuel supply. All you hear is the soft cranking of the manual windlass, the muffled rustling of chain in the hold, and the faint morning breeze as you raise the main, unfurl the genoa, and quietly waft out of the anchorage toward open water. This was the method of setting sail eons before modern engines and electric motors, and it is still a pleasant way to set sail today—if you have a manual windlass.

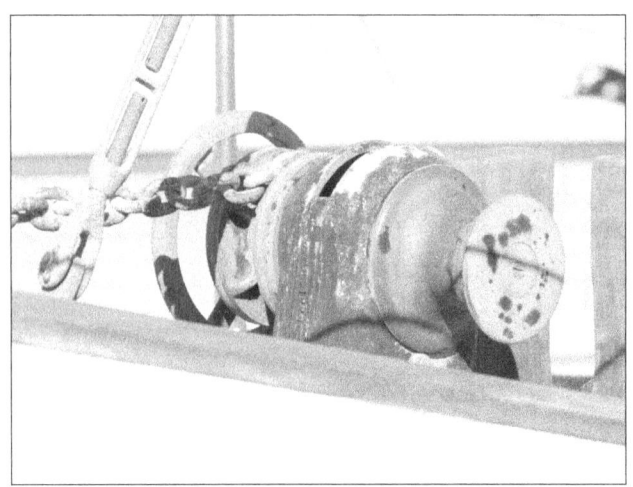

This classic bronze manual windlass was manufactured by Ideal Windlass Company of East Greenwich, Rhode Island.

A major problem you avert with a manual windlass is the fire danger inherent in all electric windlasses. Old wiring, undersized cables, or an excessive load can overheat either the cables or the drive motor to the point of igniting a fire that can devour a boat in minutes. If the polyester resin in fiberglass boats gets hot enough, it burns faster and hotter than wood. More commonly, though, electric windlasses simply stop working altogether. Once saltwater finds its way into the electric motor, it quickly lays waste to the copper wire windings and leaves the crewmember no other option but to hand-crank the windlass slowly and painfully because it is not optimized for manual operation.

A manual windlass, on the other hand, will last for decades with very little maintenance. Durable alloys and long-lasting polymer bushings go into the manual windlasses found on the market today, but the units naturally do incur wear, so keeping up with periodic lubrication is essential to their survival. It will not catch fire, and it will not impose any other physical hazard to the vessel or the operator as long as the unit is used within the limits of its maximum pull. Pushing the manual windlass beyond its rated limit theoretically could cause damage to the unit. More than likely, though, this will just wear out the operator. I once raised a 33-pound claw anchor with 170 feet of 5/16 BBB chain plus 300 feet of 5/8 nylon rode in water 220 feet deep (2.4:1 scope—yikes!) with the old Simpson-Lawrence 510 Hyspeed that is still bolted to *Saltaire's* foredeck. I was fifteen years younger, and I hope I never have to do that again. The venerable Hyspeed, having been rebuilt a few years back, is still as capable as ever.

Another advantage offered by a manual tool over its electric counterpart is the direct mechanical contact you make with the job you are doing. Just as you can feel the condition of a screw head and the density of a plank of wood through a manual screwdriver, you can feel the bottom of an anchorage as the chain drags across the sea floor, sending up signals through the windlass handle into your hands. A manual windlass affords a feeling of intimacy and control with the anchorage bottom, while an electric windlass blocks the

---

Manual Windlass Safety Tips

• After setting the anchor, use a snubber line between the anchor chain and bow cleat to protect the windlass from shock loads.

• A chain stopper helps to protect the windlass; however, it does not take the place of a snubber line.

• Use only a deck winch or the handle provided by the manufacturer to operate the windlass in order to prevent personal injury.

• Avoid using the windlass to pull the boat up to the anchor spot; instead, motor or sail up to the anchor.

• For safer, easier operation of a horizontal windlass, stand with one foot forward of the windlass and the other foot aft so you are facing the port side of the vessel, and then move the crank back and forth with both hands.

• If raising the anchor is unusually difficult due to strong winds or a very deep anchorage, take frequent breaks to catch your breath and restore your strength.

• After pulling the anchor onto the bow roller, remember to lock the wildcat with the pawl.

• Avoid depending on the wildcat to retain the anchor while under way; instead, lock the anchor chain with a chain stopper or a short length of line made fast to a deck cleat.

• Using an anchor chock will protect the deck and keep the anchor stable while on passage.

anchor chain's scrapes and grumblings from reaching the operator. With an electric windlass and either a deck button or a remote wand, you are insulated from the forces at work beneath the hull. Sensing the anchor chain's vibrations lets you know if the chain is wrapped around a rock or coral head, or if it is hooked on another anchor chain. You can actually get an idea of the size and shape of the obstruction lying several fathoms beneath the water's surface by feeling the chain with your hands and through the handle and listening to the sound amplified by the hull. This information tells whether you need to move the vessel to the other side of the obstruction, or whether it is time to don mask, fins, and snorkel to get a closer look. All of this is sure to add up to a great workout, but it certainly beats burning out an electric motor due to complete ignorance of the seabed.

Horizontal manual windlasses are designed to reduce the job of weighing anchor to a straightforward, routine procedure without the aid of hydraulics or an electric motor. Internal reduction gearing makes it possible for an adult of average strength to pull, depending on the model, up to several hundred pounds of ground tackle in a stiff breeze. With rare exception, the manual windlass mounted on the bow of a cruising sailboat has a horizontal drive shaft with a wildcat and a rope capstan, each mounted on either side of the unit's gear box. Virtually all of these units have the wildcat mounted on the starboard side directly aft of the bow roller, permitting the chain to make a solid connection with the teeth of the wildcat. Three or four wraps of nylon rode around the capstan ensure a solid grip, even at an angle of 10 to 15 degrees. And I must admit, in deep water, those last few feet leading up to the chain will burn a lot of calories as you struggle to keep the rode around the capstan while you crank with the other hand. Having an extra pair of hands to take up the slack in the rode will make the job much easier. After you have done this a few dozen times, it doesn't get any easier, but at least you will get used to it. Pace yourself, tie off the rode frequently to give yourself a rest, enjoy the exhilaration of pumping up your biceps and forearms, and then reward yourself with a cold beer after the anchor is secure and the vessel is under way.

The best way to avoid using the nylon rode is to anchor in shallow water, if that is possible, so that you use only chain. At a minimum scope of 3:1, a 150-foot length of chain is good up to 50 feet in settled conditions. The best scope is 5:1, but that may be difficult in a tight anchorage where everyone is using only a bow anchor. So it is best to have a well-practiced method of retrieving nylon rode and switching over to the wildcat while not losing grip on the rode. Try tying off the rode to a deck cleat and then holding the chain in place with a snubber line made fast to another deck cleat. This should permit you to wrap the chain over the wildcat before dropping the nylon rode in the chain locker and cranking up the anchor chain.

This manual windlass, believed to be of Chinese origin, has served on the bow of this owner-built Westsail 32 through tens of thousands of miles of ocean cruising and has yet to be serviced, yet still performs flawlessly.

Muir's two-speed manual windlass, built in Australia, is similar to the Simpson Lawrence 555, and constructed to serve on many mid-sized yachts today.

Using an excessive amount of scope, by the way, may seem prudent but can actually create new hazards. If a squall passes through and the wind suddenly shifts 180 degrees, vessel speed can be great enough to pull the anchor free, allowing the boat to sail downwind until the chain and rode are stretched out enough to reset the anchor. If vessel speed is up to two or three knots, the anchor may not set at all. A safe but conservative 5:1 scope in good holding (e.g. mud, mud and gravel, sand and rock) should reset in up to 30 knots of wind with minimal slippage without allowing the vessel to build up enough momentum to break away.

Manual vertical windlasses, such as the old Simpson Lawrence Anchorman, are intended for coastal and inland sailing vessels up to 30 feet LOA anchoring in depths of no more than 25 to 30 feet. This depth limitation is based not on any product literature but on personal experience. A manual vertical windlass is a direct-drive machine, which means for every revolution of the handle, the capstan or wildcat makes one revolution. The only added mechanical advantage is an off-center mounting hole, which effectively adds another inch or so of leverage to the winch handle. A pair of spring-loaded pawls keeps the revolving drum from unwinding whenever you stop for a rest. Kneeling on the foredeck with your knees scraping the surface grit, and your head, arms, and back swinging wildly around the little stainless canister is every bit as painful as it sounds.

This solid bronze, single-action, double manual windlass, manufactured by the former Moritz Foundry in Costa Mesa, California, offers an antique touch to any classic yacht.

To be sure, the vertical device is helpful in shallow depths and in settled conditions. Or at least, they are one step above having no mechanical advantage at all. And they are beautiful little things, shiny and nautical looking, about the size of a small deck winch. But if you are on a 25-foot vessel anchoring in a maximum of 20 feet of water and you are using a 13-pound anchor with ¼-inch chain, you probably do not need a machine to help you. Pulling up the anchor by hand will be faster and less painful than grinding a vertical manual windlass.

The Simpson-Lawrence Legacy

When Simpson Lawrence sold out to Lewmar in 2000, one of the most lamentable casualties of the transaction was the complete closure of the Simpson Lawrence line of manual windlasses. Simpson Lawrence had been credited for inventing the combination rope and chain gypsy, or wildcat, a familiar component on virtually all brands and models of yacht windlasses today. Their cast aluminum gear boxes on the Hyspeed 510 and Sea Tiger 555, plus their unique, lightweight bicycle chain gearing in the 510, revolutionized an industry that had struggled for generations to meet adequately the needs of crews on small sailing vessels. A former Simpson Lawrence employee purchased the production tooling and the rights to distribute parts, but he soon closed the business. Parts for the 510, 555, and Anchorman windlasses can be found on the Internet, and here and there you might even find a brand-new 510 or 555 still in the original box. Fortunately, there is a thriving cottage industry dedicated to producing replacement parts for the old Simpson Lawrence machines.

If you take a stroll through any North American cruiser marina today, more than a decade and a half since the demise of Simpson Lawrence, you will see that at least half of the offshore-bound vessels are still equipped with a 555 windlass, the enduring standard for the various copy cats of this device. The 555 is designed to convert both forward and backward motion of the windlass handle into a one-way rotation of the horizontal drive shaft, to which both the capstan and wildcat are connected. The double action turns spur reduction gears, two

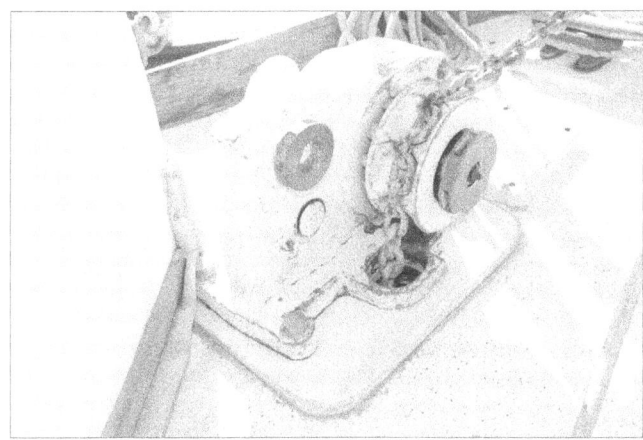

The two-speed, dual-action Simpson Lawrence 555 Sea Tiger, seen here mounted to the bow of a Cheoy Lee 35, has been the preeminent windlass of mid-size cruising boats for decades.

of which are spring loaded to alternate in and out of the meshed sequence, keeping the drive shaft moving in its single direction. The 555 features a high-speed gear with a handle fitting on the port side and a low-speed gear fitting on the starboard side. Having separate handle fittings for the two gears rather than a selector switch ensures simpler operation, lighter construction (40 pounds), and fewer components to fail under extreme conditions.

The 555 was designed for yachts measuring up to 56 feet on deck and, depending on the wildcat (there were six from which to choose), for chain sizes ranging from 5/16 to ½ inch BBB, high-test, or proof coil. This machine can handle up to 385 pounds of pull at high speed with a mechanical advantage of 12:1, and an astounding 1,100 pounds at low speed. The 555 has such high purchase that with the unit in low gear (33:1), you will be surprised at how easily you can retrieve a 44-pound anchor with 200 feet of 3/8 BBB chain in a stiff breeze with white caps spraying spindrift over the bow. It will take a while, but it will not break your back. To release the anchor or let out more scope, turn the wildcat cap counterclockwise with the handle to loosen the cone clutch. After tightening the clutch, drop the locking pawl between two cogs on the wildcat to prevent accidental disengagement of the clutch. And, as with all windlasses, mechanical or electric, always use a snubber line between the anchor chain and the bow cleat to free the windlass of torque. This machine was designed to pull a prescribed maximum load, not to absorb the violent bucking of a bow in storms over many days or weeks.

The 25-pound Hyspeed 510 is decidedly not a miniature of its big brother, the 555. As a matter of fact, beyond their horizontal design and aluminum gear box, they have little in common. The 510's one-speed drive system, which has a mechanical advantage of 12:1, is comprised of two bicycle chains and two sprockets mounted in opposite directions to permit one-way rotation of the drive shaft. Unlike the 555, which is lubricated internally with grease, the 510's chain and sprockets require a bath of heavy gear oil to keep them from rusting and binding up. The one irksome annual chore with this machine is uninstalling the unit from the foredeck, removing the clutch and cover plate, and inspecting the gear oil. Milky sludge indicates water intrusion. If the gasket is shot, you will have to cut a new one from a sheet of cork or thick paper gasket material, taking care not to break the fragile, narrow piece while you poke holes for the screws. After reassembling the unit, remove the bronze NPT plug from the base of the port side and fill with gear oil to the top of the thread. The cone clutch operates in the same manner as that of the 555, and both clutches require occasional lubrication through the grease nipple to keep them operating smoothly.

The SL Anchorman vertical windlass mentioned above may not be the easiest machine to operate, but it is, for all intents and purposes, indestructible. And amazingly, it remains a highly popular windlass on many small sailing vessels, including cruising boats under 28 feet LOA. This little beast contains only a handful of parts, none of which are likely to require replacement. The main components are the base plate, chain stripper, a pair of spring-loaded pawls, pedestal/clutch, wildcat, rope drum, cover plate, and clutch nut, the last of which is secured with a common winch handle. And that's all there is to it. As long as you periodically daub a bit of grease on the pawl springs and pedestal, it should last forever. Hence its popularity.

You can find parts for legacy SL windlasses on numerous websites, and they are for the most part reasonably priced. One site sells new 510s without the wildcat or cone clutch, which you should be

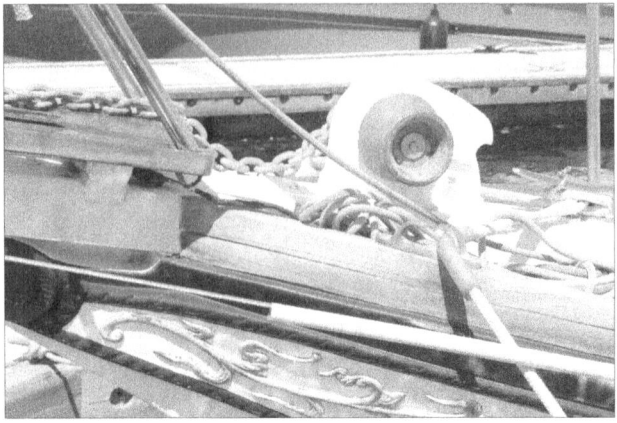

The Simpson Lawrence Hyspeed 510 windlass weighs only 25 pounds and features dual-action chain drive and sprockets.

able to find elsewhere. Used 510s and 555s can be found in all conditions, from completely frozen to nearly new. If you are mechanically inclined, you can buy an old beater for a song and rebuild it with new parts. But inspect the aluminum gear case closely. Excessive corrosion to the aluminum can mean a lost cause. The old 555s I have seen at Minney's Yacht Surplus in Costa Mesa all look intact with their aluminum gear cases free of damage, except perhaps for a few nicks and dents from the windlass handle. Cannibalizing one unit to save another is always an option, but in the case of a 510 Hyspeed, you are best advised to use only new sprockets and chains, both of which can be found either online or through an independent chandler who has the right connections. Restoring an old SL windlass will save you a small fortune and guarantee you years of dependable service, as long as you keep up with the maintenance.

New Manual Windlasses

Several American and European manufacturers continue to produce manual windlasses along with their electric or hydraulic models. One of the most frequently mentioned in dockside conversation is the Lofrans Royal, built in Monza, Italy. Available in anodized aluminum or white enamel and very reasonably priced, this one-speed, double-action horizontal windlass uses a bevel gear drive system to pull up to 430 pounds and is recommended for vessels ranging from 26 to 39 feet LOA. The Royal weighs 22 pounds, slightly less than the SL 510, and its wildcat accepts ¼ high test chain and both 5/16 and 3/8 proof coil, BBB, and high test. If anything about this windlass concerns me, it is the aluminum bevel gears performing the brutal job of raising the anchor hundreds, perhaps thousands of times over its career on the foredeck. Compared to other higher-strength marine alloys, such as super duplex stainless steel at the top end and silicon bronze a bit lower on the scale, aluminum is not prized for its high tensile strength nor for its corrosion resistance. Furthermore, since this unit's internal parts are greased internally at the factory just like the SL 555 rather than bathed in gear oil, one might be concerned about saltwater intrusion causing galvanic corrosion between the aluminum gears and the stainless shaft, along with some bronze internal fittings, potentially rendering the whole device inoperable. Granted, there are numerous grades of very fine marine-grade aluminum. However, a set of aluminum alloy gears capable of meshing flawlessly while combined with two other dissimilar metals in a warm saltwater environment over a full circumnavigation is something I would have to see to believe.

A windlass appearing almost identical to the Lofrans Royal is the Ursus horizontal windlass, produced by Vetus of the UK. Vetus supplies a wide range of equipment to the nautical industry, including engines, plumbing fixtures, bow thrusters, and fuel tanks. Built with roughly the same dimensions and mechanical operating system as the Lofrans Royal, the Ursus sells for roughly a grand and will probably last as long as the Lofrans. The wildcat accepts 5/16 proof coil or BBB chain. The company offers no literature regarding construction details, so it is advisable to find an Ursus owner, inspect the windlass, and read the product literature included with the unit before deciding whether to make a purchase.

R.C. Plath of Portland, Oregon, prides itself in high-quality precision metal spinning, which contributes to the continuing success of its simply designed and constructed manual windlass. Model 9A is cast in high-tensile, marine-grade aluminum, yielding a strong yet light machine based on the heavier bronze Model 9B. The Model 9A weighs in at 28 pounds with combination capstan and wildcat, and the Model 9B, also available in chrome plate, with the same configuration weighs a comparably hefty 45 pounds, which is still only 5 pounds more than the SL 555. Though R.C. Plath does not publish pull maximums for its windlasses, both the 9A and 9B are known to handle up to 800 pounds, and they have served well for many years on the decks of sailing vessels in excess of 35 feet LOA. The double-acting horizontal system is based on a gear drive similar to the SL 555 and therefore can last for decades with little servicing. Both the 9A and 9B accept ¼, 5/16, and 3/8 BBB chain and feature a cone clutch to hold the wildcat in place while retrieving the anchor.

The 9A and 9B are popular models seen on sailing craft throughout North America, but information regarding parts and repairs is hard to find without calling the manufacturer by telephone or dropping in for a visit. One saving grace is that the twin models have not changed in over 40 years, so you should have no trouble ordering new repair parts from R.C. Plath. When you see an old bronze windlass with its distinctive fore-and-aft slit to accept the windlass handle through the round top, it is more than likely an R.C. Plath (not to be confused with the other various Plath companies), and it is probably not as old as it looks. The green patina lends a classic look to the bronze version, making it look like it was salvaged from the Arc, but the internal design and construction include the high-tensile stainless spun parts you would expect in any other high-quality manual windlass of the late twentieth century.

The ABI 1000BR manual windlass is a spitting image of the R.C. Plath 9B, and is widely believed to be nothing more than a 9B knock-off. The ABI's weight of 49 pounds is only four pounds heavier than the R.C. Plath 9B, and the rope capstan and wildcat are also close in appearance to the 9B's. Regardless of the ABI's design origins, though, it has maintained a fairly good following among sailors. However, the author's research found no current address or telephone number for ABI, and the company is rumored to have gone out of business. No doubt a number of new and like-new units are still available and probably for very competitive prices. Nonetheless, as with any other product no longer served by its manufacturer, you will have nowhere to turn but to a machine shop if and when the unit ever malfunctions.

Last on the list of manual windlasses known or believed to be currently manufactured is the Muir Easyweigh 500 vertical windlass, which comes in several options. You can choose a pure chain wildcat set-up, or a chain wildcat with rope capstan, or either of the two with or without a rope hawser. Similar to the SL Anchorman, the Easyweigh 500 is operated with a standard winch handle, which means you can increase leverage simply by choosing a longer handle. The price you will pay for this beautiful but labor-intensive windlass will take your breath away, but Muir windlasses are backed by a solid reputation. One more positive note is that since the Muir is still being built, you can expect a warranty, technical support, and full parts availability from this well-regarded Australian company.

Owning and operating a manual windlass on a small to medium-sized sailing vessel is a way of life for thousands of cruising sailors. Boats under 36 or 37 feet LOA generally have neither the need nor the room to store large battery banks just to haul up an anchor. And with enough new and rebuilt high-quality manual windlasses on the market to feed the demand for these machines for many decades, there is no practical reason to go electric unless the sheer size of your vessel demands such a device. One of the reasons we take to the sea is to recapture the physical life, not to replicate our sedentary land life. A well-constructed, properly maintained manual windlass provides us that extra bit of exercise we seek while at the same time guaranteeing the retrieval of our anchors, regardless of whether there is fuel in the tank or enough battery charge to start the engine. With just the right breeze and the engine cold and silent, we can weigh anchor and set sail with the exhilarating feeling of independence that drove us to cross oceans in the first place.

Chapter 16
Electric Windlasses

A COMBINATION OF FACTORS CONTINUES TO FEED THE GROWING popularity of electric windlasses on modern sailing vessels. Bigger boats, bigger battery banks, an aging boater population, and an ongoing trend away from the physical life toward a push button/touch screen lifestyle have conspired to make the electric windlass de rigeur on modern, high-tech cruising yachts measuring as little as 25 feet LOA. The latest Defender and West Marine catalogs no longer carry manual windlasses, now listing only the electric variety, although some small to mid-sized electric windlasses do include manual override capability. As you have read in the previous chapter, manual windlasses are still manufactured by a few small companies for those of us who still seek longevity and energy independence in our vessels' essential systems.

Overview of Features

The purpose of a windlass is strictly to raise the anchor and chain from the bottom of an anchorage, not to pull the boat up to the anchor, much less in a stiff breeze. We want to prevent the motor windings and the power cables leading from the battery from overheating and, in the worse scenario, causing a fire. The proper way to raise anchor with any type of windlass is to sail or motor up to the point where the chain or rode is vertical and then employ the windlass to retrieve the anchor. Nonetheless, in any North American anchorage you will see weekend sailors using their electric windlasses essentially as boat winches, their vessels actually creating small bow waves as they cross the water on approach to the anchor spot. The only time this may be necessary is when your boat has run aground and you need to kedge it off a reef or beach by manually setting the anchor in deeper water and using the windlass to pull the boat afloat as the tide rises.

The internal construction and gearing of an electric windlass, which has either horizontal drive or vertical drive, varies from one model to the next. Some horizontal windlasses may have a vertically mounted motor suspended below deck and connected directly to the drive shaft via a worm gear. Other horizontal devices have everything contained above deck with reduction gearing for easier installation. Among vertical electric windlasses, some have a motor suspended vertically below deck connecting to the drive shaft by reduction gears, while other models have the motor mounted horizontally and connected to the reduction gearing via a worm gear, taking up less space in the chain locker.

Electric windlasses are rated chiefly by their maximum pull, which Lewmar recommends to be four times the total maximum weight being hauled up at any given time. A typical 35-foot cruising vessel with a 33-pound claw anchor and 5/16 BBB

> **Electric Windlass Safety Tips**
>
> - To prevent fire, use wire that is a size larger than recommended to install the electric windlass.
> - Keep a B-1 (UL-rated B:C) fire extinguisher in the forward cabin near the chain locker in case of a Class C electrical fire, which could quickly become a larger Class A fire.
> - Always have the engine running while using the electric windlass; a fouled anchor or a chain caught around a coral head can drain a battery quickly.
> - For manual override, use only a deck winch or the handle provided by the manufacturer to operate the windlass in order to prevent personal injury.
> - Avoid using the windlass to pull the boat up to the anchor spot; instead, motor up to the anchor.
> - Use a snubber line between the anchor chain and bow cleat to protect the windlass from shock loads.
> - A chain stopper helps to protect the windlass; however, it does not take the place of a snubber line.
> - After pulling the anchor onto the bow roller, remember to lock the wildcat with the pawl.
> - Using an anchor chock will protect the deck and keep the anchor stable while on passage.
> - Always remember to turn off the main power switch to the windlass when not in use.

chain at a depth of 60 feet has a total of 101 pounds to retrieve when the anchor is hanging freely just above the bottom, so the windlass should be rated for at least a 400-pound pull. This is comfortably within the range of typical mid-size cruising yacht windlasses, some of which can pull well over a ton. While comparing weight limits, another factor to consider is amperage draw. A modestly sized Maxwell VWC 1500 vertical windlass with a 1,500-pound pull, perfect for a 35-footer, draws 96 amps, necessitating an alternator putting out at least 100 amps while the engine is idling in order to prevent the rapid depletion of the battery. A Balmar 94LY-Series 210-amp alternator, which, incidentally, retails for about $2,200, cranks out 100 amps at an alternator speed of 2000 RPM, just enough to keep the house battery safe.

Power windlasses are rated also by the speed at which they can retrieve chain, the range spanning from the 1000-pound-capacity vertical Lewmar V1 Gypsy with 5/16 BBB chain at 43 feet per minute, to the diminutive, 600-pound-rated horizontal Maxwell HRC 6, which can pull quarter-inch chain at 108 feet per minute. On larger yachts, torque is the main concern, but their big windlasses can pull at respectable speeds. The 3,190-pound capacity Lewmar V5 Gypsy, suggested for boats 60 to 80 feet LOA, pulls up 90 feet of 3/8 high test chain, plus an anchor for a combined load of up to 798 pounds, in one minute. If you can afford the 120 amps of power and the $4,000 price tag, go for it.

Another feature to consider is reversibility, the ability of a windlass to pay out chain at a controlled speed, rather than letting the anchor and chain drop by loosening the wildcat, or "chain gypsy," as is done with a manual windlass. All of the electric windlasses within the range you would use on a cruising vessel are reversible. Windlasses without this feature are for rope only and are intended for small coastal motor boats, not cruising yachts. The option to raise the anchor manually, by the way, is something to consider when shopping for an electric windlass. If the engine will not start and the battery banks are short of the power you need to weigh anchor, or if the windlass motor burns out, you need to have the option of using a winch handle to raise the hook and get under way.

Other variables to consider involve matters of convenience and ease of use, such as compatibility with the chain locker and depth of chain fall, the type of electric power switch, remote control capability, amount of space occupied on the foredeck, and appearance. To guarantee you are choosing the best windlass for your boat, take precise measurements of the space you are allowing for the device, and of the area below the deck for chain and a motor drive if you install a vertical windlass, and see what fits best. Also look at amperage draw to calculate what size alternator and battery bank you will need to power the windlass. Talk to cruisers who have experience with different models of electric windlasses to find out which ones have the best combination of pulling power, conservative amperage draw, ease of use, and durability over many years of operating in a humid, tropical setting.

Horizontal

Some cruisers prefer the profile of a horizontal windlass, dividing the wildcat and rope capstan to either side of the motor housing. Some units divide the wildcat and capstan yet have the motor mounted below the deck. Ideal and Lofrans offer high-quality horizontal electric windlasses for mid-range cruising yachts, and both offer manual override. Very large yachts, measuring well over 100 feet, also use horizontal windlasses, such as those from IDEAL Windlass.

Some of the electric windlasses with horizontal capstans or wildcats are designed for installation on motor boats. You will recognize these motor boat windlasses instantly by their single wildcat or rope capstan on one side and motor housing on the opposite side. Though some of them are built by highly reputable manufacturers, such as Lewmar, they tend to be lightly built and intended for 1/4-inch to 5/16-inch chain and 1/2-inch nylon rode, just the right package for weekend fishing trips on inland lakes and shallow coastal inlets. However, they are not intended for total submersion in breaking head seas, or for long exposure to the hot, humid conditions prevalent in tropical cruising. There is nothing inherently wrong with installing one of these inexpensive machines on a cruising sailboat, but—how shall I say this?—it just isn't done.

As with all windlasses, be they manual or electric, the gear casing should be constructed of thick, marine-grade aluminum alloy, 316L stainless steel, or silicon bronze. And since the motor is sitting up on deck, the casing should also be completely sealed from the elements to prevent short circuits and mechanical failure. Additionally, it is preferable to have a separate rope capstan and chain wildcat, not just a dual-purpose wildcat for both rope and chain. Nothing is more infuriating than trying to pull 5/8-inch, three-strand nylon rope from the inner groove of a wildcat while 150 feet of chain and a claw anchor are fighting against you in a 20-knot wind. Of course, if you are using the rope capstan as intended, the really fun part is switching over to the wildcat when you get to the chain. Deploying the snubber line and chain hook to hold the chain in place while you stow the rode should make that job much easier.

Manual override capability is a significant selling point in a well-built power windlass, but in a horizontal device, manufacturers leave us with a rather slow, dubious system. You insert a winch handle into the end of a horizontal capstan, pull it half a turn, reinsert the winch handle, pull another half turn, and repeat this a jillion times until you have retrieved the anchor. Manual override on an electric horizontal windlass might make a good marketing ploy, but you might have better luck just by pulling the anchor up by hand and getting it over with.

One saving grace of most horizontal electric windlasses is the ease of installation as compared to a vertical device. Since the whole unit is mounted above deck, all you need to do is drill four bolt holes and a larger hole for the chain drop, and you are ready to install the windlass and run the wiring back to the house battery. An exception is the Lofrans Kobra 12-volt manual windlass, which has its motor mounted vertically below the deck, resulting in a smaller, less obtrusive profile above deck.

When installing a horizontal windlass, manual or electric, take care to see that the center of the wildcat lines up perfectly with the center of the

The electric Lofrans Tigres windlass features single-action manual override and a snubber cleat.

bow roller to ensure proper meshing of chain links with the sections, or teeth, on the wildcat. If you read popular advice on chain fall in the locker below decks, it may seem as if all you need is 12 inches of clearance. The product manual should be clear on this point. While the anchor is secure in its roller, there should be a one-foot clearance between the underside of the foredeck and the top of the pile of chain in the hold because the pile of links and three-strand rode itself could be a foot high. If the chain peeks too high in the middle of the pile, reducing fall excessively, have a strong stick ready to jab through the hawse hole and knock the stack down a bit.

As for the availability of electric horizontal windlasses for mid-size sailing yachts, Lewmar offers its H2 and H3 heavy-duty windlasses, which are designed and built with the cruising yacht in mind. These two models feature worm gear drive; a sealed, white enamel, marine-grade aluminum case to reduce weight; a starboard-side wildcat; and a port-side rope capstan, conforming to the traditional shape and function of a cruising windlass. Though built as 12-volt machines, you may purchase either model in a 24-volt version through special order. For an extra few hundred bucks, you can order a Manual Recovery Upgrade Kit, which you install directly onto the wildcat. A spring-loaded toggle in the upgrade kit permits you to swing the windlass handle fore and aft to speed up the process of pulling the anchor, should the motor or electrical source fail.

Ideal Windlass Company in East Greenwich, Rhode Island, offers a line of horizontal and vertical electric windlasses that are not only up to the task, but appealing to the eye as well. Rugged and ornate, their wide selection of windlasses cover the boat gamut from 25-foot gunkholers all the way to 210-foot megayachts with 1-1/2-inch chain and continuous loads of 15,000 pounds. As a relatively small, independently owned company, the owners and engineers can take on custom work, creatively adapting the location of hawse holes, the mounting pattern, and even the positioning of one or more chain wildcats or rope capstans. Ideal's machines are solid evidence of how art, foundry work, and high-precision machining can come together to produce incredible pieces of tough, functional jewelry in gleaming, highly polished stainless steel. Their entry-level, horizontal, electric reversible HF-1 windlass with a port rope capstan and a starboard wildcat will handle the anchoring needs of most mid-size yachts while costing not much more than the Lewmar H2 or H3.

Vertical

Most of the electric windlasses being sold today, at least in the U.S., are of the vertical type. They are less complicated to manufacture, take up less deck space, and are easier to operate. A vertical combination capstan and wildcat, available on some models, allows you to move from nylon rode to chain much more easily than by having to switch from one side of the gear housing to the other. Also, with the motor safely below deck, it is less exposed to the elements than an above-deck motor. A counter-argument could be made, though, that a below-deck motor sits in a perennially damp environment and never really gets to dry out, as it would outside. Indeed, some below-deck windlass motors eventually fail because of this constantly damp environment. As long as the chain locker receives ample ventilation, though, the build-up of humidity can largely be avoided.

Another important feature of vertical windlasses is their manual override capability. Lewmar is known for its winch handle hole in the outer cap on the capstan or wildcat, allowing for manual operation, and Maxwell's vertical machines have a slot in the end cap and a handle specially designed for manual operation. As opposed to the cumbersome manner in which electric horizontal winches are operated manually, a vertical windlass allows a full, 360-degree swing of the handle, which means much faster retrieval. The wide turn around the top of a vertical windlass still does not compare with the greater leverage and more comfortable action of a horizontal manual windlass, but at least this back-up option gets your anchor back up on the roller in a reasonable amount of time.

Lewmar's V and CPX series and Maxwell's RC and VWC series vertical power windlasses are some of the most popular machines in their class, not only because of their competitive prices but also because of their reputation for durability

The elegant Maxwell VWC Series electric windlass is powered by a horizontal motor and worm gear mounted below decks and features a combination capstan and chain wildcat, plus manual override.

and ease of use. The profile of the Lewmar V series wildcat-only windlasses is so compact they look like small foredeck hood ornaments. Sleek and understated, they belie their pulling power, ranging from 1,000 pounds for the V1 Gypsy, to 3,190 pounds for the V5 "Gypsy/Drum" combination. Just like the V series, Lewmar's CPX series windlasses are available as gypsy-only or gypsy with capstan (drum) and also feature a distinctive chain pipe connected to the hawse hole. Lewmar's V series units are much stronger and more amperage-hungry, and as you might expect, they are pricier than the CPX series. Nonetheless, the CPX series windlasses offer more than enough power and pulling speed for most yachts. Both

The Lewmar V3GD vertical windlass is designed for boats measuring 40 to 50 feet, and has a combination capstan and wildcat, rocker switch, dual-direction contactor, circuit breaker, and handle for manual override.

of these Lewmar series have their below-deck motors mounted horizontally so as not to take up excessive space in the chain locker.

Maxwell, a well-known manufacturer of vertical electric windlasses, offers several low-profile, capstan-only units in its RC series and versatile capstan/wildcat combinations in its VWC series. Known for their elegant, sculpted appearance, the VWC series windlasses feature a built-in hawse pipe and chain stripper. Both the RC and VWC models include a reversing solenoid, circuit breaker panel, and in case of power loss or mechanical failure, an emergency handle for manual override.

Drawbacks of Electric Windlasses

Some of the potential drawbacks and inherent dangers of electric windlasses have been covered in the preceding paragraphs. To recap, these units draw huge amounts of power, and if the engine cannot start, you are looking at operating the windlass manually until the engine returns to life. The high level of current also imposes an obvious fire hazard, so you if you are considering such a device, verify that the power cables from the battery are rated for the amperage and the length of the cable run. Upgrading to the next size of cable to ensure safety is always recommended. Heavy-gauge welding cable is frequently used for large motors and long runs.

If you lose use of your engine or alternator and do not have a back-up generator, you will be forced to retrieve the anchor manually. On vessels less than 35 feet in length with 5/16 BBB chain, a maximum 33-pound anchor, and a depth of less than 30 feet, one fairly strong person can pull up the anchor by hand in settled weather. With manual override, depending on the windlass and the unlucky crew member assigned to this task, you might be able to increase the chain length to 40 or 50 feet. Without manual override at these depths, you will have a very difficult time raising the hook, particularly in rough weather.

Electric Windlass Advantages

If you are outfitting a very large yacht, well over 50 feet on deck, you will probably be best served by an electric or hydraulic windlass. Since this book targets short-handed crews on small to mid-size yachts, the advice is intentionally biased in favor of saving crews on small vessels from undue headache and expense due to the installation of unnecessary electric appliances. I rather doubt there is a modern manual windlass that can handle a 200-pound anchor on a 150-foot sailing yacht. That job is for a hydraulic windlass operated by someone adequately trained to handle the job.

For owners of large yachts who may have a difficult time employing a manual windlass, an electric windlass can make cruising life much more feasible. Operating a deck button or a remote wand makes light work of weighing anchor quickly before a storm hits, potentially saving lives that otherwise could be threatened if manual anchor retrieval were the only means of pulling away from a rock-strewn lee shore.

In comparing manual and electric windlasses, I have indicated that manual windlasses equate to savings in fuel that otherwise would be spent on generating power for the windlass. This may not be totally accurate. With rare exception, whenever I retrieve *Saltaire's* 22-pound claw anchor and 5/16 BBB chain with the manual windlass, the first thing I do is start up the engine so that it warms up before we motor out of the anchorage. Since it takes me longer to pull up the hook with a manual rather than electric windlass, I waste more fuel getting my morning workout than the skipper who pushes a button, quickly ships the anchor, and gets under way in a few short minutes. The only time I can claim ecological and ideological purity is when there is a very light breeze blowing towards open sea, permitting me the luxury of weighing anchor and setting sail without starting the engine. This is rare, of course. So one could argue convincingly that an electric windlass is actually the green alternative. But I'm still sticking with the manual windlass—I love the workout!

Chapter 17
Tools, Spare Parts, and Maintenance Supplies

YOUR LIST OF TOOLS AND SPARE PARTS FOR THE POWER PLANT, electrical system, and alternative charging sources is a critically important facet of preparing for a long-term voyage. The choice to carry, say, one or two brand-new spare raw water pumps or just extra shaft seals to rebuild the unit while underway needs to be ferreted out before leaving port and heading for the tropics. Suppose your propeller gets severely bent by a heavy mooring line in some far-flung South Pacific anchorage, and you think you can hammer it back into shape well enough to reach your next major port of call for a professional repair. Do you have a prop puller, or will you swing your ball-peen hammer underwater while holding your breath, hoping to restore those complex curves back to some useful shape? I was forced to do this at anchor shortly after leaving Vuda Point Marina in Fiji en route to New Caledonia. The results were at least minimally functional, but a prop puller would have allowed me to produce much better results. Having the necessary tools on hand to carry out emergency repairs while underway or hove to can be the decisive factor in arriving at your next port of call without serious equipment failure.

Most cruising sailors possess basic hand tools, such as those found in virtually every garage in the developed world (screwdrivers, socket and end wrenches, etc.), but some specialty variations for marine use, along with some basic electrical test equipment, deserve special mention. In addition, a healthy assortment of spare parts is crucial to the full operability of your vessel when you are half an ocean away from the nearest decently stocked chandlery. Drawing up a list of essentials with an eye to eliminating unnecessary, space-hogging items will help you sort out your vessel's tool box and spare parts list during the havoc of those last few weeks before slipping the mooring lines and setting out for your dream cruising ground.

Engine and Drive Train

Preventive maintenance is the key to survival for your vessel's engine and transmission. Before leaving port, stow at least three of the following: oil filters, primary and secondary fuel filters, and air filters. Pack these delicate items in sealed plastic bags and store them in a clean, dry place where they will not be crushed or dented. Delo and Rotella-T oil for diesel engines is available in virtually any place of human habitation, but you should still carry enough for at least one oil change. Two or three bottles of biocide will allow you to prevent algae from growing in the diesel fuel tank, especially in a tropical environment. By adding only small amounts of biocide to the fuel tank, following the directions on the bottle, you can keep your fuel filters clear of scum that could otherwise cut off the fuel supply.

Automatic transmission fluid is also readily available throughout the world, but stow enough for at least one fluid change, particularly if you are staring down the bore of the northern Red Sea or the coast of Baja California, where long hours of motoring into gale-strength winds and towering seas can turn the gear box into a maraca. In preparing for such a long, daunting motor bash, it is recommendable to change the transmission fluid along with engine oil and filter and both fuel filters. Failure of either the engine or the transmission on such a voyage can expose vessel and crew to extreme hazards along a dangerous coast, so preparation is the best way to prevent disaster.

Amazingly, if you are anchored in a major cruising port, such as Maeva Beach, Tahiti, where there may be 300 or more vessels swinging at the hook, you would be hard pressed to find a single boat with a prop puller. Yet chances are that half of them will need one before returning home. Save yourself a lot of grief by laying out some money for a prop puller. The popular Pro-Pull is available in two sizes, both well under $300 and worth every penny: small, to fit a 1" to 1-1/2" shaft, and large, to fit 1-5/8" to 2."

Other miscellaneous power train items that come to mind are raw water pump impellers and shaft seals (or a new replacement raw water pump), propeller shaft packing, packing extractor, packing nut wrench, clevis pins for the propeller, an extra prop nut, several shaft collar zincs, and a large supply of heat exchanger pencil zincs. You can expect to find none of the preceding items outside of North America, Australia, New Zealand, or Western Europe, so determine your needs before leaving home and stock up accordingly. Otherwise, be prepared to pay big and wait long if you need any of these or other specialty items shipped to your idyllic atoll in French Polynesia.

Electrical

The degree of complexity of each vessel's electrical and multi-input charging system will dictate the list of spares and repair materials to be packed in the electrical kit. Common to all vessels are copper or lead battery cable fittings, spare LED or halogen bulbs, coax cable connectors, eye and snap connectors, cable ties, and various gauges and colors of marine grade wire. Check the spare parts lists of individual pieces of equipment to ensure you can respond to routine problems quickly while under way. Such items may include extra blades and a spare nose cone for the wind generator, a

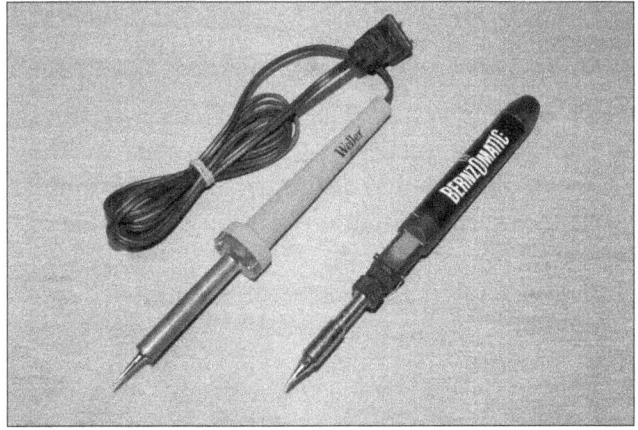

Pencil soldering irons, both electric and butane, are often necessary for making durable splices in thin electrical wire.

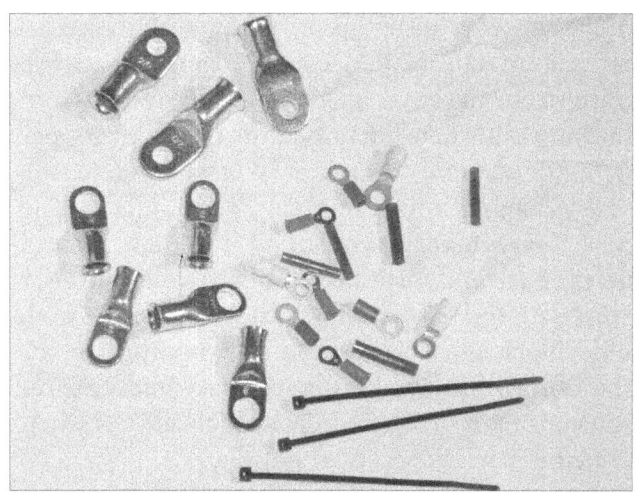

A healthy supply of marine-grade eye connectors and butt connectors, along with wire ties, will come in handy many times during your cruising career.

spare turbine and pre-cut length of line for the hydro generator, extra fasteners for the solar panel and wind generator mounting structures, spare fuses and replacement switches for the electrical panel, a spare alternator belt, and perhaps a spare alternator.

If you feel confident working on an alternator, you might want to take along a spare for each of the most vulnerable parts, including a rectifier diode assembly, slip rings, a new mounting bracket and adjustment bracket (they can break), and fasteners for the mounting structure. Also, if the individual manufacturers of your alternative energy systems offer standard spare parts kits, consider purchasing them, even if they are rather costly. Murphy's Law is alive and well on cruising boats.

Soldering irons with two or three sizes of soldering wire, plus acid-free flux and a set of soldering tools, are essential items for the cruiser's electrical toolbox. You can choose from a variety of inexpensive butane soldering irons, which heat up metal surfaces faster than electric soldering irons and avert the need for AC electrical current. Before setting sail, do yourself a big favor: think out exactly how and where you will perform soldering jobs without burning yourself or that beautiful teak table top, the pride of the salon. A one-square-foot piece of plywood with a holding device for your work will make soldering safer, faster, cleaner, and eminently less frustrating.

Another must-have is a high-quality digital multi-function tester, or "multimeter." I had to replace my cheap (under $10) analog unit twice, once from internal oxidation, the other from burning out when I bypassed the fuse with copper wire to measure alternator voltage. Before the second analog unit's untimely death, the needle never gave precise, consistent readings, instead arcing back and forth between 10.5 volts and 14.5 volts with the passing of each wave under the hull. The Fluke 28 II is the ultimate multimeter for the offshore yacht, fully waterproof and impact-resistant up to a 10-foot drop. It also floats when stored in its yellow rubber holster.

The Fluke 28 II measures up to 1,000 volts AC and DC, and up to 10 amps (20 amps for 30 seconds). With too many features to list here, this

Photo courtesy of Fluke Corporation

The Fluke 28 II digital multimeter is pricey yet fully waterproof and dustproof and can withstand the impact of a 10-foot drop.

is the little beast you can trust to measure high levels of current from a wind generator or water generator with little worry about blowing out a fuse in the multimeter. Running on three AA batteries, the Fluke 28 II boasts "backlit keypad buttons, large display digits, and two-level bright white display backlighting for easy visibility in low-lit areas," said Larry Wilson of Everett, Washington-based Fluke Corporation. The unit sells for just under $500, a bit pricey for the shoestring cruiser, but on second thought, a real lifesaver when the health of your vessel's electrical system depends on consistently accurate measurements. At the lower end of the digital tester price spectrum is the Sperry 7-Function Digital Multimeter, capable of measuring up to 660 volts AC and 500 volts DC. Though not rated as waterproof, the unit sells for under $40, making this a real bargain for cost-conscious voyagers.

In producing a clear signal from a ham or marine single-sideband radio, the two most critical yet likely to fail components are the antenna feed cable and the ground plane. Cleaning the green oxidation from the tip of the antenna feed does little good. When the wire oxidizes, it all turns green at the same time. Likewise, copper ground plane foil gradually turns green and flakes apart in the bilge, crippling the transmitter's ability to bounce a clear signal from the water into the ionosphere. Stow enough unshielded copper wire to replace the feed cable between the tuner and backstay antenna once every two or three years, plus a generous supply of Gordon West's copper foil to replace oxidized sections of the counterpoise and ground connection.

Plumbing

A healthy assortment of plumbing supplies not only guarantees fresh water to the galley and head sinks, it also means keeping your vessel afloat and the engine properly cooled. Crevice corrosion is the mortal enemy of every stainless hose clamp ever made, so carry a pile of these in every size to be encountered in your precious floating castle. A wooden plug should also be tied to each through-hull for easy deployment in case one of the cast bronze fittings breaks from corrosion. Also worth carrying are complete rebuild kits for the head, faucets, and manual bilge pumps. Electric utility pumps have changeable impellers similar to those in engine raw water pumps, but 12-volt bilge pumps can also die from water intrusion and subsequent motor failure, so it is best to carry a new spare.

Whether to purchase one or two complete new engine raw water pumps, which can drain your cruising kitty of several hundred dollars each, or a couple of new sets of shaft seals at a fraction of the price, is a topic of frequent discussion among cruising sailors. Switching out a whole unit for another saves you at least a half hour of work, and that wedge of time may be crucial to the safety of vessel and crew in some very urgent situations. Shoestring cruisers on small vessels with limited storage space opt for the extra couple of pairs of seals because "rebuilding" for all practical matters simply means changing the shaft seals, which is easy to do on a typical Jabsco raw water pump. Once you see water dripping from the pump, you have little time before the seals completely fail, allowing water to gush into the bilge. As soon as you are able, turn off the engine, close the intake ball valve, remove the pump, and switch out the seals in order to prevent taking on more water and to provide adequate cooling for the engine.

Extra lengths of hose for engine cooling may be recommendable, but if you change these before embarking on your cruise, they should last for many years. The exception is in the case of high-abrasion areas on the cooling hoses. If any part of the hose vibrates against another object, restrain that hose from the adjacent object if possible and carry enough hose to replace that length twice if needed during your sojourn. Less critical are extra hoses for the potable freshwater system. If they look cloudy inside from lack of use, pump clean water with a little chlorine bleach through the hoses and faucets. Frequent use will keep the hoses free of algae growth.

Hand Tools

Have you ever had a pair of pliers, wire cutters, or channel locks freeze up from rust? Long periods of neglect at the bottom of a salty tool box can render garden variety hand tools useless in a matter of months. One preventive strategy is to coat each tool in light machine oil, remembering to work the screw mechanisms in Crescent wrenches back and forth. Make a habit of checking your non-stainless tools on a regular basis. Cleaning and oiling tools is one of those satisfying little pastimes that keep us occupied while sailing across great expanses of sea for weeks on end. For those who are less enthusiastic about scraping rust and coating tools in oil, marinized hand tools forged from stainless steel guarantee operability at the very moment you need them.

Marinized hand tools—that is, regular hand tools manufactured for marine use—will cost you somewhat more than the standard variety, but they will pay off over the long haul in durability. Stainless steel pliers and wrenches are available online and in brick and mortar chandleries at affordable prices. And what of screwdrivers falling into the bilge? Purchase a set of screwdrivers with floating handles and stainless shafts, just the thing for working near water. These and other floating tools, some stainless, some vanadium steel, are available from

A Partial List of Tools

- Screwdrivers
- End wrenches
- Socket wrenches
- Socket extensions
- Breaker bar
- Pliers
- Channel locks
- Vice Grips
- Circlips
- Crescent wrenches
- Ball peen hammer
- Rigging tension gauge
- Awl
- Prop puller
- Oil and fuel filter wrench
- Grease gun
- Soldering irons
- Soldering platform
- Multimeter (digital or analog)
- Packing gland wrenches
- Packing extractor
- Drill motor
- Manual drill
- Drill bits
- Dremel tool
- Jigsaw and blades
- Random orbital sander
- Spare clutch belts for sander
- Orbital sanding discs
- Lifting magnet (200 lb. capacity)
- C-clamps
- Small furniture clamps
- Transformer (220VAC to 110VAC)
- Bolt cutters
- Wire cutters
- Swage tool
- Rigging fid
- Sewing needles
- Waxed nylon thread
- Palm aid

a variety of manufacturers. The only possible disadvantages in stainless tools are a propensity for crevice corrosion and the lower tensile strength of stainless as compared to vanadium alloy steel. Socket wrenches, sockets, extensions, breaker bars, and torque wrenches are available only in chrome vanadium steel or chrome molybdenum steel because of the tensile strength required of them, particularly in engine work. For the lighter tools, consider carrying both stainless and non-

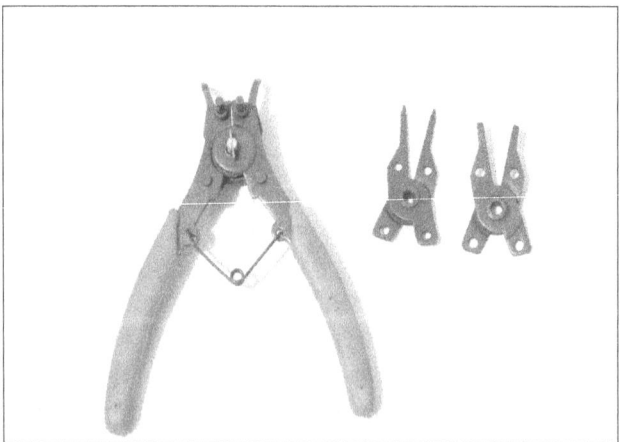

An inexpensive pair of circlip pliers will help you keep your sanity when replacing the bearings in a windvane self-steering gear.

This Stanley manual drill is the author's version of going cordless.

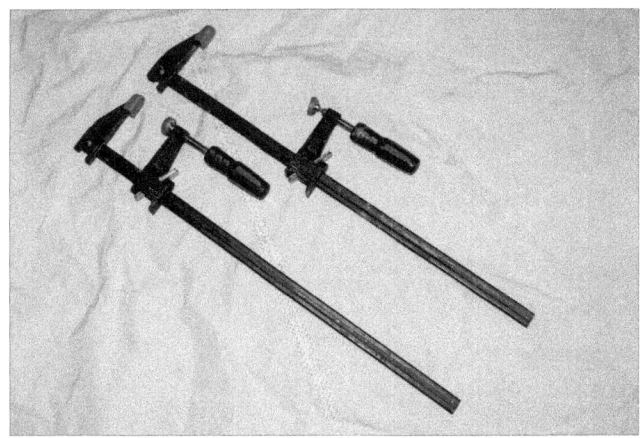

These well-used aluminum furniture clamps, each costing about $10 at Harbor Freight, have an 18-inch span and rubber clamp pads.

stainless—redundancy in hand tools is always a good idea. High-quality, brutally strong tools made of chrome-vanadium-molybdenum steel will retain their shine almost as well as stainless tools. Genuine Crescent wrenches, for example, are made of this grade of steel, which is why we spare the extra few bucks for this level of quality.

A powerful, rubber-coated magnet with a handle comes in handy when fishing for ferrous items that take a dive into a deep, murky bilge or calm anchorage. Keys are made of brass, and most marine fittings are made of bronze or 316 stainless steel, so a magnet is useless in searching for those items. However, engine parts and standard hand tools are made of ferrous steel, which is attracted by magnets. A word of caution: powerful magnets can damage or distort such sensitive devices as aneroid barometers, compasses, clocks, wristwatches, computer hard drives, and most likely cell phones and tablet computers. A hand-held magnet with 200-pound capacity can easily degauss, or even destroy, a hard drive right through a laptop's plastic exterior.

Power Tools

Powerful gensets and AC inverters on today's cruising boats have made drill motors, jigsaws, handheld circular saws, and Dremel tools ubiquitous on even the tiniest of pocket cruisers. Drill motors with battery packs are in such abundance in terms of brands and models, it is pointless to review them here. Call me old-fashioned, but my trusty Skill 110-volt AC 3/8" reversible drill motor served me honorably around the globe and still does today, even after falling from the mast head straight into the brine while *Saltaire* was docked in Mooloolaba Harbor, Queensland. A freshwater bath and some WD-40 had it back in service the same day. The one big advantage? I never have to worry about recharging, or about replacing the battery pack on some far-flung isle. My version of a cordless drill is a Stanley hand-crank drill, which I fastidiously keep lubricated and ready for use. If all you need to do is drill a few 1/8-inch holes in mahogany or teak to mount a small piece of hardware, a hand-crank drill will serve the purpose well. For drilling through metal or using bits larger than ¼ inch for wood, I switch over to the electric drill motor.

Cruisers looking for one small tool taking the place of several larger devices appreciate the versatility of Dremel's pair of multipurpose power tools: the Dremel 2-Speed Rotary Tool, ideal for cutting and sanding small surfaces, and the Dremel Multi-Max Tool Kit with its right-angled oscillating head, which can be used as a vibrator sander, hacksaw, or multipurpose saw for wood and plastic. Dremel tools retail for under $100 but face stiff competition from lower-priced knock-offs. Whichever you choose, the compact Dremel-style tool, particularly the oscillating head model, will find endless use aboard your vessel for cutting small planks to precise measurements and sanding corners where your fingertips do not fit.

In order to operate your 110-volt American tools in boatyards outside the Americas, you will need to find a high-quality transformer that converts from 220 to 110 volts. Step-down transformers are inexpensive and readily available in North America and abroad, but converting from the American system of 60 hertz to the 50 hertz found virtually everywhere else is another matter. Such systems exist, but carrying that type of sensitive equipment on your vessel is impractical and unnecessary. Converting from 60 to 50 hertz will cut your power about 20 percent, which means incandescent light bulbs will burn a little yellower, and motors will be a bit slower, but you can still use your orbital sander and other power tools. Just be patient with the somewhat slower speed. Your laptop computer and various other personal electronics are designed

Spares and Maintenance Supplies

Engine and Drive Train
- Oil filters
- Engine oil
- Fuel filters (primary and secondary)
- Diesel biocide
- Pencil zincs
- Shaft collar zincs
- Automatic transmission fluid
- Alternator belt
- Adjustable alternator bracket
- Propeller shaft packing
- Propeller nut

Electrical
- Wind generator rotor blade
- Wind generator blade cap
- Hydro generator rotor blade
- Wire (black and red, 14 gauge and 16 gauge)
- Battery cable fittings
- Eye connectors
- Snap connectors
- LED bulbs
- Halogen bulbs
- Cable ties
- Fuses
- Panel switches
- Alternator diode assembly
- Solder
- Acid-free flux

Plumbing
- Hose clamps
- Engine water hose
- Raw water pump impellers
- Raw water pump shaft seals
- Bronze ball valves
- Galley water pump rebuild kit
- Toilet rebuild kit

Hull and Deck
- Polysulfide bedding compound
- 3M 5200 or 4200
- Splash Zone Epoxy
- West System epoxy kit
- Fiberglass mat, cloth, and tape
- Touch-up paint
- Spar varnish
- Titebond III waterproof glue
- Sandpaper
- Random orbital sanding discs
- Random orbital hook & loop pad

Rigging
- 1 × 19 wire for stay or shroud
- Rigging wire compression fittings
- Strut compression fitting
- 7 × 19 halyard wire
- Wire thimbles
- Oval ferrules
- Blocks (swivel and fixed)
- Monel seizing wire

for world travel, automatically adapting to either 110 or 220 immediately upon start-up, saving you that worry.

Hull and Deck

To aid with repairs to the hull and deck, remember marine sealants like the multi-purpose polysulfide bedding compound Life-Calk, and for installations warranting a tougher bond, 3M 5200, or its less-than-permanent version, 4200. Splash Zone Epoxy, that amazing stuff you knead with your bare hands and press into a hole in the hull where it hardens underwater, comes in a 2-quart kit for about $135 and a 2-gallon kit for a little under $300. If there is one problem with carrying large amounts of Splash Zone, paints, or other substances in steel cans, it is the tendency for the cans to rust at the bottom, where you are least likely to notice it. The solution is to transfer these products into sturdy plastic containers with tight-fitting lids and label them with a permanent marker.

You will find polyester resin in 4-liter cans all around the globe, but fiberglass cloth and tape can be in terribly short supply, so take along a few yards of 6-ounce cloth and a roll or two of tape, along with a yard or so of woven roving, and seal them from moisture. West System epoxy and fillers are generally available only in North America, the U.K., American Samoa, New Zealand, and Australia, although you might have some luck in Greece and Spain as well.

Few of us leave home planning major wood construction projects aboard our cruising vessels, but changes in lifestyle along the way could demand a collection of C-clamps, small furniture clamps, a healthy assortment of stainless fasteners, and Titebond III waterproof wood glue for cabinetry. For prepping and finishing, you will need a random orbital sander with spare hook and loop pads and clutch belts, the little rubber bands that control motor speed. When it comes time to haul out halfway through a circumnavigation, you will thank yourself to no end for having your random orbital sander ready to press into service.

Rigging wire failure often occurs just above the bottom swage fitting. The author cut the swage off this lower shroud and replaced it with a used terminal extension he bought in the Dominican Republic.

Rigging Materials

The harrowing possibility of losing the mast from a failed stay or shroud is one of the deepest fears of the cruising sailor. If the individual wires are breaking at the edge of a swage or compression fitting, the time to change that length of rigging wire is NOW. As each of the 1 x 19 wires is severed, the strain on the remaining wires is compounded, rapidly leading to rigging failure. Any vessel embarking on a major cruise of six months or more should carry, as a minimum, a spare length of 1 x 19 wire to replace the longest piece of standing rigging. Installing 1 x 19 rigging wire requires a pair of Norseman, Hi-Mod or Sta-Lok terminals (commonly an eye fitting and a threaded stud). A neat trick for saving a stay or shroud frayed just

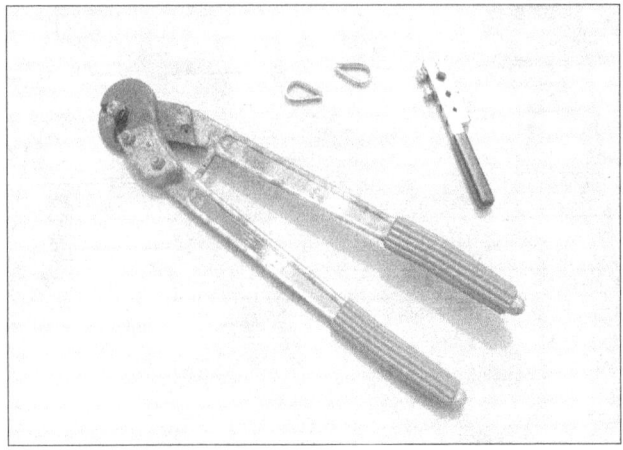

This Swage-It Tool and pair of bolt cutters have produced countless sail pendants and other expedient cables from used 1/8-inch halyard wire, thimbles, and crimp sleeves for the author and for many of his cruising friends.

above the stud fitting at the deck is to cut off the short damaged piece of wire, along with the terminal, and replace both with a long extension stud terminal. Avoiding the complete reinstallation of 1 x 19 wire permits faster, easier rigging repairs while hove-to at sea.

A rigging tension gauge is indispensable in preserving the integrity of stays and shrouds and protecting turnbuckles and chainplates from excess stress. Ensuring appropriate rig tension helps to prevent premature wear and crevice corrosion resulting from working and overstretching the rigging wire, and also ensures proper mast angle and hull shape. Too much tension in the fore and back stays, particularly on lightly built hulls, pulls the bow and stern upward, forcing excessive rocker into the hull and exerting potentially destructive pressure on the mast and mast partner.

Also pack an extra halyard and double-braided replacement sheets for each sail. In reality, high-quality sheets can last many years, sometimes through multiple circumnavigations, but better to err on the safe side. Take along a coil of thin, inexpensive nylon rope to act as a messenger line to change halyards. In addition, if your vessel uses servopendulum windvane self-steering, have available a couple of pairs of pre-cut double-braided lines to replace those controlling the helm.

Another indispensable item is a fid for making eye splices in three-strand rope. If you are accustomed to paying someone to make eye splices or rope-to-chain splices with three-strand line, now is the time to wean yourself off those services and master these traditional rope techniques. A related skill is making rope-to-chain splices in order to eliminate the clunky galvanized rope thimble and shackle that often join rope and chain. A clean, even transition from rope to chain allows you to continue weighing anchor with the windlass wildcat without having to risk losing a couple of fingers while shifting the three-strand rode from the capstan to the wildcat.

If you have an old coil of 7 x 19 flexible halyard wire lying around, do not throw it away. This wire, along with a handful of stainless thimbles and zinc-coated copper oval ferrules, enables you to fashion sail pendants, temporary replacement lifelines, hold-down wires, and long cables for securing such valuables as a pair of oars, the outboard, and the dinghy. When you leave the dinghy at the customs dock in Pago Pago, a long length of 7 x 19 wire with a padlock securing your valuable equipment will increase the likelihood of their being available for you on your return from the village.

Wire cutters for rigging are available in a range of sizes. The small, one-handed cutters are great for snipping seizing wire and thin electrical wire, but for stainless rigging your best bet is a pair of bolt cutters, worth every penny when you need to

Using a fid to make eye splices and chain-to-rope splices in three-strand rope is a skill every sailor should learn.

chop through thick 1 x 19 rigging wire. For hand swaging tools, you can choose either the Loos Lifeline Fitting Hand Swage Tool, which is easy to use yet quite large and expensive (nearly $300), or the pocket-size Swage-It Tool, available in two sizes, small (1/16", 3/32", 1/8" diameter wire) for just under $30, and the larger unit (1/8", 5/32", 3/16", 1/4" diameter wire) for just under $60. The long-handled Loos Swage Tool has one drawback: it generally requires two people to operate the device, one squeezing the handles together while the other holds the wire in place, unless you have a bench vice handy to hold one handle stationary. Both tools, the long-handled and the pocket size, are intended for making eye splices in wire with stainless thimbles and copper oval ferrules.

Developing a list of parts and tools for your ocean passage will compel you to learn more about your vessel and about your own talents and capabilities as an ocean passage maker. The success of your ocean voyage will hinge on your pre-cruise planning and ability to anticipate potential problems on your vessel before they occur. Many items not listed here will inevitably end up on your last-minute shopping list, but as long as you leave with the essentials, you can add or replenish tools and other supplies as needed along the way. During your travels, you may have the occasional opportunity to acquire exotic tools, fasteners, hardware, and fittings, which can be just as fascinating as the items you purchase in souvenir shops.

Chapter 18
The Essence of Green Voyaging

THOSE OF US WHO ARE COMPELLED TO CROSS OCEANS UNDER SAIL, SAVING energy and money as we explore distant seas and remote islands, generally are receptive to the need to protect the natural balance of our fragile biosphere. We understand that our actions have a ripple effect, causing physical and chemical reactions that can benefit, damage, or have zero effect on the natural setting in which our vessels roam. Therefore, we willingly accept responsibility for our actions, even when there is no one else around to enforce local laws.

Energy independence, and the small footprint it leaves on the places we visit, is a critically important component of green voyaging. Yet equally important is how we manage the other, less glamorous aspects of our vessels: the bilge, the holding tank, oil disposal, garbage, and other such mundane realities of sailing life. Our ability to deal with these issues will ensure not only a null or minimal effect on the environment, but also a more comfortable lifestyle on the water.

Bilge

The rule with emptying bilges is easy enough to put in words, but far more difficult to follow. No oil overboard means precisely that. So why can't we use soap to break up oil in the bilge and pump it overboard the way we toss out a stale cup of coffee? And why does the U.S. Coast Guard call soap a "dispersant"?

When soap breaks up oil, it does not chemically convert it into a less harmful substance. All the soap does is break up, or disperse, the oil into tiny droplets, forming an emulsion—what I call the "mayonnaise effect." In short, the oil is still oil. While it is true that diesel and gasoline eventually evaporate, they can still cause extensive harm to aquatic life while they are still floating on the water's surface. Heavier petroleum distillates, such as motor oil, also gradually evaporate, but in saltwater they first emulsify to form a thick sludge that gunks

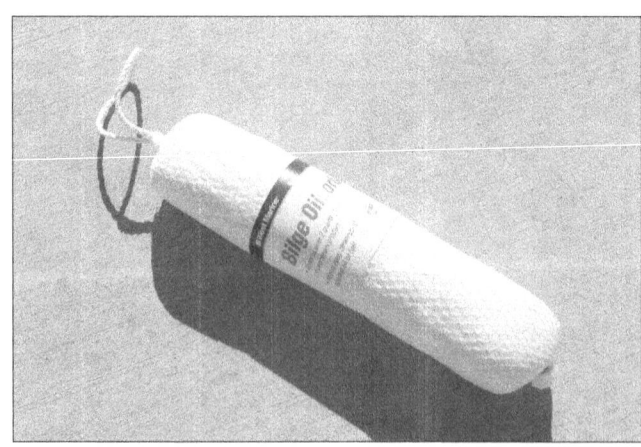

This inexpensive oil absorber is capable of extracting over a half gallon of oil and diesel from the bilge.

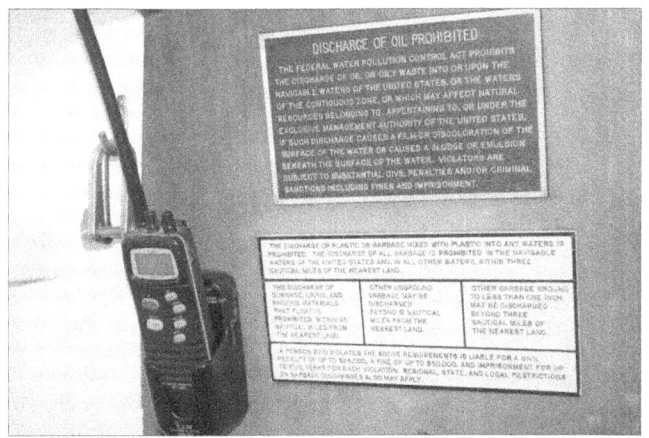

The conscientious cruiser on a U.S.-flagged vessel follows USCG and international regulations regarding the dumping of oil and sewage wherever the boat may roam.

up beaches, reefs, and boat hulls. Evaporation after that point can take many years.

If your bilge contains oil or fuel, place oil-absorbing mats in the bilge to soak up the residue. The white mats have an affinity for oil, allowing you to pump the remaining water safely out of the bilge once all the oil has been removed. Even more effective is a BioSok Oil and Fuel Absorber from Johnson Pump, which biodegrades petroleum residue in the bilge, allowing you to pump the bilge into open water after the oil or fuel sheen has disappeared.

Marine Sanitation Device

Most experienced sailors are well-acquainted with the rules governing marine toilets, Y-valves, holding tanks, and related fixtures. One big question sailors on older boats will ask is, "What do I do if my boat has no room for a holding tank and was built before holding tanks became mandatory?" The answer is simple. While the boat is within three miles of the coast, close the toilet discharge seacock and store the handle in a drawer. Whether you choose to adhere to the letter and spirit of the law regarding human solid waste is up to you. If you have second thoughts, think of it as a moral imperative, not some arbitrary rule. As for urine, it is probably harmless in limited amounts, even in a small harbor. In a survival situation, you can even drink it. Most of the male sailors I know urinate directly into the ocean while under sail (remember your harness, mates) and from the marina dock at night.

Solid waste, however, is quite a different matter. Human feces, unlike bird or fish effluent, contains highly infectious coliform bacteria. Far offshore, macerated waste discharged into the water is exposed to intense UV light and is then broken down by myriad microorganisms. But even if the law is not enough to convince us, common sense tells us not to dump fecal sewage into coastal waters. Just for the record, USCG regulations forbid discharging toilets within three nautical miles of the coast. Use your holding tank as designed, and empty it in accordance with the law.

An alternative solution for toilet waste is composting toilets. The toilet bowl on this device has separate portals for urine and feces in the bowl, requiring men and ladies alike to sit in order to urinate. Liquid waste is collected in a separate tank for disposal, while fecal waste is allowed to dry and decompose in its own tank. A cup of peat moss may be added to provide extra biological material to aid in the decomposition process. After a few weeks of collecting and composting, the solid waste may be deposited at a pump-out facility.

The Air Head, manufactured by EOS Design in Westbrook, Massachusetts, is a completely self-contained apparatus with its own holding tank and a ventilation system to dry out waste. A bit smaller than a standard land toilet, the Air Head can be used regularly by two people for a whole month before necessitating disposal. Other manufacturers of similar systems include Biolet of Fresno, Ohio; Nature's Head of Van Buren, Ohio; and Sun-Mar of Tonawanda, New York. Composting may not work for everyone, but it seems better than sailing with 20 gallons of sloshing sludge and risking a disconnected hose or ruptured tank beneath the v-berth.

Gray Water

Small amounts of food waste dumped offshore through gray water from cruising yachts have a negligible effect on the ocean's health. Mangrove leaves, coconuts, and careless land animals have been dropping into the oceans for eons and are all part of the ecological process. Inside a protected, crowded harbor, though, a high concentration of organic waste causes eutrophication, a process by which bacteria and algae deplete the water of dissolved oxygen as they multiply and break down the waste. As a consequence, fish and crustaceans die through paralysis and asphyxiation, particularly at greater depths.

The destruction wrought by eutrophication in portions of Long Island Sound and Los Angeles Harbor, to say nothing of our lakes and rivers, was front-page news in the 1960s and 1970s. Lake Erie, once known as the "Dead Sea of North America," saw the spread of Aphanizomenon flosaquae algae, which resembles green paint floating on the water. In recent years, owing to greater controls of urban water run-off and a ban on phosphorous-based dish soaps in more than a dozen states, the health of Lake Erie, along with U.S. ports and coastal waters, has gradually been improving.

When using the galley sink, filter out as much solid waste as possible before allowing the water to drain into an anchorage. Also, avoid the use of phosphorous-based soaps, at least while your vessel is in an anchorage or harbor. On many larger yachts, gray water from sink, shower, and washing machine drains empties into a large holding tank, which can be pumped out offshore or at a dockside pump facility in the same manner as a toilet holding tank.

Garbage Overboard

U.S. law allows us to dump pretty much any material other than oil or plastic at various distances from shore, depending on the substance. Nonetheless, some cruisers understandably feel guilty about dumping glass bottles, aluminum cans, and odd pieces of metal overboard, even while sailing hundreds of miles of offshore. Glass bottles, ironically, are made of molten silica sand, the same sand you find on most beaches. After making sure they have no plastic connected to them, fill them up with seawater and drop them into the briny deep for their return home.

The metals commonly found on an ocean-going yacht, except lead, are generally harmless to marine life. Throwing an old stainless steel or bronze fitting overboard will cause no harm. But if it makes you feel any better, you can save your aluminum cans for recycling once you reach shore. Good luck finding a buyer for your big bag of aluminum beer and soda cans in the Tuamotus, though. When you are well offshore, cut up the cans or simply fill them with ocean water before casting them overboard. Aluminum gradually corrodes and disperses in sea water.

A good way to cut down on garbage is to change the way you purchase and store provisions. Whenever possible, avoid foods packed in excessive plastic, such as meats in Styrofoam and plastic wrap and drinking water in small plastic bottles. Once you leave the brand-name, supermarket culture behind, circumstances will conspire to wean you off bottled water, a huge source of plastic waste in the industrialized world. You will fill the tea kettle from the tank of freshwater, which will come from either the watermaker or from a rusty faucet on some far-flung tropical island. Don't worry, your stomach will adapt.

Dry foods, such as oatmeal and breakfast cereal, are best stored in sealed plastic containers. A sealed container reduces the amount of plastic and paper packaging carried onboard, and most of all, it keeps the contents dry, tasty, and free of rice weevils. For purchasing eggs, use a plastic egg holder instead of a plastic or paper bag. The egg holder will result in less trash onboard and keep your eggs safer on the trip back from the village open-air market.

Anchoring and Mooring

Some of us die-hard purists turn our noses up at moorings, preferring to do it the old fashioned way by dropping the hook and claiming our little territory for ourselves. We don't seem to mind the old practice of swinging around in a variable breeze, with our neighbors arcing into our swing zone and shaking their fists at us as the wind unexpectedly changes direction. I admit that I too have been one of those fiercely independent skippers, gambling at anchorage roulette rather than paying to park at one of those orange balls. Moorings are placed not just to protect sensitive coral reefs and kelp beds, but also to spare skippers the hassle of retrieving anchors from submerged rocks and debris.

Using a stern line in a cramped anchorage prevents vessel damage and ensures a good night's sleep. In the background, moorings keep boats safely apart while protecting the delicate seabed from scarring by anchors at Little Fisherman's Cove, Catalina Island.

There are two logical defenses for anchoring: (1) you know the limits of your own ground tackle but have no idea of what is holding that mooring ball in place; and (2) using your own ground tackle, you are free to weigh anchor and set sail whenever you wish. When the wind is up, it helps to know exactly what is keeping your precious floating palace from landing on the rocks. A frayed piece of cheap polypropylene line haphazardly knotted to an undersized mushroom anchor in loose sand does not instill the feeling of security we seek in a sustained, 50-knot Red Sea gale. With an anchor, we are free to choose the best place to wait out a storm, and we can pay out as much chain and nylon rode as we deem necessary to ride out the tempest. And of course, when it comes time to get a jump on the next short weather window, we do not want to be waiting for some overfed, underworked port officer to sputter over in his inflatable dinghy to collect the mooring fee, strike up a conversation, and finally let us go at 4:30 in the afternoon. With an anchor, we are free to leave at the very moment we see fit. If you absolutely must anchor, find a wide clearing in the coral or submerged vegetation where there is only sand, mud, or rock. And make sure your anchor chain has room to swing 360 degrees at low tide without scraping over vulnerable areas.

A mooring, on the other hand, offers obvious advantages. First, fore-and-aft mooring guarantees our space without the need to worry about slamming into another vessel. Also, many skippers prefer not having to go through the trouble of setting and raising the anchor, cleaning the chain as it emerges from a muddy bottom, or worse, losing the anchor. In environmentally sensitive anchorages, moorings limit the damage boats can do to coral beds, kelp forests, and colonies of crustaceans.

In most corners of the world, the question of whether to anchor or take a mooring is not a matter of choice, so it is a good idea to review your pilot book before making landfall. In a Venetian harbor in the Mediterranean, you moor and anchor simultaneously. To Med-moor to a sea wall, throw a stern line to someone on shore, then motor out to set the bow anchor, and then haul in the stern line until you are fairly close to the wall. Finish up by cranking in enough anchor chain to keep the bow pointed away from the wall while allowing enough slack for high tide. In a world that seems to be getting smaller by the day, we need to sail farther and farther afield of the normal routes to find those idyllic anchorages where we are free to come and go as we please, unencumbered by mooring, Med-mooring, or competing for anchorage space.

Sailing Versus Motoring

Each cruising skipper seems to have his or her own rule about when to crank on the iron jib. For some, a sailing speed of less than 5 knots means it's time to motor. At the more humble end of the spectrum, having enough wind to operate the windvane self-steering is the cut-off point. We all want to save fuel, but we all want to get the voyage behind us at some point as well. If you are truly committed to saving fuel and working toward the shared goal of a cleaner planet, the best rule seems to be keeping the boat under sail as long as there is navigable wind. After all, we are out there to enjoy passage-making rather than to bemoan this rarified experience.

When light winds are sustained for long periods, such as along the Pacific coast of central Mexico out 600 nautical miles, you have no choice but to use the engine, at least sparingly, as you venture farther offshore in search of wind. The need for speed becomes more critical in late May when a tropical depression, or worse, a full-blown hurricane, can begin forming in the Gulf of Tehuantepec. You will need to divide your time between slow sailing in light breezes and motoring through flat calms to get out to where the wind is blowing if you are headed north along the Clipper route, where a southwesterly current can erase your gains while you try to make headway.

Weather windows generally cover a five-day period, which is usually enough time to pull away from a continental shelf and get safely into the trade winds where the weather is steady and predictable. The worst weather conditions are almost always within 300 miles of the coast, which means all of the Mediterranean and the coasts of every large land mass in the world. On the 600-mile sail from Gibraltar to Lanzarote in the Canary Islands, a southwester can throw you up onto the rocks along the west coast of Africa in little time. If you are sailing south along the Moroccan coast and the wind starts dying while cirrus clouds are passing overhead from the southwest, you need to be motoring as fast as your engine can manage until reaching safe harbor, or you risk facing a deadly gale that can last up to a week. The safety of vessel and crew is far more important than our worries over carbon emissions.

Going Ashore

It is truly amazing to watch a frustrated sailor hunched over an outboard motor, pulling the starter rope under the hot, tropical sun, his inflatable dinghy bouncing against the side of his yacht's hull for a full 20 minutes until he finally gives up and climbs back onboard. And the dinghy dock in front of the local bar is only a couple of hundred yards away. Rarely do we see anyone grabbing a pair of oars to pull his way to shore anymore. Even more rarely do we see a cruiser using a hard (non-deflatable) dinghy. Rowing is one of the most relaxing, exhilarating, satisfying things one can ever do on the water, yet we have traded our oars for a noisy, smelly, capricious gasoline bomb that gives us little pleasure.

Oars give us complete control of the dinghy. We pull away from hazards instantly, turn around, stop, hover over shallow water to study a reef, ghost past a yacht where we rain-checked a dinner invitation, or pull up to a beach without destroying the prop—all in complete, blissful silence. With our hands gripping the finely varnished ash handles, we feel the deep satisfaction of converting muscle power into motion, imbuing ourselves with a profound sense of inner peace on the water. We stay trim, save fuel, prevent oil slicks in our pristine anchorage, and of course, save money. And while our neighbor is reporting the theft of his dinghy and outboard to the local policía or village chief, our oars and hard dink, which have little monetary value, carry us past the yelling, the finger pointing, the blaming, and the loss assessing while we go on our merry way.

Nonetheless, for those who still feel they need an outboard motor, a lot of engineering has been invested into designing and manufacturing motors that require little maintenance and produce very low emissions. Be warned, though: small outboard motors are the life blood of poor fishing villages the world over, so don't be surprised if you wind up replacing it at least once during an extended cruise.

In both the U.S. and E.U., the trend in outboard motors is gradually moving away from two-stroke engines toward four-stroke gas and propane motors. This trend is due in part to the gradual outlawing of two-stroke motors on inland waterways. That being said, two-stroke outboard engines, some of which produce fewer harmful emissions than same-sized four-stroke engines, continue to be popular for their lower

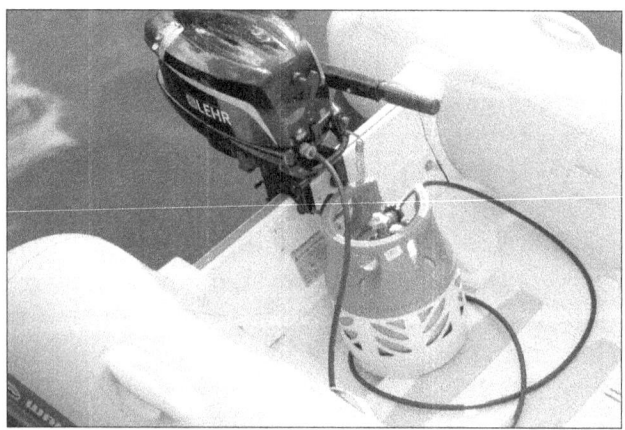

Photo courtesy of Lehr

A Lehr propane-powered outboard with a composite tank is a safe, clean alternative to a smelly, leaky, and highly volatile gasoline-powered motor with plastic tank.

weight and greater power. And since there is no current movement to control the use of two-stroke outboards on coastal waters anywhere in the world, we can expect them to remain in use for many years.

A more ecologically correct alternative is the four-stroke propane-powered outboard, such as that built by Los Angeles-based Lehr. Designed by Captain Bernardo Herzer, a cruising sailor, the Lehr is currently available in five sizes: 2.5hp, 5hp, 9.9hp, 15hp, and 25hp. Lehr outboards use a standard propane connection hose, the same we use for our barbecues, and can run on a one-pound camp stove tank, a 20-pound barbecue tank, or one of several impact-resistant composite tanks offered by Lehr.

And last, there is always the electric alternative. Sevylor and Torqeedo are industry leaders in electric outboard motors, producing incredibly powerful and efficient, if not rather pricey, alternatives to gasoline and propane motors. The Torqeedo Travel 1003 produces 3hp but costs roughly twice the price of a comparably powered four-stroke outboard produced by Lehr or any of the various gasoline outboard manufacturers. However, Torqeedo also markets a flexible 45-watt solar panel capable of charging the Torqeedo 4.0 from 0 to 100 percent charge in 13 hours. So while there is a higher initial cost, one can easily imagine the fuel savings, not to mention the enhanced safety and ease of use, from using a purely solar-charged outboard motor. Whether you are going ashore or trolling for reef fish, the last thing you should be worried about is the efficiency and cleanliness of your dinghy's outboard. Who wants to eat fish from an oil-slicked reef?

Responsible Fishing

Sport fishers love to boast about the size and quantity of fish they kill. One sport fisher can catch and slaughter a half-dozen or more tuna, each one weighing in excess of 100 pounds, in one day. But what does he do with the fish? Eat it? Really? Maybe he donates it to an orphanage.

When we cruising sailors fish, it is because we want to eat the fish. But be careful. In general, the larger the lure you troll, the larger the fish you are liable to catch. Imagine hauling a 300-pound ahi into the footwell of a 30-foot sloop in 12-foot seas. Fortunately for the fish, you can give up that dream. You have no choice but to cut the line and let it go—if Jaws has not already saved you the trouble. Test your lures to see what they bring up, and then determine the best size. For a couple with no refrigeration onboard, an 8-pound tuna, wahoo, or dorado should more than suffice for a day of sumptuous dining. A freezer, of course, allows you to store excess catch. The bottom line is either to catch and release, or catch only what you know you can eat.

As for lobstering and crabbing, follow U.S. and state rules, even in developing countries where you can catch what you want with impunity. Our fish and game regulations are established with the idea of maintaining and managing wildlife populations. Bagging juvenile crustaceans, as well as fish, only sounds the death knell for future generations of affected species. In many poor countries, local fishermen will approach your anchored vessel with the morning catch of whatever they can find: juvenile lobster, undersized fish, all fresh but no longer able to be thrown back into the water. So herein lies our moral dilemma: do we help to support a destitute family by purchasing their shockingly underpriced merchandise, or do we turn down the opportunity in hopes of reducing the demand for undersized catch?

We cannot expect local and foreign law enforcement agencies to shoulder full responsibility of protecting our world's oceans and coastal waters. In some cases, we need to impose on ourselves certain rules of behavior that reach beyond the law. Let us agree to police ourselves, not just to avoid legal tangles, but to promote a sustainable planet for future generations of ocean navigators.

Establishing Personal Standards

Of the many traits shared by cruising sailors, one of the most admirable is a shared need for personal accountability. Thousands of miles from home, you will observe cruisers refusing to purchase 5-inch-long lobster, throwing their undersized catch back into the brine, and treating workers in developing countries with the same respect we would show workers back home. There is also a palpable, commonly felt commitment to improving the way of life in coastal communities, manifesting itself in myriad ways: beach cleaning parties, clothing donations to local orphanages, medical assistance for villagers from cruising physicians and nurses, gifts of toys and children's books to schools and families, and the list goes on. If we can contribute but one thing to the many places we visit, it is leaving those places either exactly the same as we find them, or slightly better.

When considering our individual commitment to protecting the world's oceans and coastal communities, we can defer to the words of Clyde W. Ford, author of *Boat Green: 50 Steps Boaters Can Take to Save Our Waters*. Ford challenges us fellow cruisers to create "a personal vision statement of what protecting the marine environment means." Whether written or internalized, our personal statement can be a summary of our personal values about the significance of our oceans in the overall health of Earth's biosphere, a thin, fragile film roughly 15 miles thick covering a planet 8,000 miles in diameter. Our personal commitment to protecting this delicate environment drives our interaction with the oceans we cross, the wildlife we encounter, and the people we meet along the way. Let us resolve to do everything in our power to protect the health and sustainability of our little planet and of every living thing around us, including each other.

Chapter 19
Energy Efficiency: Three Cruising Yachts

U P TO THIS POINT, WE HAVE ANALYZED THE ESSENTIAL COMPONENTS of an energy-independent, offshore sailing platform. We know how much electricity can be produced by a variety of different generating devices, we understand some of the key points in installing such devices, and we know how to develop an energy plan to make the best use of all of this equipment. What remain to be discussed are the platforms themselves, the vessels whose design and construction best favor a successful ocean crossing, and how these boats might be best equipped to harness energy from sun, wind, and water.

Going the Distance

All cruising sailboat designs offer ample opportunities for installing renewable energy sources capable of generating charging amperage for the house battery banks. Some smaller boats may have less battery storage space than larger yachts, but skippers on smaller boats are also less likely to perceive a need for such extensive reserve power. At the other extreme, very large yachts consume more amp hours than can be met by an array of solar panels, a pair of wind generators, and a hydro generator, so their skippers generally eschew windvane self-steering gears on their posh yachts, even if a Hydrovane, Windpilot Pacific Plus, or Saye's Rig could save them a fortune in fuel and in repair costs for their hydraulic steering and autopilots. Despite the contributions alternative energy sources can make toward a large yacht's electrical storage demand and toward a cleaner ocean environment, owners of these yachts generally prefer the ease of using a diesel generator and its attendant lack of clutter above decks. On boats less than roughly 50 feet LOA, skippers overwhelmingly prefer the fuel-saving advantages of petroleum-free electrical charging, saving not only money but also space otherwise needed for fuel storage. Let's face it, though we are proud of doing right by Mother Nature, the main goal of cruising skippers is to complete voyages without spending our life's savings on diesel or weighing the boat down excessively with extra fuel.

The easiest boat to fit with non-combustive electrical generating equipment is the standard, no-frills masthead sloop or cutter with an aft cockpit. The long, wide expanse of deck area offers itself to a large solar panel array atop an arch or a large bimini, and the low, even deck structure allows use of a servopendulum windvane self-steering gear with most main steering systems. Some yacht crews prefer a center cockpit, particularly on boats more than 40 feet LOA, because it yields more usable cabin space, as there is usually a cabin sole around the engine compartment allowing access to the full length of the cabin. However, center cockpits are generally, but not always, considered off-limits to servopendulum self-steerers, instead necessitating the installation of a Hydrovane, Wind Pilot Pacific Plus, or trim tab such as Scanmar's Auto-Helm. Complicating matters more, a hatch over the rear cabin coupled with a limited amount of walk space will make the installation of solar panels particularly challenging without some help from an arch or other raised structure, such as a pair of free-standing mounting masts.

The variety of solidly built cruising yachts capable of circling the globe and making use of alternative energy is steadily expanding. Naturally, any attempt to cover a large sampling of these vessels and the ways they have been outfitted for ecologically correct power generation and consumption in one chapter would be impractical if not impossible. That said, of all the boats available on the new and used market, three stand out as well-designed, solidly constructed, proven passage makers, all of which have made multiple circumnavigations with the aid of alternative energy. Each of the three vessels presented here was selected to represent a given size range: pocket cruiser, mid-sized yacht, and larger yacht. These three yachts, as legendary as the designers who created them, are David Sadler's Contessa 32, Robert H. Perry's Tayana 37, and Germán Frers' Hallberg-Rassy 46. Size is the least of the differences among these three yachts, as each represents a design philosophy unique to its designer and builder.

Contessa 32

When Jeremy Rogers made the decision to build a larger version of the renowned Contessa 26, made famous by circumnavigator-author Tanya Aebi in *Maiden Voyage*, David Sadler's Contessa 32 design became an overnight success. Rogers took first place in the Cowes Week Regatta at the Isle of Wight on *Red Herring*, ushering in a generation of Contessa 32s that went out of production in 1983 but resumed in 1995. The Contessa passed the ultimate test of her seaworthiness when she was the only vessel in her category to survive the 1979 Fastnet Race disaster, in which 14 lives were lost.

With a ballast-to-weight ratio of .473, a relatively deep draft of 5 feet, 6 inches, and a conservative beam of 9 feet, 6 inches, it is easy to see how capsizing this vessel is no easy feat. Adding to the low center of gravity is a relatively low shear that reduces hull exposure to wind and wave; if the Westsail 32 is a combat boot, the Contessa 32 is a jogging shoe. The Contessa 32's strong, simple masthead rig and fin keel with skeg rudder render her an easily managed offshore sailor for single-

Contessa 32 Specifications

Designer:	David Sadler	L/B:	1.33
Builder:	Jeremy Rogers	Hull Mat:	Fiberglass
Keel type:	Fin keel	Fuel:	12 gallons
LOA:	32'	Water:	18 gallons
LWL:	24'	P:	35'
Beam:	9' 6"	E:	10'
Draft:	5' 6"	SA (main):	175 sq. ft.
Disp:	9,500 lbs.	I:	40' 8"
Ballast:	4,500 lbs. lead	J:	12' 8"
Rig:	Masthead	SA (fore):	258.45 sq. ft.
Aux:	Yanmar 3GM30F	SA:	433.45 sq. ft.
B/D:	.473	SA/D:	15.51

Photo courtesy of Scanmar

Deck fittings help to accommodate a Monitor windvane on the small transom of the Contessa 32 Spirit of Amport.

Photo courtesy of Joe McCarthy

A flexible solar panel is permanently installed on Calypso's *coach roof.*

Photo courtesy of Joe McCarthy

Calypso's *gleaming, well-appointed interior is bedecked with generous portions of the sustainable manufactured hardwood Kebony.*

Photo courtesy of Mark Jennings

Kebony sustainable manufactured hardwood adds both elegance and low maintenance to Calypso's *deck and toe rail.*

or short-handed crew. The cockpit's moderate size allows for a fuller cabin, plus plenty of room for a pair of side-mounted solar panels and a mast for a wind generator.

The latest generation of the Contessa 32 is an eco-friendly yacht built and equipped with the latest energy-saving and energy-producing technology. For starters, the hull is lined with thick Thinsulate insulation protecting the crew from severe cold and also acting as a noise muffler. Next, all of the interior and exterior trim, including the side decks, is cut from Kebony, a maple-based, manufactured hardwood substituting for the tropical hardwoods mahogany and teak, which have been severely depleted throughout the developing world where they are grown. The impregnated hardwood is actually stronger than teak and keeps its shape better than untreated natural wood, making it ideal for shaping and finishing. Below the waterline, Jeremy and his son Kit have switched from poisonous cuprous oxide bottom paint to the environmentally safe Hempel, a rubbery paint with a slimy residue that resists barnacles and seaweed, and adds to hull speed, owing to its low-inertia surface. Whereas standard ablative bottom paint has a surface comparable to 400-grit sandpaper, Hempel poses virtually zero resistance to forward movement, a boon to ocean racers.

Another feature of the new Contessa 32's is a hybrid, parallel, diesel-electric propulsion plant designed and built by Graeme Hawksley of Hybrid Marine on the Isle of Wight (see Chapter 1). The

Photo courtesy of Mark Jennings

Yacht Builder Jeremy Rogers sails the newly launched Contessa 32 Calypso *in her home port of Lymington, UK.*

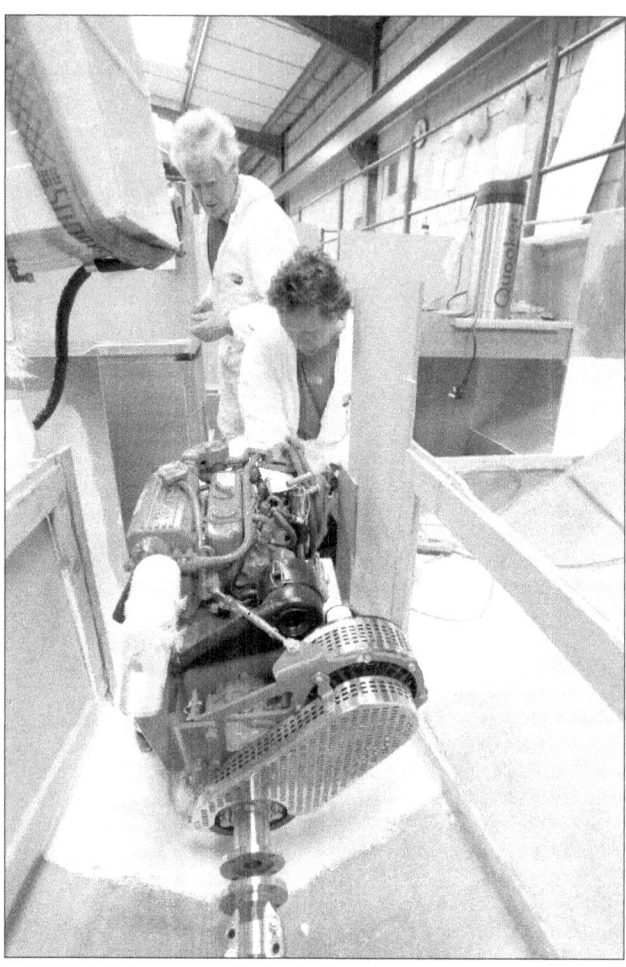

Photo courtesy of Joe McCarthy

Kit Rogers of Jeremy Rogers Yachts checks the installation of a hybrid diesel-electric engine from Hybrid Marine, Island of Wight, UK, on the new Contessa 32 Calypso.

Photo courtesy of Joe McCarthy

Kit Rogers fits energy-saving Thinsulate to the interior of Calypso's *hull.*

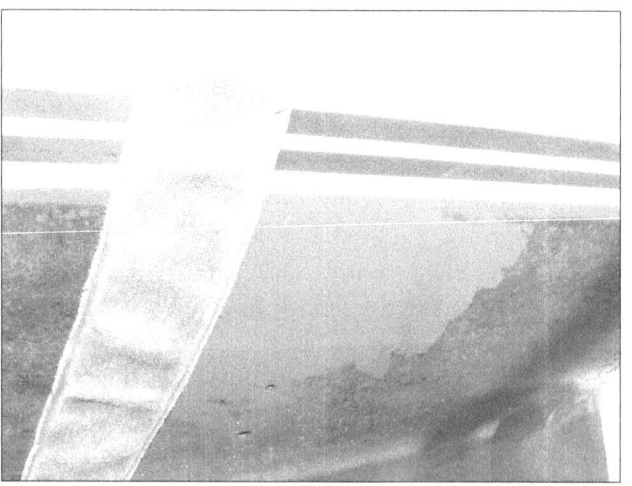

Photo courtesy of Kit Rogers

Calypso's *undersides have been painted with Hempel, a slick, rubbery paint to which marine life cannot firmly attach.*

hybrid design permits the helmsman to choose from five different modes to employ the power plant: diesel propulsion, engine-powered electric propulsion, battery-powered electric propulsion, combined diesel-electric propulsion (rarely used), and generator mode by using the propeller to power the motor-generator for battery charging.

Of all the yachts available on today's market, Jeremy Rogers' Contessa 32 with its combination of Sadler's highly stable offshore sailing platform, the Rogerses' solid construction, and innovations from Hybrid Marine and a variety of other products, is unquestionably one of the most soundly built small cruising boats available anywhere on the world market.

Tayana 37

It is said that at any given time, there are more of Robert H. Perry's Tayana 37s crossing oceans than any other boat. With a total count of nearly 600 built, many of them having completed full navigations of the earth, this heavily built, full-keeled design has earned its popularity through its dependable performance in everything from light airs to sustained full gales. Despite its rugged design, though, this venerable ocean cruiser offers its crew a pleasant, roomy, teak-lined interior and a very sea-kindly motion on open water. Perry designed

Photo courtesy of Hydrovane

Sailing with two outboards, an arch with solar panels, and a deck enclosure blocking wind from the Hydrovane cannot be easy, but it appears to work for the skipper of this Tayana 37.

Tayana 37 Specifications

Designer:	Robert H. Perry	L/B:	3.16
Builder:	Ta Yang Yacht	Hull Mat:	Fiberglass
Keel type:	Full keel	Fuel:	90 gallons
LOA:	36' 8"	Water:	100 gallons
LWL:	31'	P:	45' 4"
Beam:	11' 7"	E:	15' 6"
Draft:	5' 8"	SA (main):	351.08 sq. ft.
Disp:	22,500 lbs.	I:	50' 10"
Ballast:	8,000 lbs. iron	J:	19' 6"
Rig:	Cutter	SA (fore):	495.3 sq. ft.
Aux:	Perkins 4-108M	SA:	846.38 sq. ft.
B/D:	.32	SA/D:	17.06

A pair of steering lines lead from a Monitor windvane to the wheel adaptor on this Tayana 37.

A Hydrovane self-steerer shares a custom mounting bracket with a Duogen air and hydro generator.

the Tayana 37 as a faster, roomier alternative to the popular Westsail 32, which popularized offshore sailing in the early 1970s. The Tayana 37 was one of the early "performance cruisers" in the true Perry tradition, which started with the Valiant 40. The iron ballast on the Tayana 37's full keel was kept to 32 percent of the total design weight of the craft, while the somewhat deep draft of 5 feet 8 inches guaranteed enough righting movement to compensate for the moderate ballast. This combination of generous draft and moderate ballast yields a fast, comfortable yacht in all weather conditions, from light winds to a sustained full gale.

Still built by Tayana Yachts in Taiwan, the 37 remains a blend of modern yacht-building and old-world craftsmanship, combining modern deck and hull laminates with gobs of hand-carved hardwoods just about everywhere you look, from the honey-colored bowsprit to the gunwale trim and, of course, the varnished wood interior. Besides the pronounced bowsprit, her rounded stern, or "buttocks" as Perry calls them, are her most eye-catching feature. And though the stern may offer a somewhat more complex surface than a flat transom for mounting alternative power-generating devices, the typical cruising Tayana 37 carries, as a minimum, a windvane self-steerer and a pair of solar panels. Other sister ships may also carry a hydro generator or a wind generator. Installing this equipment requires careful attention to the mounting structures, the stainless steel tubes of which must be carefully cut and fitted to accommodate the canoe transom.

The adjustable tube fittings on the Monitor windvane servopendulum make transom mounting a fairly easy affair. The tubes are precut by the manufacturer to fit the transom, so all the installer has to do is drill holes in the transom for the mounting brackets and then bolt the unit

Phovto courtesy of Bob Johnson

A Monitor windvane steers this Tayana 37 with control lines leading through swivel blocks to a wheel adaptor on the helm.

into place. A Hydrovane will come with mounting tubes and adjustable mounting brackets, but the upper mounting structure may also be ordered as a custom-welded stainless structure, depending on the owner's wishes. Of all the windvane self-steering mounting structures on the market, Hydrovane seems to offer its clients the most creative array of tube and bracket arrangements, which can be offset from the centerline if necessary. Owing to the sheer number of Tayana 37s undertaking extended cruises, it is difficult to pinpoint a particular style or trend in outfitting these vessels for alternative

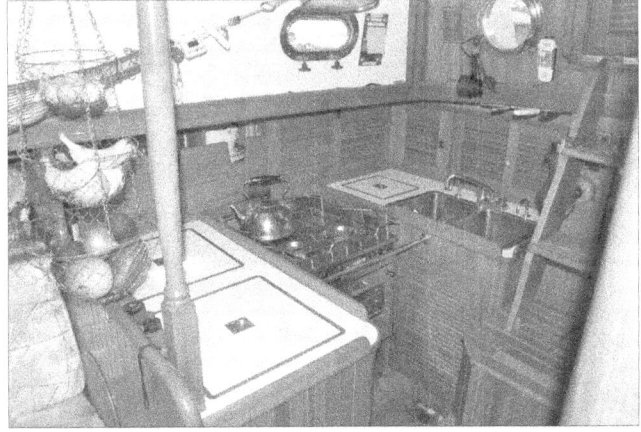

Photo courtesy of Bob Johnson

The separate top-opening fridge and freezer are connected by a narrow opening (not visible), allowing both sections to share the same compressor, condenser, and evaporator.

energy; the options for equipment and mounting styles are wide and varied.

Hallberg-Rassy 46

The elegant yet tough passage maker Hallberg-Rassy 46 lies towards the upper end of the standard range of yacht size to be found circling the globe. Designed by Germán Frers of Argentina and built by Hallberg-Rassy of Sweden, the 46 has all the earmarks of a large luxury yacht, yet with solid, respectable sailing performance in all weather conditions as proof of her worth as a world cruiser. This is the boat that has gained fame as *Mahina Tiare III*, owned by author-cruisers John and Amanda Neal. Their vessel serves as the platform for their ocean cruising school, Mahina Expeditions, which they operate from the Arctic Circle to French Polynesia and New Zealand. Student cruisers learn to deal with a variety of challenges, from reefing in gale conditions to giving wide berth to coastal obstructions, while trusting their safety to a pair of highly experienced instructors and a safe, solid vessel.

A short list of the Hallberg-Rassy 46's essential features depicts just the kind of boat every sailor dreams of, if you can afford it. For starters, the 46 displaces 35,264 pounds with 14,106 pounds of ballast, which translates to a hefty ballast-to-displacement ratio of 40 percent. The generous 6-foot, 2-inch keel might be a tad too deep to claim "shoal draft" status, but the heavy ballast and low center of gravity yield a great deal of righting movement, meaning you can expect the rail to stay out of the water while sailing to weather single-reefed in a light gale. Offering protection above decks is the signature Hallberg-Rassy four-section tempered glass windshield, making life a lot more bearable when bashing to windward, and the center cockpit adds an extra measure of safety for crew, as well as cozy seating for above-decks dining in settled conditions. When it comes time to climb the mast, the 46's strong, straightforward masthead sloop rig keeps things really simple; imagine having to do that with a fractional rig, particularly in the middle of a gale.

The 46's bigger sibling, the Halberg-Rassy 55, is fitted with a Mastervolt diesel generator by

Photo courtesy of Tor Johnson

Mahina Tiare III sails through pristine waters off Tavarua Island, Fiji.

the builder, but the more compact 46 does not include this convenience. However, the 46's large engine compartment has ample room to fit a small generator in the general size range of a 2-cylinder Fischer Panda Mini 8, which measures 23.2 × 17.3 × 21.5 inches and weighs 350 pounds. The 46 also features a highly efficient Frigoboat keel-cooled fridge and freezer with holding plates. Plus, with all the spare deck space aft of the center cockpit, there is plenty of room to install and access alternative charging sources to keep the fridge and other onboard systems running faithfully around the clock. On *Mahina Tiare III*, explained John Neal, "We use an Ampair towing generator on passages, and that has been very amazing, meeting 90 percent of our power needs." Neal also pointed out that some 46s employ "fold-down solar panels" along the lifelines to provide easy access to sunlight while keeping them off-deck and out of the way of crew members. Other equipment easily finding a home aboard the Hallberg-Rassy 46 are one or two wind generators, free-standing solar panel masts, and a transom-mount hydro generator, such as a Watt & Sea or Duogen combination wind and water generator.

Installing a wind-powered self-steering mechanism on a large yacht with a center cockpit may appear daunting at first glance, but at least one Hallberg-Rassy 46 has been fitted with Scanmar's Monitor servopendulum and signature SwingGate system, with steering lines routed over the aft cabin to a wheel adapter on the helm. Another popular option for the 46 is the Hydrovane, a stand-alone steering system that leaves the helm free of steering lines and extra blocks. The Hydrovane requires only minor steering adjustments at the unit's control box to keep the vessel on course.

Making the best choice of an offshore sailing vessel and equipping it for an extended offshore cruise entail some serious soul-searching that all ocean sailors must face before we lay out our life savings to fulfill our dreams. Our decisions take into account not only our pocketbooks, but also our need for comfort and speed, and our personal

Hallberg-Rassy 46 Specifications

Designer:	Germán Frers	L/B:	3.27
Builder:	Hallberg-Rassy	Hull Mat:	Fiberglass
Keel type:	Fin keel	Fuel:	172 gallons
LOA:	46' 3"	Water:	239 gallons
LWL:	38'	P:	52' 2"
Beam:	14' 2"	E:	18' ½"
Draft:	6' 2"	SA (main):	470.48 sq. ft.
Disp:	35,264 lbs.	I:	59' ½"
Ballast:	14,106 lbs.	J:	18' 6 ½"
Rig:	Masthead Sloop	SA (fore):	547.39 sq. ft.
Aux:	Volvo Penta TMD 31	SA:	1017.88 sq. ft.
B/D:	.40	SA/D:	15.21

An Ampair water generator mounted to the stern rail of the Hallberg-Rassy 46 Mahina Tiare III.

John Neal prepares to launch the rotor of the Ampair water generator from the stern of the Hallberg-Rassy 46 Mahina Tiare III.

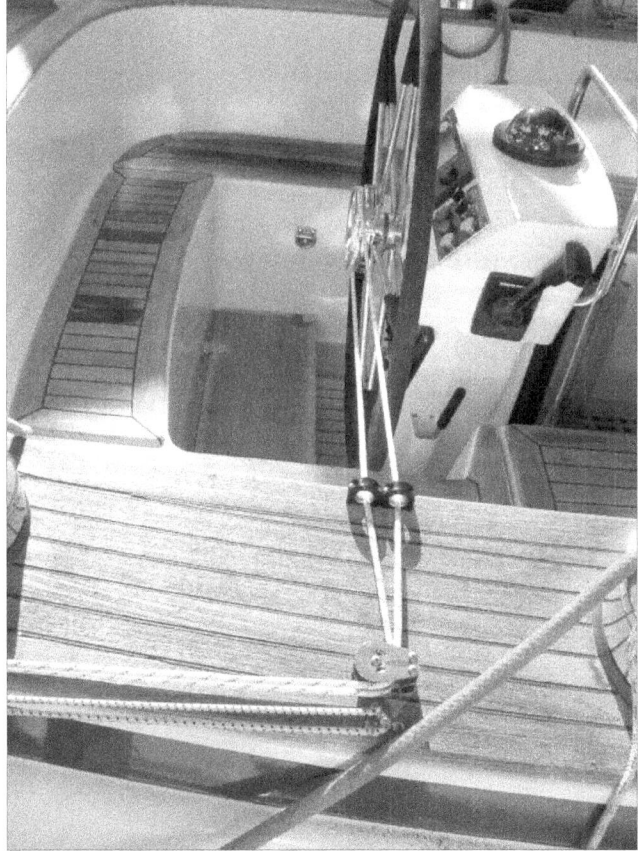

A Monitor windvane's steering lines are routed through blocks and fairleads to the center cockpit helm on a Hallberg-Rassy 46.

A Monitor Swing Gate is installed to this Hallberg-Rassy 46, permitting easy access to the transom swim step.

philosophy about what is most important in a boat capable of crossing oceans in nearly all kinds of weather short of a hurricane. While we fuss over the details of design and construction, we also need to consider how to make our vessels energy independent, allowing us to survive for months on end in the Tuamotus of the South Pacific or Cocos Keeling in the Indian Ocean without access to diesel fuel or fresh water. Survival under such conditions requires the use of alternative energy available through the harnessing of power from the sun and wind, and while under sail, from the water itself. Settling on a general preference of boat design and a list of equipment and charging systems is by no means an easy task. But by sailing in familiar coastal waters, reading widely on sailing and ocean piloting, and hanging out in sailor dives to hear what experienced passage makers have to say about various yacht designs and alternative energy systems, we gradually gain a picture of where our needs and values—and finances—fall within the grand scheme of offshore voyaging.

References

Boat U.S. (2011, October). Ultra-low-sulfur diesel: anything to worry about? Seaworthy.

Brotherton, Miner K., and Edwin R. Sherman. (2003). The 12-volt bible for boats. Camden, Maine: International Marine.

Calder, Nigel. (2005). The boatowner's electrical and mechanical handbook. Camden, Maine: International Marine.

Collins, Daniel. (2014, November). Silent running: re-powering a 36-foot ketch with an electric motor. Blue Water Sailing.

Dear, Ian, and Peter Kemp. (1987). The pocket Oxford guide to sailing terms. New York: Oxford University Press.

Fitzpatrick, James J. and Dominic M. Di Toro. A history of eutrophication modeling in Lake Erie. Retrieved May 9, 2015, from http://www.ijc.org/php/publications/html/modsum/fitzpatrick.html

Jeffrey, Kevin. Independent energy guide. (1995). White River Junction, Vermont: Orwell Cove Press.

Kettlewell, John J. (2009, October 5). Composting toilets: a green approach to dealing with voyaging waste. Ocean Navigator.

Lawrence, Keith, ed. (1988). Outfitting: equipping a boat for performance, comfort, and safety. Riverside, Conn.: Belvoir Publications.

Lawrence, Keith, ed. (1988). Do-it-yourself improvement projects. Riverside, Conn.: Belvoir Publications.

Lochhaas, Tom. Uses of a voltmeter on a boat. Retrieved December 24, 2015, from http://sailing.about.com/od/equipmentgear/a/Uses-Of-A-Voltmeter-On-A-Boat-On-Your-Boat.htm

Morris, Bill. (2006). Bluewater gear. Ocean voyager: annual handbook of offshore sailing.

Morris, Bill. (2011, May/June). Efficiencies of a genset. Ocean navigator.

Morris, Bill. (2009, September). Green voyaging. Ocean navigator.

Morris, Bill. (2009, January/February). Managing alternative energy. Ocean navigator.

Morris, Bill. (2007, May/June). Power plucked from the air. Ocean navigator.

Morris, Bill. (2004). The windvane self-steering handbook. Camden, Maine: International Marine.

Morris, Bill. (2012, November/December). Voyager's toolbox. Ocean navigator.

Mustin, Henry C. (1994). Surveying fiberglass sailboats: A step-by-step guide for buyers and owners. Camden, Maine: International Marine.

Pardey, Lin and Larry. (1987). The capable cruiser. New York: W.W. Norton & Company.

Perry, Robert H. (2008). Yacht design according to Perry: my boats and what shaped them. Camden, Maine: International Marine.

Sherman, Edwin R. (2007). Advanced marine electrics and electronics troubleshooting. Camden, Maine: International Marine.

United States Coast Guard. (2015). Fire extinguishing systems. Retrieved from http://www.uscg.mil/hq/cg5/cg5214/fesys.asp

United States Environmental Protection Agency. (2011). Detroit River-Western Lake Erie Basin indicator project. Retrieved from http://www.epa.gov/med/grosseile_site/indicators/algae-blooms.html

United States Environmental Protection Agency. (2012). Diesel fuel. Retrieved from http://epa.gov/otaq/fuels/dieselfuels/index.htm

U.S. Energy Information Administration. (2015). How much ethanol is in gasoline and how does it affect fuel economy? Retrieved from http://www.eia.gov/tools/faqs/faq.cfm?id=27&t=10

Wing, Charlie. (2006). Boater's illustrated electrical handbook. Camden, Maine: International Marine.

Appendices

Appendix 1: AWG Battery Cable Sizes

12 Volt; Vessel Current in Amps (3% Drop)

Round-Trip Length in Feet	Amperage							
	60	80	100	120	140	160	180	200
15	4	4	2	2	2	1	1	1/0
20	4	2	2	1	1	1/0	2/0	2/0
30	2	1	1/0	2/0	2/0	3/0	3/0	4/0
40	1	1/0	2/0	3/0	3/0	4/0	4/0	
50	1/0	2/0	3/0	4/0	4/0			
60	2/0	3/0	4/0	4/0				
70	2/0	3/0	4/0					
80	3/0	4/0						
90	3/0							

Appendix 2: AWG Wire Gauge Sizes

12 Volt; Vessel Current in Amps (3% Drop)

Round-Trip Length in Feet	Amperage								
	5	10	15	20	30	40	50	60	70
15	16	12	10	10	8	6	6	4	4
20	14	12	10	8	6	6	4	4	4
30	12	10	8	6	4	4	2	2	2
40	12	8	6	6	4	2	2	1	1/0
50	10	8	6	4	2	2	1	1/0	1/0
60	10	6	6	4	2	1	1/0	2/0	2/0
70	10	6	4	2	2	1/0	2/0	2/0	3/0
80	8	6	4	2	1	1/0	2/0	3/0	3/0
90	8	4	4	2	1/0	2/0	3/0	3/0	4/0

Appendix 3: Beaufort Scale

Force	Wind Speed in Knots	Description
0	<1	Flat calm
1	1-3	Light airs; slight rippling on water's surface
2	4-6	Light breeze; small, glassy waves
3	7-10	Gentle breeze; waves 1 to 4 feet; some glassy foam
4	11-16	Moderate breeze; waves 4 to 8 feet; whitecaps with spray;
5	17-21	Fresh breeze; waves 8 to 12 feet with white-capped seas and spray everywhere; first reef
6	22-27	Strong breeze; long waves with white foam; second reef
7	28-33	Near gale; waves 12 to 18 feet; streaks form on breaking waves; third reef
8	34-40	Full gale: waves 14 to 18 feet with breaking crests and sprindrift; sailing under trysail or storm jib
9	41-47	Strong gale: waves of at least 18 feet with dense streaks of foam and reduced visibility from foam and spray; hove-to under trysail or storm jib
10	48-55	Storm: waves 20 to 30 feet; heavily rolling seas with white foam; sailing downwind under bare poles, towing a drogue
11	56-63	Violent storm; waves 30 to 45 feet; greatly reduced visibility from foam and spray
12	64 and over	Hurricane/cyclone: waves topping 45 feet; air filled with foam and spray; very little visibility

Appendix 4: Cruiser's Ham Bands

by FCC License Level (Voice Only)

40 Meters

Amateur Extra	7.125-7.3
Advanced	7.125-7.3
General	7.175-7.3

20 Meters

Amateur Extra	14.150-14.350
Advanced	14.175-14.350
General	14.225-14.350

17 Meters

Amateur Extra	18.110-18.168
Advanced	18.110-18.168
General	18.110-18.168

15 Meters

Amateur Extra	21.200-21.450
Advanced	21.225-21.450
General	21.275-21.450

Appendix 5: Marine Fire Extinguishers

Extinguisher and Purpose	Type of Fire	Extinguishing Agent
A — Ordinary combustibles	Paper, wood, fabric, trash, rubber, and plastics, including cured polyester resin in deck laminates.	Water, foam, dry chemical
B — Flammable liquids	Gasoline, oil, grease, oil-based paints and varnishes, and solvents, including mineral spirits and acetone	Foam, dry chemical, carbon dioxide
C — Electrical equipment	Energized ("hot") electrical equipment, electrical appliances, computers, and circuitry	Dry chemical, carbon dioxide

Appendix 6: Sailboat Specifications Decoded

Designer:	Naval architect	L/B:	Length/beam ratio
Builder:	Company name	Hull Mat:	Hull construction material
Keel type:	Fin keel, full keel, etc.	Fuel:	In gallons
LOA:	Length overall	Water:	In gallons
LWL:	Length on waterline	P:	Mainsail luff
Beam:	Maximum width	E:	Mainsail foot
Draft:	Deepest point of keel	SA (main):	Mainsail area
Disp:	Total design weight	I:	Height of jib
Ballast:	Weight of keel ballast	J:	Distance between mast & bow
Rig:	Sloop, yawl, ketch, etc.	SA (fore):	Jib area fore of mast
Aux:	Engine make & hp	SA:	Total sail area
B/D:	Ballast/displacement ratio	SA/D:	Sail area/displacement ratio

Special Thanks

The author wishes to thank the following business establishments for their technical assistance and cooperation in the research for this book.

AC/DC Marine
23316 South Normandie Ave.
Unit D
Torrance, CA 90502
(310) 864-3131
megan@acdcmarineinc.com

Balmar DC Charging Systems
15201 39th Ave. NE
Marysville, WA 98271
(360) 435-6100
balmar@balmar.net

Captain's Locker
194 N. Marina Drive #100
Seal Beach, CA 90803
(562) 598-6611

Chula Vista Marina
550 Marina Parkway
Chula Vista, CA 91910
(619) 862-2835
boatslips@cvmarina.com

Clean eMarine
311A Third Street
Annapolis, MD 21403
(410) 353-2597
info@c-e-marineamericas.com

Coastal Climate Control
P.O. Box 4535
Annapolis, MD 21403
(301) 352-5738

Elco Motor Yachts
21 S. Water Street
Athens, NY 12015
(877) 411-3526
info@elcomotoryachts.com

Electric Yacht
5042 Lowry Terrace
Golden Valley, MN 55422
(855) 339-2248
info@electricyacht.com

Hallberg-Rassy Varvs AB
Hallberg-Rassyvägen 1
SE-474 31 Ellös
Sweden
+46 - (0)304 54 800
info@hallberg-rassy.se

Hamilton Ferris
3 Angelo Drive
Bourne, Cape Cod, MA
(508) 743-9901
sales@hamiltonferris.com

Heritage Yacht Sales
829 Harbor Island Drive
Newport Beach, CA 92660
(949) 673-3354

Hybrid Marine
11 Melville Street
Sandown, Isle of Wight, UK
P036 8LF
+44 1983 403236
info@hybridmarine.co.uk

Hydrovane
2424 Haywood Avenue
West Vancouver, BC
V7V 1Y1 Canada
(604) 925-2660

Jeremy Rogers Limited
Lymington Yacht Haven
Kings Saltern Road

Lymington
Hampshire
SO41 3QD
Tel: +44 (0)1590 646780
mail@jeremyrogers.co.uk

Lehr
8922 Ellis Ave
Los Angeles, CA 90034
(310) 839-9009

Mahina Expeditions
P.O. Box 1596
Friday Harbor, WA 98250
(360) 378-6131
sailing@mahina.com

Sailomat USA
5933 Avenida Chamnez
La Jolla, CA 92037
(858) 454-8550
contact@sailomat.com

Scanmar International
432 South 1st Street
Richmond, CA USA 94804
(510) 215-2010
scanmar@selfsteer.com

SES Flexcharge
Seelye Equipment Specialists
1217 State Street
Charlevoix, MI 49720
(231) 547-9430
sales@flexcharge.com

ThunderStruck Motors, LLC
2985 Dutton Ave. Ste 3
Santa Rosa, CA 95407
(707) 578-7973
connect@thunderstruck-ev.co

Index

A

Alternators 21, 23, 69, 71, 73, 75
    N-type 15, 46, 73
    Prestolite 17
    Prestolite 105-amp alternator 15
    P-type 15, 46, 73
    selecting an alternator 16
    spike protector 15, 17
        Balmar Transient Spike Protector 17
    stock alternator 16
Ammeter 64, 72
    analog meter 80
    digital meter 80
Anchoring 142–143
    over vulnerable areas 143
Automatic identification system (AIS) 89
Autopilots 101, 104, 107, 111, 112, 114, 116
    components 111–116
    linear drive 112–115
    operating theory 111
    rotary drive 112–116
    tiller pilot 102–104, 107, 109, 112, 113
        Raymarine EV-100 Tiller autopilot 112
        ST2000 Tiller Pilot 112
    tiller ram 113
    wheel pilot 113, 114
        Raymarine EV-100 Wheel autopilot 113

B

Batteries
    Absorbed glass mat batteries *See AGM batteries*
    AGM 39, 71
    amp hours 37, 40
    AWG Battery Cable Sizes 45
    Battery Chart, 12V, 8D 38
    carbon foam 39, 40
    chargers 47
    charging 46–48, 63, 69–76
    cold cranking amps (CCA) 37
    consumption 53, 78, 88, 93
    cranking 16, 18
    cranking amps (CA) 37
    deep cycle 43
    Trojan T-125 43
    dual purpose 36, 39
    flooded 40–43
    fuel cells 9, 10
        Hydromax 150 hydrogen fuel cell 42
    gel 50, 71, 73
    golf cart 16, 37, 39, 43, 56
    house 20, 27, 46–49, 70, 72, 74–76, 86, 92–95, 97, 99, 115, 116, 125, 126, 147
    installation 70, 107, 115, 137, 152, 154
    lithium-ion 40, 41
        OPE Li-3 lithium battery 41
    marine cranking amps (MCA) 37
    monitoring 37, 69, 70, 73, 82
    reserve minutes 37, 39, 40
Biodiesel 31
    complications 31–33
    home-made 31
    performance 23, 25, 29, 31–33, 65, 73, 98, 107, 151–153, 156
    Schematic of Biodiesel Production Path 33
    vegetable oil 31, 32
Biodiesel Blends Chart 31
Butane *See Liquid petroleum gas*

C

Charting 89–93
    digital 90–93
    NOAA raster charts 90–93
    paper chart 88, 90
Control panel 25
    integrated 24, 69, 75, 102, 111, 115, 116
Corrosion 29, 49, 122, 133, 134, 138
    crevice corrosion 134, 138
    galvanic 46–52, 122–123
    in cast iron engine block 4
    in stainless steel fuel tank 8, 21–27, 131–139

D

Data Links 62–68, 89–93, 111–116
    data cable 90
    NMEA 0183/2000 90
Depth Sounder 88, 89

handheld digital sounder   88–93
Diesel Engines   3, 5, 7, 9–11
   diesel-electric power   10
   Diesel Engine Comparison Chart   6
   glow plugs   5
   operating theory   5, 111
   repowering   7, 9, 10
      diesel-electric power   10
Diesel fuel   131, 155
   low sulfur diesel (ULSD)   30

E

Electric motors   118–123, 119–123, 156–157
   Electric Inboard Motor Comparison Chart   10
   propulsion   3, 9–12
   repower   9
Emergency rudder   10–110
Energy Planning Chart   79
Engine
   cooling   4, 5, 133
   monitoring   81
   raw water pump   23, 131, 133
Ethanol   28–30

F

Fire extinguishers   100, 125–129
   dry ice   100
   Marine Fire Extinguishers chart   160
Fuel cells   41, 42
   hydrogen   41, 42
Fuel filter   134
   primary fuel filter   5, 7
   secondary fuel filter   5, 7
   water separator   8
Fuel flash points   4, 32, 34
Fuel tanks   21, 131
   aluminum   8
   composite tank   144
   fiberglass   8
   polyethylene   8
   stainless steel   8

G

Garbage, the proper handling of   142
Gasoline   4, 8, 20, 26
Gasoline engines   3–5
   replacement   5

Gauges
   analog gauges   78, 80–82
      engine control panel   83
   digital gauge   84
   temperature gauge   80
Generators
   on main engine   13, 14, 18
Generator sets
   asynchronous   26
   Beta Marine 7kW genset   23
   coupling   23
   Entec West 4200-D,   25
   gasoline   26
   Marine Genset Comparison Chart   22
   Nexgen UCM1-3.5   26
   portable gas-powered   20
   sound shield   25
   speed control   26
Gow plugs   5, 43
GPS (Global Positioning System)   46, 64, 72, 86, 88–93
   101, 111, 112, 115, 116
   handheld GPS   88, 90, 92, 101, 135
   permanent-mount   88
Gray water   141
   eutrophication   142
   filtering   142

H

Ham Radio (SSB)   91–93
   antenna   91–93
   counterpoise   91–93 133–139
   tuner   91–93
Hose clamps   5, 7
Hoses   5, 7
Hydro generators
   Francis turbine   67
   retrieval   66
   rotor   66
   towed   67
   transom-mount   67
   wind-water conversions   64
Hydromax 150 hydrogen fuel cell   42

J

Junction box
   electrical   47–49
   rotor   61–66
   towed   63, 64, 67, 68

transom-mount 63, 66–68
wind-water conversions 64–66
WP-200 generator diagram 65

K

Kerosene 87

L

Lights
cabin 87
halogen 87
incandescent 86, 87
LED (Light Emitting Diode) 86–89
navigation 86
Liquid petroleum gas
butane 131, 132
conversion from gasoline 35
impurities 34
outboard motors 144, 145
propane 96, 144, 145
regulators 34

M

Marine sanitation device (MSD) *See Toilets*
Mooring *See also Anchoring*
Multimeter (volt meter)
analog 132
digital multimeter 132–139
Fluke 28 II digital multimeter 132

O

Oil
absorber 141
dispersant 140
dumping 141
oil pressure 25
Outboard motors
electric outboard 145
gasoline outboard 145
propane-powered outboard 145

P

Petroleum distillates 28
Photovoltaic energy 46, 47
Propane *See Liquid petroleum gas*

R

Radar
amperage draw 89
Radios
Ham (SSB) *See Ham Radio (SSB)*
Cruiser's Ham Bands 160
Refrigeration 94, 96–98
air-cooled 97
compressor 95–97, 99, 153
condenser 23, 94–99, 153
cycling 94, 96–98
dry ice 100
freezer 27, 94–98, 145, 153, 154
heat exchanger 98
holding plate 96, 97, 99
ice box conversion 95, 99
insulation 95, 99, 149
keel-cooled 98
portable ice maker 92, 95, 99, 100
refrigerant 96
water-cooled 97
Repowering
with a diesel engine 7–9
with an electric motor 118, 119, 156
with hybrid electric 27, 149–151
Rigging
1 × 19 wire 136–138
7 × 19 wire 138
spares and maintenance supplies 136
swage tool 139
terminals 138

S

Seals
junction box 47–49, 52
raw water pump 131
Solar panels
blocking diode 58
controller 47–50
flexible 48
installation 49
mounting 50
non-marine 48
photovoltaic theory 46
rigid 47
Solder 49
acid-free flux 132
Soldering irons

butane soldering irons 132
electric soldering irons 132
Sound Shield 25

T

Tachometer 9, 80, 81
Toilets
   composting 141
   discharge 141
   holding tank 141
   marine sanitation device (MSD) 141, 141–146
Tools
   cordless 135
   hand tools 133
   power tools 135
Transformers 135

V

VHF *See VHF Radios*
VHF Radios 86–93
   digital selective calling 90–93
   VHF base-mount 27, 89–93
   VHF handheld 90–93
Voltage regulators 50–52, 69–76
   external 71
   mechanical 69
   monitoring 69, 70
   rectifier 71
   shunt 71–73
   smart controllers 69, 73

W

Water separator 8
Wind Generator Output Chart 57
Wind generators
   Betz' Law 53
   cavitation 46
   radio interference 48
   theory 53
   vibration 54
Windlasses, electric
   amperage draw 125
   chain gypsy 125
   construction 124
   ease of use 125
   electric windlass safety tips 125
   horizontal 126, 127

   Lofrans Tigres 126
   manual override 126
   reversibility 125
   speed 125
   vertical 124
      Lewmar V3GD vertical windlass 128
      Maxwell VWC Series 128
   wildcat 125–129
Windlasses, manual
   chain drive 122
   chain gypsy 120
   double action 120
   durability 117
   gear drive 122
   horizontal 122
   manual windlass safety tips 118
   Safety tips 118
   vertical 120
   wildcat 119–123
Windvane self-steering
   double-rudder system 103
   emergency rudder capability 108
   matching vane gear to vessel 107
   matching windvane to boat 105
   servopendulum
      Servopendulums: Pros and Cons 104
   servopendulum-trim tab
      Trim Tabs: Pros and Cons 104
   wind-powered auxiliary rudder 105
Wire
   AWG Battery Cable Sizes 45
   AWG Wire Gauge Sizes 45

About the Author

Circumnavigator-author Bill Morris, a native of Los Angeles, received his first inspiration to sail the world's oceans at the age of twelve when his father offhandedly suggested selling the house and circling the globe aboard a large yacht.

Though the proposal was soon abandoned, the idea was permanently engraved in Bill's imagination. Serving as a radio repairman and later as an outboard motor mechanic in the U.S. Army while stationed in the Panama Canal Zone during the mid-1970s, he picked up valuable skills that would help him later in life as a cruising sailor.

He went on to receive a Ph.D. in Administrative and Policy Studies in Education from UCLA, amassing nearly 30 years' experience in teaching writing at the secondary and college levels in Southern California, South Florida, and American Samoa. Bill and his wife Marilu eventually crossed the Pacific from Panama to Mooloolaba Harbour, Queensland, Australia, and then to Darwin, Northern Territory, aboard their 1966 Cal 30 *Saltaire*.

After Marilu left *Saltaire* to give birth to their daughter, Yasmin, Bill continued west back to Los Angeles by way of the two canals, surviving a Somali pirate attack in the Gulf of Aden. Bill is the author of *The Windvane Self-Steering Handbook* (International Marine, 2004), and he has written many articles on both cruising adventure and alternative energy for offshore vessels in *Afloat*, *Blue Water Sailing*, *Latitude 38*, *Ocean Navigator*, and *Ocean Voyager* magazines.

Photo courtesy of Ron Durham

Circumnavigator-Author Bill Morris

www.ingramcontent.com/pod-product-compliance
Lightning Source LLC
Chambersburg PA
CBHW082122230426

43671CB00015B/2772